The Politics of Resistance in France, 1940-1944

JOHN F. SWEETS

THE POLITICS O

A HISTOR

LIBÉRATION

ORGANE DES FORCES DE RÉSISTANCE FRANÇAISES

NOTRE TACHE

Voici notre Chef...

Le Général de Gaulle
anticipateur de Génie

Consignes aux Militants

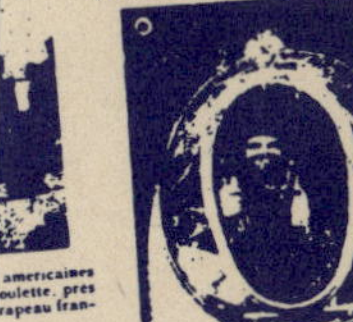

NUMERO SPECIAL ILLUSTRE

MAI 1943

UNITE

par Henri FRENAY

Dans la guerre comme dans la paix le dernier mot est à ceux qui ne se rendent jamais. Clemenceau.

ORGANE DES MOUVEMENTS DE RESISTANCE UNIS

FRANÇAIS, PRÉPAREZ-VOUS!

VERS UNE FRANCE NOUVELLE

RESISTANCE IN FRANCE, 1940-1944

OF THE *MOUVEMENTS UNIS DE LA RÉSISTANCE*

Northern Illinois University Press / *DeKalb*

All photos courtesy *Comité d'Histoire de la 2ᵉ guerre mondiale*, Paris.

Library of Congress Cataloging in Publication Data
Sweets, John F   1945-
  The politics of resistance in France, 1940-1944.
  Bibliography: p.
  Includes index.
  1. Mouvements unis de la Résistance.   2. World War,
1939-1945—Underground movements—France.   3. France—
Politics and government—1940-1945.   I. Title.
D802.F8S88   940.53'44   75-15014
ISBN 0-87580-061-0

For my Mother and Father

Contents

Preface

THE POPULAR IMAGE of the Resistance in France has been that of a paramilitary movement principally concerned with the sabotage of the German war machine. Certainly most resisters desired above all a chance to fight the Germans. In northern France, where the German occupation began immediately after the armistice of 1940, the Resistance developed and retained a distinctly military orientation. By contrast, because of the absence of German troops until November 1942, the Resistance in southern France exhibited a marked political coloration early in its existence. Opposition to the armistice led to opposition to the Vichy regime. The ultimate goal of the three leading resistance movements in the unoccupied zone, Combat, Libération, and Franc-Tireur, was to liberate French territory by driving the Germans out of France, but this aim was linked to the overthrow of Vichy. These movements accepted Charles de Gaulle as the symbol of their struggle because he promised a restoration of the traditional liberties of Frenchmen, a progressive social outlook, and a purified political regime in contrast to Vichy's reactionary social and political programs.

Perhaps the most significant aspect of the history of the Resistance was the remarkable political revolution carried out by those who supported Charles de Gaulle within France. In particular, the unique contribution of the three major movements in the southern zone, united in the Mouvements Unis de la Résistance (MUR), was to alert the Resistance to the importance of political considerations. Although fellow resisters in the northern movements complained that they were overly concerned with politics, MUR leaders, encouraged by Gaullist representatives sent from the exterior, assumed positions of national leadership within the Resistance in undermining the Vichy administration and in preparing the organizations that would take over the administration of France at the liberation.

The political consciousness of the movements in southern France, which, once unified, represented the largest component of the organized Resistance in France, explains the central position of the MUR in achieving what, it is argued, was the most important result of the Resistance's activity. When Allied troops arrived in France, they were confronted almost everywhere with local administrations loyal to de Gaulle and already functioning under the orders of the Comité Français de la Libération Nationale (CFLN), which because of this fact was recognized unanimously as the legitimate government of France.

Because this study centers on the organized movements in southern France, it is not a comprehensive history of the Resistance in France. However, the major problems the MUR confronted, from organization and political commitment to military and subversive action, were those shared by the Resistance in general. To that extent this study addresses the fundamental issues of the Resistance in France through a description of the development of the three major resistance movements in southern France, their progress toward unification, and their important role within the national resistance organizations. Individual chapters examine their relations with Charles de Gaulle and the exterior Resistance, their association with the Communist party, and their attitude toward other French political parties, notably the Socialist party. Finally, a description of the liberation of France, in which the story of the MUR necessarily merges with that of the entire Resistance, evaluates the military and political achievements of the movements and offers an explanation for the curious disillusionment of many resisters at the liberation in spite of their extraordinary accomplishments.

Most of the documentation for this study was uncovered in the archives of the Comité d'histoire de la deuxième guerre mondiale in

Paris. In the years following the liberation, the staff of the Comité d'histoire collected the témoignages of hundreds of resisters. These documents, along with the periodic reports of Gaullist agents in France, the papers of several leading resisters, and collections of numerous clandestine newspapers, form a substantial core for an understanding of the Resistance in France. Although the Comité d'histoire maintains by far the most important holdings, additional materials may be found at the Bibliothèque nationale and the Bibliothèque de documentation internationale contemporaine. In the United States useful materials are found in the Records of the Office of Strategic Services (OSS) and in the Captured German Documents, which are preserved in the National Archives at Washington, D.C.

For an extremely cordial reception and interest in my research I am indebted to many people in France: Madame Paule Letty-Mouroux, secrétaire générale of the Fédération des amicales de réseaux, renseignements & évasions de la France combattante, for her assistance in tracking down the current addresses of many former resisters; M. Henri Michel, sécrétaire général of the Comité d'histoire de la deuxième guerre mondiale, for his warm welcome and full cooperation in granting me access to the Comité's archives, and the cordial assistance of M. Michel Rauzier, the Comité's biblothécaire, as well as the other members of the Comité's staff; and those former resisters who permitted me to use the testimonies and other documents that they had deposited at the Comité d'histoire or who were kind enough to talk with me. Those resisters who allowed me to read their testimonies are listed in the bibliography, but I must express my gratitude to Madame Lucie d'Astier for permission to use her late husband's testimony, and to M. Felix Liguory, the executor of the estate of Antoine Avinin, for permission to utilize M. Avinin's testimony. A special word of thanks is due M. Alban Vistel, who unselfishly shared many invaluable documents from his personal papers—the single most important source of documentation concerning the Mouvements Unis de la Résistance—and who always responded generously to my many requests for additional information.

I am indebted to Duke University for a Danforth Fellowship and travel grant, which enabled me to conduct my research in France. I am grateful to Professors Joel Colton and William Scott of Duke University, who from its beginning discussed the project with me and offered numerous constructive suggestions for revision, and whose advice and encouragement I value highly. During its preparation for publication

Jay Luvaas of Allegheny College, Nathanael Greene of Wesleyan University, and Robert O. Paxton of Columbia University read the manuscript and contributed valuable suggestions for improvement. Thanks are due also to James Greenlee of Northern Illinois University who suggested alterations in my translation of several French passages. Finally, I am most grateful to my wife Judy, whose patience and understanding helped to carry me through the long years of my preoccupation with the Resistance in France.

I also wish to acknowledge the kind assistance of Marianne Ranson (Comité d'Histoire de la 2ᵉ guerre mondiale in Paris) in selecting photographs for the illustrations. The General Research Fund of the University of Kansas provided small grants to help defray the cost of some of the illustrative materials.

John F. Sweets

The Politics of Resistance in France, 1940-1944

CHAPTER I

The French Response to Vichy and the German Occupation, 1940-1944

THE ARMISTICE of 17 June 1940 created two Frances —the occupied zone garrisoned by German troops and the southern, free zone controlled by the Vichy regime.[1] But to divide Frenchmen an armistice had not been required. Numerous events during the thirties, including the turbulent day of 6 February 1934, the Popular Front, and the Nazi-Soviet Pact, had produced or revealed serious political divisions in the fabric of French society. A fragmented nation had gone to war in 1939 without the enthusiasm and unity of France in 1914.[2] Now, four years of German occupation would bring further discord; the geographical separation created by the armistice formed a rather superficial overlay for the more important partition that

---

[1] See Appendix for map of France according to the armistice terms.

[2] Recent studies of the "fall of France" include Guy Chapman, *Why France Collapsed: The Defeat of the French Army in 1940* (London: Cassell, 1968); Alistair Horne, *To Lose a Battle: France 1940* (London: Macmillan, 1969); William Shirer, *The Collapse of the Third Republic* (New York: Simon and Schuster, 1969); and John Williams, *The Ides of May, the Defeat of France, May-June 1940* (London: Constable, 1968). Marc Bloch, *L'étrange défaite: témoignage écrit en 1940* (Paris, 1946). English translation, *Strange Defeat* (New York: W. W. Norton & Co., 1968) remains among the best accounts.

placed in opposite camps Frenchmen who cooperated in varying degrees with the victorious Germans, and those who refused the armistice and all that it implied. One contemporary political analyst of this tragic period wrote: "Never in its two thousand years of history has the country known more tragic hours, never has its social, political, and moral fabric undergone a more terrible ordeal."[3]

In the immediate aftermath of their military disaster, there was no question where the sympathy of the overwhelming majority of Frenchmen lay. The spectacle of defeat, for which years of propaganda about the unbreachable Maginot line and about Europe's best army had prepared no one, and the humiliating rout before the relentless onslaught of German tanks and planes stunned and bewildered the French.[4] In their confusion and despair they accepted without hesitation when Philippe Pétain offered himself as a shield for France in her misfortune.[5] Who better than the venerable Marshal, the Victor of Verdun, could rally confidence and, hopefully, limit the inevitable German exactions? Two months after the German invasion, the National Assembly voted by a decisive majority (569 to 80) to bury the Third Republic and grant Pétain full powers to draft a new constitution for a proposed National Revolution. Senator Marcel Astier's desperate "Long live the Republic come what may"[6] found little echo in the resigned Assembly, and the slogan "Work, Family, Fatherland" soon replaced the Republic's "Liberty, Equality, Fraternity."[7]

---

[3] André Siegfried, "The Rebirth of the French Spirit," *Foreign Affairs* 23, no. 4 (July 1945): 556.

[4] In *L'Exode de mai-juin 1940* (Paris: Presses Universitaries de France, 1957), Jean Vidalenc presents the interesting thesis that the exodus was for many their first act of resistance, a contention that is perhaps more pleasing as an afterthought than valid for 1940. *L'Exode* is nonetheless an excellent description of the massive exodus of civilians and military personnel in the face of the invader.

[5] The text of Pétain's speech of 17 June 1940 is reproduced in Emmanuel d'Astier, *De la chute à la libération de Paris* (Paris: Gallimard, 1965), p. 235.

[6] Shirer, *Collapse*, p. 942.

[7] A detailed discussion of the Vichy regime is beyond the scope of this study, but a bare outline is essential in order to understand the motivations of the resisters, who opposed Vichy's ideology as well as its policies. Among the most valuable studies of the Vichy regime are: Robert Paxton, *Vichy France* (New York: Alfred A. Knopf, 1972), now the essential starting point for anyone studying France in this period; Yves Durand, *Vichy 1940-1944* (Paris: Bordas, 1972), an excellent short synthesis; Henri Michel, *Vichy: Année 40* (Paris: Robert Laffont, 1966), excellent for the regime's first months; Fondation Nationale des Sciences Politiques, *Le Gouvernement*

An essential fact about the new French government, the ramifications of which it would never surmount, was its birth in humiliating defeat. The natural first step for Vichy was an attempt to come to terms with Germany. In December 1940, after an interview with Hitler at Montoire, Pétain appealed to the French people: "It is with honor and to maintain ten-century-old French unity in the framework of the constructive activity of the new European order that *I embark today on a path of collaboration. . . .* Follow me: keep your faith in *la France éternelle.*"[8] The policy of collaboration adopted by Pétain at Montoire, as well as the first actions of his government in internal affairs, set the pattern for Vichy's future development.[9] Beyond simply preserving France from harm, the leaders at Vichy hoped to demonstrate the regime's legitimacy by taking every possible initiative to assert an independence of action. Having accepted the fact of defeat and assuming that Germany would soon dominate all of Europe, Pétain and Pierre Laval and their colleagues hoped to gain for France the best possible place in Hitler's new order. They believed that they could at the same time satisfy Hitler and serve France.[10]

Collaboration in international relations soon had its corollary in an internal regime compatible with National Socialism. Not that Vichy ever approached the German model: it had no such unity or coherence, and its inspiration was predominantly French,[11] despite some

---

de Vichy 1940–1942 (Paris: Armand Colin, 1972); the first three chapters of Stanley Hoffman, *Decline or Renewal?* (New York: Viking Press, 1974). Robert Aron's *Histoire de Vichy 1940–1944* (Paris: Fayard, 1954) should be used with caution.

[8] D'Astier, *De la chute*, illustration number 19, "Appel aux français" of December 1940; my italics. Aron, *Histoire de Vichy*, chap. 5, discusses the limited interpretation Pétain placed on the word *collaboration*, but concludes (pp. 308–10) that the psychological effects were nevertheless disastrous. See also Michel, *Année 40*, pp. 295–353; and Geoffrey Warner, *Pierre Laval and the Eclipse of France* (New York: Macmillan Co., 1968), pp. 231–43.

[9] Michel, Année 40, presents a convincing case for this interpretation. Paxton, in his *Vichy France* and in "Le Régime de Vichy en 1944," (Paper presented to the International Colloquium on the Liberation of France, Paris, October 1974) stresses a similar view. See also Yves Durand, *Vichy 1940–1944*.

[10] That they were deluded in this belief is convincingly demonstrated in Eberhard Jäckel, *Frankreich in Hitlers Europa* (Stuttgart: Deutsche Verlags-Anstalt, 1966), a well-documented study, which indicates that Hitler could never have been satisfied short of a complete catering to his every whim.

[11] See particularly the articles by Henri Michel, "La Révolution Nationale Latitude d'Action du Gouvernement de Vichy," *Revue d'histoire de la*

slight similarities in ideology and tone. The new political regime was in many respects the triumph of the prewar anti-republicans, their revenge for the Popular Front. Early in its existence Vichy exhibited marked clerical, militaristic, anti-Semitic, and authoritarian tendencies.[12]

Such a regime was installed with surprising ease in part because the dead Republic had few defenders, even among the republicans, in the immediate aftermath of the defeat. Léon Blum, the former Socialist Premier and leader of the Popular Front of 1936, retained his strong republican faith but admitted that the Third Republic's parliamentary system had had serious faults.[13] The presidents of the two legislative bodies, Édouard Herriot and Jules Jeanneney, later were disturbed by the suppression of republican liberties, but in 1940 they praised Pétain for securing the unity of the French people.[14] One of the bitterest of Vichy's critics, the head of the Free French in London, Charles de Gaulle, certainly had no great regret at the passing of the Third Republic, "a moral, social, political, and economic regime," which he said, "had abdicated in defeat, after having paralyzed itself in licentiousness."[15] Only the passage of time, the occupiers' exactions, and the degeneration of Vichy would restore some of the prestige of the lost Republic, and even then few would desire a simple return to the organic laws of 1875.

It is unlikely that many Frenchmen thought carefully about the nature of the new regime. In the anguish and shock of unanticipated defeat, the Republic and its hapless political chiefs, along with alleged Communist fifth column activities, became handy scapegoats for the disaster, while the Marshal appeared to most citizens as a kindly father

---

deuxième guerre mondiale, no. 81, 21ᵉ *Année* (January 1971); Stanley Hoffman, "Aspects du Régime de Vichy," *Revue Française de Science Politique*, 6 (1956); and Robert Soucy, "The Nature of Fascism in France," *Journal of Contemporary History* 1, no. 1 (1966).

[12] Michel, *Année 40*, passim. Siegfried, "The Rebirth," p. 559, argues that many civil servants worked to ease the effects of the government's policies; "The Marshal, however, was thinking too much of disciplining the French people to be thinking of France."

[13] Léon Blum, *À l'échelle humaine, Oeuvre*, vol. 5, pp. 429–38, and his letter to General de Gaulle, 15 March 1943, *Oeuvre*, vol. 5, p. 398. See also Joel Colton, *Léon Blum* (New York: Alfred A. Knopf, 1966), pp. 389–91.

[14] Marie Granet and Henri Michel, *Combat* (Paris: Presses Universitaires de France, 1957), p. 15.

[15] Charles de Gaulle, *Discours et messages*, vol. 1 (Paris: Librairie Plon, 1970), p. 205.

and savior. It is difficult to exaggerate the Marshal's popularity.[16] He was genuinely admired and revered by most Frenchmen. Even the most ardent Gaullists acknowledged the strength of Pétain's following. In one of the early "Fighting France" pamphlets designed to attract support for the Gaullist cause, Pierre Tissier admitted: "There can be no doubt that Marshal Pétain did, at first, have behind him the support of very nearly the whole nation."[17] Particularly in the southern zone, where there were no German troops to sully his prestige, a cult devoted to the Marshal soon emerged. Youth and military groups swore their fealty to the grand old man, and Pétain photographs, medals, stamps, and busts were distributed in shops all over southern France.[18] After all, something had to replace Marianne as an acceptable symbol for the new France. The new regime flooded the countryside with Pétain propaganda suitable for all ages. The Paluel-Marmont comic book *Il était une fois un Maréchal de France* began:

> Once up a time, there was a Marshal of France whose manners were so noble, look so straight and voice so soft that all—going beyond admiring him—loved him, and even those who had been his adversaries held him in great esteem.
>
> His name was Philippe Pétain. But no one ever called him that; like they said Vercengetorix or Pasteur, they said simply: Pétain.[19]

The immense and undeniable popularity of the Marshal was partially derived from the myth of the "double game" that Pétain was allegedly playing. Many felt that his apparent cooperation with the Germans was merely a cover for his behind-the-scenes activity. When the proper moment came the wise and crafty Marshal would issue a call for a rising that would expel the Nazis from French soil.[20] This

---

[16] Henri Michel, *Pétain, Laval, Darlan,* trois politiques? (Paris Flammarion, 1972), pp. 73–76.

[17] *Fighting France Pamphlets,* no. 1, *The Nazification of Vichy France* (London: Oxford University Press, 1942), p. 5.

[18] The Comité d'histoire de la deuxième guerre mondiale in Paris has preserved several cartons full of Pétain propaganda, Pétain calendars, etc. In future citations the *Comité* will be abbreviated CHG. Henri Amouroux, *La Vie des Français sous l'occupation* (Paris: Fayard, 1961). Chapter 17, "La Mystique du Maréchal," offers many colorful details and stresses the personal rather than the political nature of this attachment to the Marshal.

[19] Propaganda files in the archives of the Comité d'histoire de la deuxième guerre mondiale.

[20] Louis-Dominique Girard's *Montoire, Verdun diplomatique* (Paris:

Posters distributed in November 1940 at Lyon announcing a visit by Marshal Pétain. The notice quotes passages from Pétain's speeches which blame France's recent defeat on a shortage of men, arms, and allies, and adds that Frenchmen had been too concerned with personal pleasures and had failed to make necessary sacrifices in the national interest.

faith in Marshal Pétain was of surprising longevity, even if old idols are rarely shattered in a day. From the first the tendency was to separate Pétain from his ministers, who drew all of the blame for unpopular measures they had supposedly tricked or forced the good Marshal into underwriting.

Even some resistance journals in the southern zone made this distinction. In August 1941, *Vérités*, predecessor to the largest clandestine journal and resistance movement in southern France, wrote: "Monsieur Marshal, we beg you: Listen to the voice of tens of thousands of Frenchmen who love their country, respect you personally, but have no confidence at all in your collaborators. . . ."[21] A few months later, the same journal added: "We hope that the Marshal will be able to defend the interest of the country against

---

André Bonne, 1948) is one of the most elaborate attempts to justify Vichy's actions according to the thesis of an alleged *double jeu*.

[21] *Vérités*, no. 9 (25 August 1941).

his ministers."[22] But outside Pétain's popularity the new regime and its proposed National Revolution, attractive to certain categories of Frenchmen (particularly conspicuous among the ranks of former opponents of the Popular Front), struck relatively few responsive chords in a people who had been nurtured in a long-standing republican tradition. In the home of the Declaration of the Rights of Man, a country that had finally opted for Dreyfus and the individual against anti-Semitism, the Church, and the Army, many were repelled by anti-Semitic legislation, a catering to clerical interests, suppression of the right of assembly, dissolution of the trade unions, and a tightly controlled press.[23]

Although Vichy failed to engender great enthusiasm in the populace and was, according to some, "of all the regimes under which modern France has lived . . . the most ephemeral and possibly the least significant,"[24] still dislike was slow to develop into outright opposition. It is clear, as some of the best recent scholarship has established,[25] that most Frenchmen were neither heroic resisters nor villainous collaborators. Surely most people were principally concerned with holding a secure job to assure their next meal.[26] After all, with German troops patrolling over half of the country, thousands of refugees from the combat zones to be resettled, and a million and a half French soldiers in German prisons, was this the time to worry about parliamentary niceties? In the circumstances, most Frenchmen tried to provide for themselves and their families as best they could and probably hoped for brighter days.

In the meantime was not Pétain, who made his reputation in World War I through his concern for the lives of his men, the best hope for an early return of the prisoners? So soon after the defeat, how many families with relatives captive in Germany could be expected to pro-

---

[22] *Vérités*, no. 15 (25 October 1941).

[23] Jacques Delperrie de Bayac, *Histoire de la Milice* (Paris: Fayard, 1969) argues that all collaborationist groups were forced to draw recruits from the same limited manpower pool. See Robert Paxton, *Vichy France*, 234–41, for distinctions made between Pétain and his regime and for a view of shifts in public opinion toward Vichy.

[24] Gordon Wright, "Vichy Revisited," *Virginia Quarterly Review* 34 (1958): 501.

[25] The third chapter of Stanley Hoffman's *Decline or Renewal?*, a commentary on Marcel Ophüls's film, *The Sorrow and the Pity*, is a particularly good reflection of the personal dilemmas facing Frenchmen in this time.

[26] Granet and Michel, *Combat*, pp. 5–8.

test vigorously a political regime that promised to "bring back the boys," even if they secretly disdained its policies? Finally, was there a viable alternative? In the popular mind responsibility for the debacle fell on the former political elites as well as the generals. All of the political parties were shattered, their leaders either silent or supporters of Vichy. In short, the path of Vichy appeared inescapable. To choose resistance in 1940 seemed neither logical nor prudent. Indeed, few Frenchmen made that choice, and many months passed before the Resistance, under the influence of complex and changing circumstances, became in any sense a mass movement.

Yet, a few intransigent individuals did rebel, refusing to accept the defeat as final and rejecting collaboration with the victors. Best remembered was the call of a renegade French general in London who evoked an unyielding France that would not brook collaboration. On 18 June 1940 the BBC broadcast this historic appeal:

> I, General de Gaulle, now in London, call on all French officers and men who are at present on British soil, or may be in the future, with or without their arms; I call on all engineers and skilled workmen from the armaments factories who are at present on British soil, or may be in the future, to get in touch with me.
>
> Whatever happens, the flame of the French resistance must not and shall not die.[27]

Charles de Gaulle had decided on a "clear and terrible mission." In his own words his task was no less than "to assume the burden of France."[28] The ramifications of de Gaulle's appeal would have a tremendous impact on the later development of the interior resistance movements, but of greater immediate significance were the independent decisions of others in France. These men, no less than de Gaulle, were imbued with a sense of mission, a charge voluntarily assumed to retrieve the lost honor of their country.

Edmond Michelet, who before the war had belonged to the Cercle Duguet, an antifascist organization that aided German Catholic refugees in France, was proud to have authored one of the first Resistance tracts. On 16 June 1940 Michelet made 500 copies of his *Simple Ad-*

---

[27] De Gaulle, *Discours et messages*, vol. 1, p. 4.

[28] Charles de Gaulle, *Mémoires de guerre*, vol. 1 (Paris: Librairie Plon, 1954), p. 74.

vice on Trying to See Clearly, which warned against the impending armistice. Later Michelet recalled that his manifesto had been "absolutely spontaneous, inspired by his most profound patriotic and anti-nazi sentiments."[29] In the fall of 1940 Albert Camus expressed eloquently the feelings that led several sincere pacifists such as he to join the Resistance.

> Nothing is less excusable than war and the recourse to national hatreds. But once the war is here, it is vain and cowardly to stand aside under the pretext that one is not responsible for it. The ivory towers have fallen. Complacency is forbidden for oneself and for others.
>
> To judge an event is impossible and immoral from the outside. It is in the midst of this absurd calamity that one retains the right to despise it."[30]

For Alban Vistel, a leader of the resistance movements near Lyon, the Resistance had been a "reaction of individual honor,"[31] a stand for certain essential human values, "a victorious refusal of any historical determinism,"[32] and an affirmation of faith in a France that had incarnated the principles of liberty and the dignity of man.[33] From the Vichy government's first anti-Semitic measures, many Frenchmen who turned to the Resistance had sentiments similar to those expressed in the message that the Archbishop of Toulouse, Mgr. Jules-Geraud Saliège, on 28 August 1942 ordered read in all of his parishes.

> There is a Christian morality, there is a human morality which imposes duties and recognizes rights. These duties and rights are derived from the nature of man. . . . It is in the power of no mortal to suppress them.

---

[29] *Témoignage* of Edmond Michelet, Archives, CHG.

[30] Albert Camus, *Carnets (May 1935–February 1942)* (Paris: Gallimard, 1962), p. 172.

[31] Alban Vistel, *Héritage spirituel de la Résistance* (Lyon: Éditions Lug, 1955), p. 63. Vistel's book, especially pages 56–90, is among the most profound discussions of what motivated individual resisters in their reactions to the defeat and the Vichy regime. A shorter version, "Fondements spirituels de la Résistance," appeared in Esprit 20ᵉ Année, no. 195 (October 1952): 480–92.

[32] Vistel, *Héritage,* p. 81.

[33] Vistel, *Héritage,* p. 80.

> Children, women, men, fathers and mothers are treated like a vile herd, members of the same family are separated from each other and shipped off to an unknown destination; it has been reserved to our times to see these sad spectacles.
>
> Why does the right of asylum exist no longer in our churches? . . . In our Diocese horrible scenes have taken place. . . . Jews are men and women. Foreigners are men and women. There is a limit to what can be permitted against them; against these men, these women, against these fathers and mothers. They belong to the human race. They are our brothers like so many others.
>
> France, beloved country, France, you bear in the conscience of all your children the tradition of respect for the human person. . . . I am sure you are not responsible for these errors. . . .[34]

It is of course impossible to analyze completely the motivations of every resister, but some general comments about these first recalcitrants are possible. In attempting to explain their actions, the pioneers of the Resistance, convinced of its necessity from the first and so creators of the first organized opposition, return time and again to the twin themes of patriotism and humanism.[35] Their natural patriotic reaction to the German occupation was closely linked to a belief in the value of the individual human being. These two ideas tended to merge into a conception of France as the traditional champion of individual human worth. At the liberation the mayor of Toulouse suggested that despite their evident political divergences all the resisters had a "common patrimony" that consisted of "a profound feeling for human dignity."[36] They had carefully weighed the meaning of their patriotism and had voluntarily chosen to engage in a rather noble crusade, not so much as fanatics but instead, as one observer

---

[34] Copy of the letter reproduced in *Ville de Toulouse Bulletin Municipal* (Numéro spécial consacré à la libération de Toulouse, October 1944 [Marseille: Imprimerie Gaussel & Cie.]), p. 28.

[35] Since the war the Comité d'histoire de la deuxième guerre mondiale has collected an invaluable series of interviews with hundreds of resisters, whose *témoignages* are found in the Archives CHG. Those I have consulted are listed in the bibliography.

[36] *Ville de Toulouse Bulletin Municipal* (Numéro spécial consacré à la libération de Toulouse, October 1944), p. 12.

recalled, *"des convaincus,"*[37] with the comforting certitude that justice and honor were on their side.[38]

Changing conditions later brought to the Resistance many men simply compelled by circumstances to enlist in the underground, but most of the early organizers were men who had made a conscious choice. That the ranks of the Resistance held its quota of adventurers, oddballs, and persons on the margins of society should not obscure the seriousness of purpose that characterized its leading architects.

A later generation conditioned to scoff at idealism might be tempted to discount such an explanation, but without it no valid understanding of the original Resistance is possible. Yet their idealism should not be portrayed as mindless romanticism. Pierre Bertaux, an early resister at Toulouse, insisted: "Make no mistake, what we did was not done out of romantic spirit . . . but simply because we thought it had to be done. When one sees that there is no one there to do it, no more talk: one does what must be done."[39] In much the same manner Max Juvenal, chief of the Resistance in the region of Aix-en-Provence, remarked that many resisters felt simply that they could not leave to future generations "the heritage of a France which had accepted without opposition, the defeat, the humiliation, the injustice."[40]

Those men who took this stand for honor and justice were a mixed lot. Men and women of every class and ideological persuasion were represented in the first organizations. Adherents of the Communist party and of the Action Française were among the members of the southern zone's largest resistance movement, Combat. Although the resisters ranged over the full spectrum of society, certain elements were noticeably more prominent than others. Completely satisfactory statistics on the social composition of the Resistance are lacking, but

---

[37] Xavier de Virieu, *Radio journal libre (Juillet 1943–Août 1944)* (Paris-Lyon: Éditions Jean Cabut, 1947), p. 503.

[38] Albert Camus's "Lettre à un Allemand qui fut mon ami," published clandestinely in *La revue libre,* no. 2 (February 1944), offers an excellent illustration of the resisters' self-assurance in the justice of their cause.

[39] Pierre Bertaux, "Comment je suis devenu résistant," *Histoire de notre temps,* no. 1 (Spring 1967) (Paris: Librairie Plon), p. 212. René Cerf-Ferrière, *Chemin clandestin* (Paris: Julliard, 1968), p. 178, adds: *"Non et non,* we were not adventurers in the vulgar, pejorative sense."

[40] Max Juvenal, *Un résistant parmi tant d'autres parle à la jeunesse de son pays* (Paris: La Fédération nationale des anciens de la résistance, 1965, Supplément au Journal N° 79, 1965), p. 12.

available evidence provides a good estimate of the nature of the leadership elite.[41] The leaders were largely from the middle class, and members of the liberal professions played a major role in the early organization. Because the production of a clandestine newspaper was normally the first evidence of a movement's existence, journalists, editors, publishers, and writers were naturally prime recruits. At Lyon, the capital of the Resistance in southern France, the office of Yves Farge at the *Progrès de Lyon*, a legally published paper, was a favorite meeting place of resisters from several movements.[42]

Since public school teachers and intructors at the lycées and universities had been among the staunchest supporters of the Republic (particularly after the laicization of public instruction early in the century), they along with outspoken journalists were among the early targets of Vichy's purges and were quickly cast into the opposition. Many of the early resistance organizations in the unoccupied zone were located in such university towns as Clermont-Ferrand, which housed numerous refugees from Alsace-Lorraine, Toulouse, and Montpellier, and where both professors and students were actively engaged.[43]

As the movements began to expand, the work of organization required men who could travel from one area to another without arousing suspicion. So administrators, such as inspectors of finances, bank officials, and inspectors of public health or education, often served as recruiters and liaisons because of their relative freedom of travel.[44] Christian Pineau, a prominent prewar trade union figure and one of the founders of Libération, a northern zone movement, was delighted when Vichy appointed him to a position in the Ministry of

----

[41] See chart in Granet and Michel, *Combat*, pp. 229–30, which is the best statistical estimate of the leadership's composition. Nicholas Wahl, "De Gaulle and the Resistance" (Ph.D. diss. in Political Science, Harvard University, 1956), pp. 208ff., offers another estimate based on a survey of 114 top resisters from both zones.

[42] Yves Farge, *Rebelles soldats et citoyens* (Paris: Éditions Bernard Grasset, 1946), pp. 9–10.

[43] *Témoignages* of Albert Coste-Floret, François de Menthon, Henry Ingrand, Claude Bourdet, Henri Frenay, and André Hauriou.

[44] Document 137673 R, Records of the Organization of Strategic Services, National Archives, Washington, D.C. This report, written shortly after the liberation, also notes that doctors' and dentists' offices often were used as meeting places because they could set up appointments without arousing suspicions, even if their phones were monitored. In future citations these records will be cited as OSS Document No. ——.

Provisions (ravitaillement) that enabled him to extend his contacts for intelligence gathering.[45]

Despite years of training that had emphasized Germany as the hereditary enemy of France, surprisingly few professional military officers joined the Resistance. Among the exceptions was Henri Frenay, whose natural patriotic reaction had been to refuse compromise with the Boche and who was perhaps the single most important resistance chief in the Vichy zone, where he conceived of and organized by far the most solid resistance movement. But generally the military caste was bound by its loyalty to Marshal Pétain. Some officers in the small armistice army that the Germans allowed Vichy probably hoped that Pétain would eventually give the signal for a renewal of hostilities. Such men may well have interpreted Vichy's orders for the camouflage of certain war matériel as resistance to the conquerors. Nevertheless, after the total occupation of France in November 1942 and the birth of the first Maquis groups, which sorely lacked military cadres, most of the officer corps abstained from commitment to the Resistance. Even during the last two years of total occupation, when it was increasingly apparent that Pétain would issue no call for armed resistance, few officers were able to overcome their distaste for irregular units organized for guerrilla warfare or their suspicions about leftist political influence in the Resistance.[46]

The elite of the Resistance generally were young and rarely experienced in politics. Several of the founders of Franc-Tireur, smallest of the three major movements in southern France with which this study will be primarily concerned, had been active in the Jeune République, but this involvement was exceptional. Among the founders of Combat and Libération, the other two principal movements, few men had been active in political parties; none were professional politicians. Nevertheless, the resistance movements soon assumed a marked political cast. Since they were in opposition to both the Germans and Vichy, the movements naturally were leftist from the beginning. It could not have been otherwise, since from their viewpoint Vichy was clearly a champion of the Right, the home of conservatism and reaction. Although they adopted no party label—

---

[45] Christian Pineau, *La Simple vérité* (Paris: Julliard, 1961), p. 224.

[46] Henri Michel, "The Psychology of the French Resister," *Journal of Contemporary History* 5, no. 3 (1970): 161–64; Robert O. Paxton, *Parades and Politics at Vichy* (Princeton, N.J.: Princeton University Press, 1966), pp. 399–409, "Officers and the Underground, 1943–44."

indeed, they were most often violently opposed to the Republic's former parties—the movements stood for antifascism, republicanism, and a vague form of socialism that became more clearly defined as the months passed.[47]

The composition of the rank and file greatly strengthened this tendency. The leadership was essentially middle class, but recruitment of militants stressed the little man. Libération, which included on its directing committee representatives of the Socialist party and the Confédération Générale du Travail (CGT), was most obviously oriented toward the Left; but, the other movements also placed a major emphasis on attracting workers, students, artisans, and small shopkeepers.[48] It was precisely these groups that were most threatened when Vichy began a forced labor draft in the fall of 1942, and the Maquis formations were composed mostly of workers, students, and farmers. Thus for many the Maquis represented at first a haven from deportation. But once the movements had organized these persons, the Resistance also offered them a vision of a world in which *"liberté," "égalité,"* and *"fraternité"* would become finally *"réalité."*

Before we begin a detailed examination of the resistance movements, it is desirable that their role be viewed in its proper perspective. The resisters began their activity as a very small fraction, an "infinitesimal minority"[49] of Frenchmen. Even in its maturity the active Resistance represented only one or perhaps two of every hundred citizens.[50] The effectiveness of this small minority was greatly enhanced, of course, by the sympathy and occasional aid of many Frenchmen who took no active part in organized resistance formations. But early developments must be seen against the backdrop of

---

[47] Henri Michel, *Jean Moulin l'unificateur* (Paris: Librairie Hachette, 1964), p. 42, notes that the Resistance, especially in the South, was at first oriented toward "an antifascism *un peu in abstracto.*" We shall examine the thought of the resisters in more detail in a later chapter.

[48] OSS Document 19307 C, a report dated 3–5 July 1942, noted that this tendency was strengthened when the workers' opposition to Vichy's labor charter became evident.

[49] Henri Michel, *Histoire de la Résistance* (Paris: Presses Universitaires de France, 1950), p. 32.

[50] Peter Franklin Barnes, "The French Movements of Resistance, Portrait of a Transient Elite" (Honors thesis [B.A.], Harvard College, 1962), p. 8; Wahl, "De Gaulle and the Resistance," p. 194; and Gordon Wright, "Reflections on the French Resistance," *Political Science Quarterly* 77, no. 3 (September 1962): 337–39, concludes about 2 percent of adult Frenchmen, something over 400,000, were active in the Resistance.

an indifferent and at times hostile populace. Many Frenchmen believed that the Germans would not have shot hostages and taken other repressive measures without the provocation of resistance agitators.[51] In the early months of the Occupation, German and Vichy propaganda was fairly successful in portraying most actions of the Resistance as the work of foreigners and Communists, who, many believed, were also partially responsible for the defeat through their alleged sabotage activities.[52]

Claude Bourdet, a major leader of the movement Combat, recalled: "In the beginning, one must say, the Resistance had been the affair of an extremely small and nonconformist minority . . . for reasons accidental or fundamental, this first organization of the Resistance was the work of a handful of isolated individuals, a minority that had no contact with the masses and therefore utilized as a base small groups of comrades or friends."[53] Still, Bourdet adds the interesting observation that they really need not have been more numerous. In the early days they had no arms and no real capacity to stage effective demonstrations. In fact, they could hope for no more than that people listen to Radio London (BBC) and be favorable to the Allies.[54]

Had the Resistance remained the property of these isolated few, their sacrifices, if not in vain, would have been essentially symbolic, a martyrdom for truth, liberty, justice, and honor, enough perhaps to allow those who had participated to "look at a Russian, English or American soldier without blushing,"[55] but too little to be considered a phenomenon that touched a whole nation. The crucial factor for the

---

[51] "Rapport" of Jacques Bingen, January and February 1944, Archives, CHG.

[52] See propaganda files, Archives, CHG. The Germans almost always labeled acts of sabotage as the work of "Kommunists." This terminology appears throughout the Captured German Documents, National Archives, Washington, D.C., in the situation reports of various German occupation authorities in France. The bibliography includes a list of the reels of the Captured German Documents used for this study. Jacques Delperrie de Bayac, *Histoire de le Milice*, pp. 165–71, stresses the importance of the Communist bogey for Vichy, as does Paxton, *Vichy France*, pp. 223–28 and passim.

[53] Claude Bourdet, "Histoire de la Résistance française" (text of a lecture given 3 May 1960), in *Après-Demain*, nos. 30–33.

[54] Bourdet, "Histoire de la Résistance française." Yves Farges, *Rebelles*, p. 21, wrote: "At that time, one man per square kilometer was quite sufficient to maintain France."

[55] Roger Stéphane, *l'Observateur*, no. spécial, "Huit ans après (no. 120, 28 August 1952), p. 16.

Resistance in France was a dramatic shift in public opinion from 1940, when it was predominantly Pétainist, to 1944, when it had become clearly Gaullist and pro-Resistance.[56] The author of a study of the Resistance in the departement of l'Allier (near Vichy) suggested: "Let no one kid himself: the Resistance, in the sense of a total engagement, was the work of a small number in proportion to the whole. But the increasing, tacit adhesion of the masses seemingly 'carried' the Resistance."[57] It was extremely important that at the time of the liberation de Gaulle and the resisters took power with the enthusiastic support of and not against the will of the people.

One perceptive commentator advised:

> One cannot in fact understand the development and organization of the Resistance in France, if he does not recognize first of all that it was not a willful creation ordered from above, but a spontaneous surge from the base. From the time of the Armistice, the most perceptive and most courageous had understood the necessity for it, but being an elite, they were few in number. The numbers came afterwards: certain people enlightened by the events; many pushed by necessity, discomfort, menaces weighing on this or that category of citizens, the requisition *en masse* of the workers; finally a few attracted by a spirit of adventure that need not be considered reprehensible in the slightest.[58]

In often unexpected ways a combination of factors sometimes beyond the control of the Resistance contributed to its development. The exactions of the Germans, Vichy's conduct, the changing fate of the war, de Gaulle's activity, the actions of the resistance movements—all had a part in the evolution of public opinion.

It is probable that patriotism was the first inspiration for most in-

---

[56] Marcel Baudot, *L'Opinion publique sous l'occupation* (Paris: Presses Universitaires de France, 1960), passim. Jacques Touzeau, *La Propagande radiophonique en France pour la relève et le Service du Travail Obligatoire* (University of Paris: Diplôme d'Études Supérieures, Faculté des Lettres et Sciences Humaines de Nanterre, under Professor René Rémond), examines this process with special attention to the importance of Vichy's labor policies in the evolution of public opinion.

[57] Georges Rougeron, *La Résistance dans le département de l'Allier* (Montlucon: Typocentre, 1964), introduction.

[58] Colonel Costa de Beauregard, "Vercors 1944," *L'Armée,* no. 6 (September 1960), p. 8.

dividual commitments to the Resistance;[59] therefore, the German actions in Occupied France—indeed, their mere presence—was a primary spur to recruitment for the resistance organizations. Occupation toops and German police in the northern zone made resistance activity extremely dangerous, but their presence clearly defined the enemy. Resistance in the occupied areas meant resistance to the Boches, and from the first the resisters probably had the sympathy of a substantial part of the population. Although initially surprised by the proper conduct of most of the occupying troops, few Frenchmen were seduced by the German officers' carefully cultivated "Korrect" attitude. Financial sleight-of-hand cleverly camouflaged the economic pillage of France. With the exception of the railroads' rolling stock and war matériel, the Germans paid for almost everything they took, but the unlimited supply of *Reichskreditkassen* with which they paid was charged to the French government,[60] and the valuation of the currency was inequitable (one mark equaled twenty francs).[61] To this problem was added the indemnity the armistice required and the lodging and upkeep of the Occupation troops. The results were hard times, rationing, and an insidious black market.[62]

In addition to aggravating the economic problems of France, the line of demarcation between the two zones separated numerous families, whose correspondence was closely regulated.[63] Acts of the theoretically sovereign state at Vichy were promulgated in the northern zone only after German approval.[64] A rigorous press censorship gave rise to a new Franco-Germanic dialect, which occasionally

---

[59] Michel, "Psychology of the French Resister," pp. 168–69.

[60] Pierre Arnoult, *Les Finances de la France et l'occupation Allemande 1940–1944* (Paris: Presses Universitaires de France, 1951), especially pp. 1, 2, and 7. See also Alan Milward, *The New Order and the French Economy* (London: Oxford University Press, 1970).

[61] Henri Amouroux, *La Vie des Français*, p. 8, contains a chart indicating that the franc in 1944 was worth less than half its 1940 value, so a serious inflation added to the dislocation caused by the inequitable valuation of the franc.

[62] Jacques Delarue, *Trafics et crimes sous l'occupation* (Paris: Fayard, 1968). Première Partie: "Les dessous du marché noir"; and *Les grandes énigmes de la Résistance*, vol. 3 (Paris: Éditions Les Amis de l'Histoire, 1968), pp. 103–52: "Le livre blanc du marché noir."

[63] See *Le Journal de la France* ("De l'occupation à la libération," no. 118, 23 August 1971), p. 637, for a reproduction of the standard postcard required for correspondence across the line of demarcation.

[64] Michel, "La Révolution nationale latitude d'action," pp. 11 and 14.

amused but generally disgusted the readers of daily newspapers.[65] Despite the legacy of a strain of anti-Semitism in certain regions of France, the myth of a master race held little appeal to most Frenchmen; aside from the governing circles at Vichy and the marginal bands of fanatic collaborators in Paris led by Doriot, Déat, and Deloncle, few were pleased by the treatment of the Jews.[66] Virtually all Frenchmen were horrified by the mass executions of hostages that began in the fall of 1941.[67]

Adding insult to injury, the daily parade of German troops around the Arc de Triomphe and down the Champs-Élysées in Paris, if intended to impress or frighten the Parisians, undoubtedly served mainly to enrage them. No one was fooled; these Germans were indeed not tourists.[68] Powerless to throw out their conquerors, the people of the occupied territory would not be forced to welcome their uninvited guests. One of the great clandestine novels, *Le Silence de la Mer*, by

---

[65] The best treatments of press control include: E. Dunan, "La Propaganda-Abteilung de France: taches et organization," *Revue d'histoire de la deuxième guerre mondiale*, no. 4 (October 1951), pp. 19–32; Claude Lévy, "La Presse de collaboration en France occupée: conditions d'existence," *Revue d'histoire de la deuxième guerre mondiale*, no. 80, 20ᵉ Année (October 1970), pp. 87–100; R. G. Nobecourt, *Les secrets de la propaganda en France occupée* (Paris: Fayard, 1962); and Hans Umbreit, *Der Militärbefelshaber im Frankreich* (Munich, 1968), pp. 150ff.

[66] An "Überblick über die Betätigung politischer Vereinigungen im besetzten französischen Gebiet," Paris, 15 March 1942, in Captured German Documents, T-501, Roll 144, Frames 166–72, includes a listing and brief descriptions of the various collaborationist groups active in Paris. The conditions for French Jews in the occupied zone were clearly more hazardous than in the South, at least until the total occupation. See Michel, *Année 40*, pp. 141–45; also *Verordnungsblatt des Militärbefehlshabers in Frankreich*, vol. 2, for decrees of the occupation authorities concerning the mandatory wearing of a yellow star and other measures never extended to the southern zone. Paxton, *Vichy France*, pp. 173–85, discusses Vichy's anti-Semitism, emphasizing the special responsibility of the government in this area.

[67] Even some members of the German military expressed fears that this policy, as well as the treatment of the Jews and the economic exploitation, was unwise in that it might increase resistance to the occupant. See Captured German Documents, T-78, Roll 457, Frames 6435189–92, 6435212–3, and 6435230–33 for complaints of General von Stülpnagel about the activities of the SS in France and the intervention of Heydrich in the affair. Also Michel, "La Révolution Nationale Latitude," p. 10, notes Stülpnagel's fears that the German policies might force Pétain to resign.

[68] Colonel Passy (André Dewavrin), *2ᵉ Bureau Londres* (Monte-Carlo: Éditions Raoul Solar, 1947), pp. 114–19, reproduces some of the first clandestine tracts, the *Conseils à l'occupé*, circulated in Paris under the Occupation.

4 July 1940, German Occupation troops parade down the Champs-Élysées, a daily occurrence until the Parisian insurrection of August 1944.

Vercors (Jean Bruller) impressively portrayed a silent disdain expressed through the refusal to associate with the Germans. Vercors captured the attitude of many silent Frenchmen who felt, "these men will disappear under the weight of our contempt, and we shall not even trouble to rejoice when they are dead."[69]

Conditions in southern France were more complex than those in the North. A northern zone resistance leader, perhaps exaggerating the carelessness of the southern resisters, recounted his trip through the unoccupied zone in early 1941.

> The Resistance leaders go about openly, meet in cafés and busy restaurants, not making the slightest effort to hide. They all but have calling cards made bearing their underground titles. What they lack is a few Germans in the street. . . . In most of the tracts circulated among workers of Lyon

---

[69] Vercors, *The Silence of the Sea* (New York: Macmillan Co., 1944), p. vii. This novel was the first in a series of *"Cahiers de silence"* published by Les Éditions de Minuit, the most famous clandestine publishing house.

> factories, Germans were not even mentioned. They were so far away![70]

In fact, the absence of Occupation troops meant that the southern Resistance early developed a political nature, an appreciation of the political significance of their opposition that differed markedly from the more purely military conceptions of their northern comrades. The implications of this difference for organization of the Resistance became evident later, but before German troops arrived in November 1942, it encouraged the southern resisters to emphasize opposition to Vichy policies rather than a strictly anti-German stand.

The existence of a theoretically sovereign French government at Vichy and, more importantly, Pétain's evident popularity created an equivocal situation for the resisters. For example, some army officers, acting as patriots, undeniably camouflaged arms and ammunition, fully expecting to use them one day under Pétain's orders against the Germans.[71] We have seen that even the resisters, despite their opposition to his policies, were hesitant to attack Pétain personally, but it is perhaps worthwhile to reemphasize the personal nature of Pétain's following.

Personalities aside, the policies the Vichy regime pursued failed to evoke popular enthusiasm. Most were greeted with apathy, some with hostility. As in the response to German exactions, the resistance's ranks swelled, and sympathy for its actions grew in part as a direct result of Vichy's actions. The Marshal's prestige could not mask this general rejection of Vichy's policies. A German intelligence report, *On the Situation in unoccupied France, March, 1941,* acknowledged that Pétain's standing was "very strong"; nevertheless, it stated: "The 'average Frenchmen' are all against any collaboration with Germany." The French, asserted the German observer, would do at best the very minimum required by the armistice, and 95 percent of the people hoped for an English-American victory. Laval, "the leading advocate of cooperation with Germany," had "not 5 percent of the French behind him."[72]

Marshal Pétain's endorsement at Montoire of the policy of collaboration had dismayed many people, but many interpreted his dismissal

---

[70] Pineau, *La Simple vérité,* pp. 99–100.
[71] Michel, "Psychology of the French Resister," pp. 161–64.
[72] Captured German Documents, T-77, Roll 1027, Frame 2499476–8.

of Laval, on 13 December 1940, as a reversal of his earlier decision.[73] However, other disturbing measures were soon taken. The anti-Semitic tendencies of certain circles at Vichy resulted in legislation from the regime's first days that limited Jewish participation in the liberal professions and excluded them from any public function or any responsible position in journalism, theater, cinema, or radio. By acting in this manner *before the Germans demanded that it do so,* Vichy had hoped to affirm its administrative authority over French territory. However, in so doing Vichy provided a definition of Jew that went beyond what the Germans themselves had planned to apply at the time.[74]

Many individual Frenchmen, as human beings, were revolted by this curiously hasty anti-Semitism of Vichy, and workingmen as a class were disgruntled by the dissolution of the trade unions and the attempt by the État français to force a labor charter on all categories of workers. This Charte du Travail, a mélange of corporatism and paternalism, was a total failure, as was virtually the entire program of the so-called National Revolution.[75] One observer, who left France in November 1942, suggested that the prevailing impression was that no fundamental changes could be made legitimately while the Germans remained in France.[76] Others must have become discouraged when

---

[73] Aron, *Histoire de Vichy,* pp. 311–30; Michel, *Année 40,* pp. 359–98 and ff.

[74] Michel, *Année 40,* pp. 141–45 and Paxton, *Vichy France,* pp. 173–85. It was true that the administrators tended to apply this legislation loosely in certain areas. At the same time, however, prison camps were prepared for foreign Jews who did not receive the same sympathy given French citizens, and in North Africa, Jews were denied their traditional citizenship rights. Both of these measures went beyond any obligation imposed by the armistice. The hierarchy of the French Catholic Church, normally firm in its support of Vichy, in 1942 publicly opposed the regime's anti-Semitism.

[75] Paul Farmer, *Vichy Political Dilemma* (New York: Columbia University Press, 1955), chap. 2, and pp. 232–33; Gordon Wright, *Rural Revolution in France* (Stanford, Calif.: Stanford University Press, 1964) argues that the popular conception that the farmers supported the regime is overdrawn and that many rural elements were very active in the Resistance. OSS Documents 48195 S (24 October 1943), 19307 C (3–5 July 1942), 30321 S (6 March 1943), and 39014 C (June 1943) report the total failure of Vichy's labor policies. See also Paxton, *Vichy France,* and Durand, *Vichy 1940–1944,* passim.

[76] Émile Blamont, Report on the "Situation générale de la France à la veille de l'occupation totale," 25 November 1942, in Oudard Papers, Archives, CHG.

early hopes for a return of the French prisoners of war did not materialize in spite of Pétain's reputed concern above all for the soldiers.[77] The Marshal's reputation could not resist corrosion forever.

With Pierre Laval's return as head of government and heir apparent, in April 1942, fewer and fewer Frenchmen believed the Marshal could effectively withstand German pressure. To make matters worse, Pétain publicly announced his total support for Laval. Immediately following Laval's recall Pétain declared: "Today, at a moment as decisive as that of June, 1940, I find myself again with M. Pierre Laval with the responsibility of directing the nation's work and the European political order, the foundations of which we laid together. . . . Frenchmen, the new government will give you new reasons for belief and hope."[78] Two months later, referring to his new chief minister, the Marshal added: "There remain no clouds between us. . . . We are walking hand in hand."[79] Therefore, Pétain could not avoid incrimination along with Laval when a sizable shock-wave of public revulsion followed Laval's notorious comment on 22 June 1942: "I hope for the victory of Germany, because without it, bolshevism would tomorrow install itself everywhere."[80] Many Frenchmen may have shared Laval's fear of "bolshevism," but what most remembered and decried in his speech was the bold expression of a desire for German victory.

Finally, on 11 November 1942, after the successful American-English invasion of French North Africa, the Germans moved into southern France, meeting no opposition from Vichy. The only major

---

[77] Pierre Arnoult, and others, *La France sous l'occupation* (Paris: Presses Universitaires de France, 1959), chap. 11 by François Boudot and Jean-Marie d'Hoop, "Le problème des prisonniers et le gouvernement de Vichy," pp. 171–86.

[78] Speech of 19 April 1942, quoted in Jacques Chastenet, *De Pétain à de Gaulle* (Paris: Fayard, 1970), p. 69.

[79] Speech of 11 June 1942, quoted in Henri Noguères, *Histoire de la Résistance en France*, vol. 2 (Paris: Robert Laffont, 1969), p. 457. The return of Laval ended once and for all the southern resisters' hesitancy to criticize Pétain. In particular *Combat*, which had been the most reluctant to attack the Marshal, now bitterly denounced the myth of Vichy's double game. See *Combat*, especially the issues of May, June, July, and December 1942.

[80] G. Warner, *Pierre Laval*, pp. 301–2, notes that Pétain had personally authorized the wording of this phrase in Laval's speech, despite his later denials before the evidently averse public reaction. See *Le Procès Pétain* (Lyon: Roger Bonnefon, 1945), pp. 510–16, for Laval's explanation of this phrase and Pétain's rebuttal.

act of defiance came in the harbor at Toulon, where against the orders of Laval, the French sailors scuttled their fleet.[81] The occupation of France was now total, and Pétain had missed his last chance to play the other half of his double game. With the empire in American hands and the fleet under the waves, little justification remained for continuation of a government at Vichy. The small band of men who stayed had nothing left to bargain with; they had only to follow the orders of the Reich.[82]

It is impossible to determine the exact moment, but at some point, probably by the summer or fall of 1942, certainly by 1943, masses of Frenchmen in all parts of the country had begun to turn away from Pétain and to look for salvation by de Gaulle and the Resistance he symbolized.[83] Moreover, not content with having lost their sympathy, the Vichy regime drove many thousands of Frenchmen into active resistance with the initiation of a forced labor draft, the Service du Travail Obligatoire (STO), which entailed the deportation of Frenchmen for work in Germany. When the *relève*, a voluntary system that promised the return of one prisoner of war in exchange for three workers to man German factories, failed to produce sufficient manpower, Laval resorted to conscription, calling up complete classes of men. Work in Germany became a mandatory substitute for the former French military service.[84]

Until this time the Resistance had been largely the work of men

---

[81] Warner, *Pierre Laval*, pp. 356–57.

[82] Adrienne Doris Hytier, *Two Years of French Foreign Policy* (Paris: Librairie Minard, 1958), makes a fairly convincing case for the possibilities afforded, though missed, by the existence of a French government prior to the total occupation, but she concludes that after November 1942 no real reason justified its continuation.

[83] Yves Durand, *Vichy 1940–1944*, Part 3, "L'Évolution de Vichy," provides an excellent insight into shifts in public reaction to Vichy. Aron, *Histoire de Vichy*, says that by the summer or fall of 1942, "the vast majority of the country was hostile to the government. . . . For many French people who had been Pétainist in July, 1940, de Gaulle had now become what the Marshal had been at first: the symbol of a renascent France" (p. 507). The OSS Documents are very useful in their reflection of this evolution of public opinion. The reports are of uneven value and must be used individually with some caution, but despite a few reports to the contrary, the overwhelming impression is a very marked shift to de Gaulle, especially after the return of Laval.

[84] German observers from the Armistice Commission at Wiesbaden reported that the workers who went to Germany under the voluntary *relève* system did so in hope of material advantage more than from concern for

At Lyon's Place des Terreaux, 12 July 1942, a swearing-in ceremony for the Service d'Ordre Légionnaire, a veterans' organization committed to Pétain and the ideals of his "National Revolution." In addition to a pledge of personal loyalty to Pétain, the legionnaire's oath included the phrases "I swear to fight against democracy, Gaullist dissidence, and the Jewish leprosy."

driven by political or moral ideals. But when the STO began in the fall of 1942, the stability of many Frenchmen was first seriously disturbed. All able-bodied men from eighteen to sixty-five years of age and single women from twenty-one to thirty-five were liable for forced labor at the whim of the government.[85] Previously the city dwellers had suffered greater privations from the Occupation than had country

---

the POW's. Captured German Documents, "Lage unbesetztes Gebiet (Auswertung von Berichten der Kontroll-Inspectionen)," 31 July 1942, T-77, Roll 1027, Frames 2499982–5. Sources for the STO include the Nuremburg Trial Documents: OSS documents, Arnoult, *La France sous l'Occupation,* Jean-Marie d'Hoop, "La Main-d'oeuvre française au service de l'Allemagne," *Revue d'histoire de la deuxième guerre mondiale,* no. 81, 21e Année (January 1971), pp. 73–88; Albert Speer, *Inside the Third Reich* (New York: Macmillan Company, 1970), Alan Milward, *The New Order and the French Economy;* and Touzeau, *La Propagande.*

[85] Aron, *Histoire de Vichy,* pp. 533–35.

people, who had at least managed to eat fairly well.[86] Now, both peasants and workers were threatened. Few left for Germany of their own free will. Thousands flocked into the wooded and mountainous areas such as the Haute Savoie and the Auvergne, giving birth to the first Maquis bands. Many farmers offered food and lodging to the young refractories who were forced to live off the land as hundreds of Frenchmen passed from thought to action for the first time. The surviving resistance chiefs were unanimous in singling out the STO as the most important contributing factor in filling out the ranks of the Resistance.[87]

In January 1943, to meet the threat posed by the formation of the Maquis and the widespread opposition to the STO, Vichy created the Milice, a special repressive force composed largely of the dregs of society, but including as well some misguided patriots and even a few youths who would do anything to avoid work in Germany.[88] The Milice was headed by Joseph Darnand, a fanatical anticommunist and superpatriotic former war hero. As secretary-general for the maintenance of order after December 1943, he became the chief police officer for Vichy. Under his enthusiastic leadership the Milice showed no scruples in its pursuit of the resisters. The flimsiest suspicion warranted torture or execution for anyone suspected of aiding the Maquis. In its cruelty the Milice rivaled the Gestapo.

If the now nominal French government could thus wage a war of terror on its people, it could no longer command their support.[89] Although local administration continued to plod along,[90] apparently under the direction of Vichy, it was thoroughly infiltrated by Resistance sympathizers, and orders from above were interpreted loosely or

---

[86] Farmer, *Vichy Political Dilemma*, p. 233; Henri Raymond (alias Cesar), "Experiences of an SOE Agent in France," in *The Fourth Dimension of Warfare*, ed. Michael Elliott-Batemen (Manchester: Manchester University Press, 1970), p. 116, and Pineau, *La Simple vérité*, pp. 143–48.

[87] Cerf-Ferrière, *Chemin-clandestin*, p. 140; *témoignages* of Bourdet, Frenay, and many others; Yves Durand, *Vichy 1940–1944*, pp. 130–32.

[88] Delperrie de Bayac, *Histoire de la Milice*, pp. 172–81; Petrus Faure, *Un témoin reconte* (St. Étienne: Imprimerie Dumas, 1962), p. 137.

[89] OSS Document 62365 R, 15 March 1944.

[90] Alfred Cobban, "Vichy France," in *Survey of International Affairs, 1939–1946: Hitler's Europe*, ed. A. Toynbee and V. Toynbee (London: Royal Institute, 1954), p. 343, says: "The real government, from beginning to end of the Vichy episode, was the bureaucracy."

disregarded.[91] For example, the police were required to make random arrests in different localities with the intention of trapping resisters. A Gaullist agent reported that by early 1944 the regular French police carried out these operations very unwillingly:

> They arrest mostly those whose papers are in order and who will be released several days afterwards. I have been told of numerous cases where our comrades had been released immediately, when the police realized they were in the Resistance. . . . The regular police are violently hostile to the Milice and do everything they can against them.[92]

If slight traces of sympathy for Pétain lingered on,[93] no hint of this sentimental attachment was extended to his government. The head of government and the man generally held responsible for France's woes, Pierre Laval, was detested and almost universally condemned.[94] By the spring of 1944 the divorce between the people of France and their government was complete. As early as February 1944 an observer in Switzerland commented: "Vichy is dead . . . there is no French government in France anymore."[95]

This dramatic evolution of public opinion was largely the result of conditions within France, the product of indignation toward the occupant and its stepchild at Vichy, but the conduct of Charles de Gaulle and the fortunes of war were not without influence. De Gaulle's very obstinacy and refusal to bend even slightly where French interests were concerned, which often estranged Allied chiefs

---

[91] See Paul Durand, *La S.N.C.F. pendant la guerre* (Paris: Presses Universitaires de France, 1968), and Marcel Paul, *Histoire des P.T.T. pendant la deuxième guerre mondiale.* Four volumes (Paris: Ronéotypé by Ministère des P.T.T., 1967), for descriptions of two of the administrations most thoroughly engaged in the Resistance with accomplices at every level.

[92] Report, "L'Opinion publique," to CFLN *Commissariat à l'Intérieur* from Yvon Morandat. Received May 1944. Archives CHG; see also Warner, *Pierre Laval,* pp. 372–73, quoting a report from Knochen, a high ranking SS chief in France; also OSS Document 62365 R dated 15 March 1944.

[93] See Aron, *Histoire de Vichy,* pp. 668–70, for a description of Pétain's trip to Paris in 1944.

[94] Recall p. 22 above, a German intelligence report of March 1941 had noted the prevalence of this attitude toward Laval as early as three years before spring 1944. Paxton, *Vichy France,* p. 234, and elsewhere, cites other German testimony that Laval was "universally detested."

[95] OSS Document 56831 R.

of state, tended to win support for him among the French people.[96] From the beginning of the Occupation, de Gaulle had symbolized for many an unyielding, pure, and honorable France. His frequent speeches, along with those of the spokesman of Fighting France, Maurice Schumann,[97] were loyally followed by thousands of Frenchmen,[98] despite severe penalties for listening to the BBC.[99] Many felt that this radio propaganda was more effective and reached a wider audience than the resisters' clandestine newspapers.[100]

The first reaction of many resisters had been an attempt to join de Gaulle in London. Failing that, establishing contact with the Free French (later the Fighting French) became a primary objective of the early movements. If their viewpoints at times were sharply divergent, the interior resistance movements and de Gaulle were united in the same struggle. By 1942 all of the large, organized movements had rallied to the banner of *Fighting France*, and their loyalty to de Gaulle would remain unswerving through the liberation of France. In describing his triumphant reception at the liberation of Paris, de Gaulle was justifiably proud to recall the momentary unity of the French people, who had chosen him as the "recourse for their suffering and the symbol of their hope."[101]

A final consideration that encouraged Frenchmen to turn to the Resistance was the destruction of the myth of the invincible German armies. Certainly after their decisive defeat at the hands of the Germans, few Frenchmen had believed the British could long withstand

---

[96] Of the numerous biographies of Charles de Gaulle, those of Paul Marie de la Gorce, *De Gaulle entre deux mondes* (Paris: Fayard, 1964) and Jean Lacouture, *De Gaulle* (Paris: Éditions du Seuil, 1969) are the most satisfactory. Arthur Layton Funk's *Charles de Gaulle, The Crucial Years, 1943–1944* (Norman: University of Oklahoma Press, 1959) is excellent for de Gaulle's relations with the Allies.

[97] Schumann has published the texts of his speeches in *Honneur et patrie* (Paris: Éditions du Livre Français, 1946).

[98] Wahl, *De Gaulle and the Resistance*, pp. 179–80.

[99] *Verordnungsblatt des Militärbefehlshabers im Frankreich*, vol. 2, p. 462.

[100] Touzeau, *La Propagande*, pp. 233–35, concludes that Radio London was undoubtedly the most listened-to radio in France after 1943.

[101] De Gaulle, *Mémoires*, vol. 2, p. 311, also p. 307. Compare to Georges Bidault, *D'une Résistance à l'autre* (Paris: Les Presses du Siècle, 1965), pp. 65–67. Gordon Wright, *France in Modern Times* (Chicago: Rand McNally & Company, 1960), p. 527, notes: "The flame of the resistance seemed to have fused together all patriotic Frenchmen, producing a unity the nation had not known for a generation."

the might of the Third Reich. But England did hold, as had Russia, after absorbing horrible casualties. The Americans and British landed in North Africa and by 1943 were advancing in Italy, while the Russians began the relentless offensive that would lead eventually to the gates of Berlin. Evidently the Nazi regime was not to topple without a fight, but by 1943 hopes for that end were not without some foundation. By 1944 expectation turned to conviction, and the eventual Allied victory appeared a certainty. In a France ravaged by civil war between Resistance and Milice, only one's personal survival remained in doubt.[102]

In these conditions the final year of the Occupation brought thousands of new recruits to the Resistance, some with less than noble motivation. One Gaullist agent reported contemptuously that "there is neither a prefect nor a collaborator who does not have 'his' Jew for the postwar period . . . ,"[103] which was assumed to secure his resistance credentials in case of need. The original resisters were understandably dismayed by this influx of latecomers—the resisters of September 1944, or the *naphthalinés* (mothballs, referring to former officers whose uniforms had been packed away in cedar chests during the Occupation). A popular cartoon in the months immediately following the liberation pictured a man coming home to show his MLN (Mouvement de la Libération Nationale) card to his wife and children, with the comment: "I have just joined the Resistance."[104]

If the pioneers of the Resistance who had seen their friends and families imprisoned, tortured, deported, and murdered before the apparent indifference of many of their neighbors, may be allowed to scorn the contribution of those who turned to the Resistance at the last minute, the historian may be more charitable. A decision to join the Resistance was not a simple choice bereft of consequences. The Resistance was a dangerous game; the stakes often were life itself. By joining, one endangered not only himself but family and friends as well. It is not surprising that few possessed the uncommon courage required for such a commitment, particularly at first, when all logical estimates condemned such enterprises to futility. It was only natural

---

[102] In a report, "D'un Intellectuel résistant," to the exterior (Oudard Papers, Archives, CHG) Albert Camus urged the Allies to speed up their invasion before the elite of France was completely destroyed by severe repression.

[103] Jacques Bingen, "Rapport," November 1943, Archives, CHG.

[104] Werth, *France 1940–1955* (Boston: Beacon Press, 1946), pp. 228–29.

that for reassurance many would await changes in the war and public opinion. Furthermore, all of those whom the pioneers considered Johnny-come-latelies were not simply opportunists. Surely some, the "exploiters of the Resistance," sought economic or political advantage from their change of heart, but many who streamed into the Maquis and assisted the insurrection at the liberation were undoubtedly inspired by a feeling of patriotic duty. Perhaps they would have liked to contribute more, but limited by circumstances they were glad to have done something at least.

The interior resisters also occasionally resented those who had remained in London and Algiers, separated from the Occupation by miles of ocean, discussing the Resistance and the political future of France without a firsthand understanding of the clandestine struggle.[105] But it was clearly more difficult, for example, for a former dignitary of the Third Republic, particularly if he had been connected with the prewar Left, to organize underground activities than it was for the unknowns who composed the bulk of the clandestine leadership.[106] Indeed, some of the original resisters acknowledged the realistic limitation on their numbers, and most were less discouraged by those "resisters" of questionable motivation than they were encouraged by widespread endorsement, gratitude, and support from countless Frenchmen.

A former resister has given us a perceptive synthesis of this process in southern France. He recalls that Laval's speech of June 1942, expressings his hopes for a German victory, produced

> the great shock of revulsion among the mass of the noninvolved, who, if they were not yet ready to follow the Resistance, felt in no way desirous of a Hitlerian victory. When, in March, 1943, the STO was implemented, each family saw itself directly concerned. From then on, if the active Resistance remained the property of a minority, it was no longer isolated. Peasants could be found hiding refractories or materiel; shopkeepers supplying the Maquis; doctors caring for the injured; gendarmes and policemen warning of raids; brave people putting up in their homes those hunted by the

---

[105] Pineau, *La Simple vérité*, p. 92. Various reports of Bingen and Serreules, Archives CHG—see chap. 3 for greater detail.

[106] Bourdet, "Histoire de la Résistance française." Many prewar political leaders of the Left were either in prison or under surveillance.

police and others arriving by parachute; others offering to transmit information, to distribute tracts. . . . By tacit or formal memberships, the greatest number would make themselves accomplices. The perspectives would become those of the majority, which finished by believing itself to have always been [the majority].

And, at the end, you had more or less, in their hearts or in fact, everyone, or almost.[107]

Bearing in mind these few indications of who the resisters were, why they felt compelled to react against the Occupation and collaboration, the general political environment in which they operated, and the evolution of the public's appreciation of their activities, we shall turn to an examination of their actions—the creation of an underground nation.

---

[107] Rougeron, *La Résistance*, p. 37.

CHAPTER 2

The Mouvements Unis de la Résistance

Shortly after Pétain's request for an armistice from the victorious Germans, in cities and towns across the unoccupied zone groups of like-minded Frenchmen began to discuss the implications of their recent disaster. In the course of casual conversations, those who refused to accept the defeat as final hatched ambitious schemes for opposition to the government's policy.[1] The creation of a resistance movement usually was the work of a small band of close friends, or occasionally a family affair.

Often the creativity and leadership of one or two men made a strong impress on the movement and largely shaped its growth; indeed, for a long time the movements existed essentially in the minds of these few. Months would pass before the first resisters could transform their words into concrete actions. Rare were those who had experienced underground life. Many, if committed to action against Vichy and the Germans, simply did not know exactly what to do. One member of a small resistance movement recalled:

> Certainly we were aware of the need for action. But what action? And with whom? A long time was necessary to get to

---

[1] Germaine Tillon, "Première Résistance en Zone Occupée," *Revue d'histoire de la deuxième guerre mondiale*, no. 30 (April 1958), p. 12.

know one another, to understand one another, to establish confidence and to act between men and women who had decided to react against Pétain, against the invaders.[2]

Thus men who had specific proposals that were sufficiently bold yet credible and who possessed the will to execute their plans were destined for leadership in the nascent clandestine formations.

Inventiveness and imagination were essential to the founders of a movement. The history of the Resistance is a tale of continual improvisation. Expansion, indeed survival, of a resistance movement depended on the creative adjustments its leadership would contrive to meet the changing exigencies of clandestine life. Combat, Libération, and Franc-Tireur, the movements that during 1941 emerged as the major resistance organizations in southern France, fortunately had three leaders of exceptional quality. Of contrasting backgrounds and temperament, a serious career officer Henri Frenay, a sentimental journalist-intellectual Emmanuel d'Astier de la Vigerie, and a Jewish entrepreneur Jean-Pierre Lévy, the three founders of the Resistance in southern France, created the Mouvements Unis de la Résistance (MUR), by far the most solid non-communist resistance organization in all of France. By 1944 only the French Communist party and its appendage, the Front National, could rival the MUR's influence over the interior Resistance. But only the most sanguine observer might have suspected such a destiny from the humble origins of these movements, whose path to unity and prominence would be sometimes difficult, always dramatic.

On 13 July 1940, Henri Frenay, a young captain in the French army, crossed the demarcation line that separated Occupied France from the free zone. He had been captured during the campaign in Alsace but had escaped his German guardians and made his way through the occupied territory in time to celebrate the 14 July national holiday, Bastille Day, on unoccupied soil. Handsome, athletic, and self-confident, Frenay was a natural leader of men.[3] Instinctively

---

[2] Robert Fiat, *L'Insurgé (1940–1944)*: "Un Mouvement de Résistance Un Journal" (Essai d'Histoire pour le Diplôme d'Études Supérieures d'Histoire, 1961), Bibliothèque, CHG, p. 11.

[3] *Témoignages* of Bourdet, de Menthon, Jacqueline Bernard, Archives, CHG; Cerf-Ferrière, *Chemin clandestin* (Paris: Julliard, 1968), p. 64; Alban Vistel, *La Nuit sans ombre* (Paris: Fayard, 1970), pp. 53–55; Marie Granet and Henry Michel, *Combat* (Paris: Presses Universitaires de France, 1957), pp. 28–37.

his first steps toward underground life led Frenay to seek kindred spirits among his fellow officers at Vichy, but his approaches met with less success than he had hoped. Frenay, somewhat sympathetic to Pétain, was nevertheless resolutely opposed to the armistice that most of the officers corps felt inevitable and that some even welcomed as a blessing.[4] Frenay would not limit his opposition to the camouflage of a few weapons and await further instructions from above. His contacts with several officers at Vichy's *deuxième bureau* (the intelligence section of the French army) were fruitful in providing information for his first clandestine bulletins; but in general his military associates disapproved of his activities. On 28 January 1941 he resigned his commission to free himself for wider contacts.[5]

Imaginative but practical, Frenay wasted no time in establishing a skeleton organization of cadres. From the first, Frenay spoke with contagious enthusiasm of a mass movement to involve thousands of followers. However, Claude Bourdet, Frenay's second in command for Combat, remembered that for many months the troops were imaginary.

> Each of us was "chief" of something. Personally, I was promoted chief of Combat for the Alpes-Maritimes, and, evidently, in the beginning, I had no one under my orders.
>
> This method may appear absurd, but it was the only way possible. A clandestine situation neither permits the calling of assemblies nor the organization of elections. There was nothing to do but call oneself "chief" and set off in search of one's troops.[6]

A curious moral dilemma faced every founder of a clandestine movement. In order to secure new adherents, the pioneer chiefs were forced to lie, to exaggerate the number of their effectives, and to claim contact with the exterior and access to weapons that existed only as

---

[4] Paxton, *Parades and Politics at Vichy* (Princeton, N.J.: Princeton University Press, 1966), chap. 1, "1940: The French Army Lives On," pp. 3–38. See Philip C. F. Bankwitz, *Maxime Weygand and Civil-Military Relations in Modern France* (Cambridge, Mass.: Harvard University Press, 1967), chap. 8 and Epilogue, for the critical role of the military leadership in the demand for the Armistice.

[5] *Témoignage* of Henri Frenay, Archives, CHG.

[6] Bourdet, "Histoire de la Résistance française," *Après-Demain* nos. 30–33.

fond hopes.[7] Yet these men were pledged to a "Crusade of Truth against Falsehood, Good against Evil . . . ,"[8] and intended to brand lying in public a crime in the new France they would create.[9] But what sensible man would join a clandestine formation with no troops, no arms, no foreseeable future?

Alban Vistel, creator of La Reconquête, a small resistance organization centered in the Vienne region near Lyon and later absorbed by Libération, recalled the first meeting, in November 1940, of the fifteen or twenty volunteers who were in fact the whole movement. "If they had known that 'La Reconquête,' was they alone," wrote Vistel, "it would have been less impressive."[10] Vistel also remembered the recurrent questions from his eager young followers who as the months passed became more persistent about contact with London and de Gaulle. His ineluctable response was: "But of course we are in contact with them."[11]

Frenay's clandestine journal in 1941 bore the title *Vérités*, underscored sarcastically with a Pétain quote: "I hate the lies which have done you so much harm." One of the first and major concerns of *Vérités* and other underground papers was to offer unbiased news and opinions that could not be found in the officially sanctioned papers.[12] Surely Frenay, who signed his editorials "Véritas," must have had a somewhat troubled conscience in those early days when constant bluff and deception were essential to the expansion of his movement.

Still, Frenay's need for ruse was shorter lived than that of the other founders. Persistence and much hard work helped Combat during 1942 to clearly outstrip the other movements in southern France. The movement, directed from a central administration[13] at Lyon and

---

[7] *Témoignages* of Frenay and Bourdet, Archives, CHG.

[8] *Combat* no. 1 (December 1941).

[9] *Combat* no. 34 (September 1942).

[10] Alban Vistel, *La Nuit*, p. 36.

[11] Ibid., p. 38; Vistel, *La Nuit*, pp. 30–39, offers a very perceptive insight into the question of the psychological effects on the chiefs of their deliberate deception and resultant bad consciences.

[12] See *Vérités* no. 1, and later issues for box under the title, containing a statement of intentions, which expressed the motivations inspiring the underground newspaper.

[13] Along with Frenay, other important directors of Combat included Berthie Albrecht, Jean-Guy Bernard, Claude Bourdet, François de Menthon, Pierre-Henri Teitgen, General Bertin-Chevance, Marcel Degliame, and Guillain de Bénouville.

theoretically separated into military and political sections, was organized by national services, each headed by a national director. Among the most important political or civil services were: ROP (Recruitment, Organization, Propaganda), charged with the clandestine journal; a counterfeiting service to produce facsimiles of documents, such as ration cards, visas, or other frequently demanded personal identification; and the NAP (Noyautage des Administrations Publiques), a creation of Claude Bourdet, which sought out accomplices at all levels of the Vichy administration to sabotage and prepare the overthrow of the government from within.[14]

As one might suspect, Frenay's first thought was to build a secret military force. Much of his original effort centered on the establishment of groups of six and thirty (the *sixaines* and *trentaines*) to form the embryo of a powerful military organization that, when supplied with arms, could assume a major role in the future liberation of France. The Secret Army (Armée Secrète or AS), whose creation was decided in the fall of 1942 following agreement with de Gaulle to place all paramilitary elements of the southern movements under centralized control, was patterned with little or no alteration on Frenay's organization for Combat. Frenay's movement also provided 75 or 80 percent of the effectives in the AS.[15]

In contrast to the Secret Army, whose forces, unarmed and often untrained, were generally considered a reserve for D-day, the Groupes Francs (GF) were devoted to immediate, direct action. Originally the invention of Jacques Renouvin, a university professor violently opposed to collaboration and associated with the movement Liberté, the Groupes Francs became a service of Combat when in November 1941 Liberté fused with Frenay's Vérités (or Mouvement de Libération

---

[14] *Témoignage* Bourdet, Archives, CHG. My discussion of the origins of Combat, as well as the other two leading movements, is based to a large extent on the many *témoignages* collected by the Comité d'histoire de la deuxième guerre mondiale. They are too numerous to cite repeatedly, but a list of those I have consulted is found in the bibliography. They will be cited individually where they have been particularly valuable. Granet and Michel, *Combat,* offer a much more elaborate discussion of the movement's organization than space permits here.

[15] Granet and Michel, *Combat,* pp. 28–33 and 226–27; for statistics on the size of the Secret Army in October 1943 see table reproduced in *La France et son empire dans la guerre,* vol. 2 (Paris: Éditions Littéraires de France, 1947), p. 118.

Nationale, its official designation) to form Combat. Renouvin, a sensitive, devout Catholic, did not like the idea of killing people,[16] and the Groupes Francs' early actions were intended more to embarrass collaborators than to harm them physically. The groups issued warnings before blowing up newsstands that sold collaborationist journals, and some of their raids were more comical than destructive. For instance, at Montpellier the citizenry awoke one morning to find their statue of Louis XIV decorated with the message: "I would never have collaborated."[17] (The indelible paint resisted all efforts to remove it.) By the end of 1942 Renouvin had organized about eight hundred handpicked men in *sixaines* that carried out frequent, spectacular raids in every region of southern France.[18]

In addition to the services of the Groupes Francs, Frenay gained from the fusion with Liberté a broadened social base for his movement. Most of Frenay's early recruits had derived from his military contacts, but François de Menthon, a professor of law at the University of Montpellier and founder of Liberté, had recruited most of his following in intellectual and Christian Democratic circles. The blending of these elements and the addition of numerous working-class people by means of an intensive recruitment campaign in 1942[19] made of Combat the most heterogeneous major resistance movement in southern France. Ideologies and social backgrounds in the movement ranged from a prewar Action Française militant, Guillain de Bénouville, Combat's national director responsible for relations with the exterior, to the young Communist Marcel Degliame, head of

---

[16] *Témoignages* of Frenay, Archives, CHG; Camus, *"Lettre à un allemand qui fut mon ami," La Revue Libre* no. 2 (February 1944) expressed eloquently the feelings of many of the original resisters who found it very difficult to kill other human beings, even though they were the enemy.

[17] Granet and Michel, *Combat*, pp. 58–62.

[18] *Témoignage* of Frenay, Archives, CHG. Frenay stated: "Renouvin had accomplished a work which had no equivalent in the Resistance at that time." See also *témoignage* of Bourdet, Archives, CHG; Madeleine Baudoin, *Histoire des Groupes Francs (M.U.R.) des Bouches-du-Rhône* (Paris: Presses Universitaires de France, 1962).

[19] OSS Document 19307 C. A report dated 3–5 July 1942 noted: "Bourgeois and more or less military" in origin (that is, not issued from the working class), since the past winter the movements "are orienting themselves . . . towards the world of labor, which, against the expectations of [the movements'] founders, has become an essential element of the Resistance." Thus Libération was insisting on its ties with the workers, and Combat had a labor chronicle in its clandestine newspaper.

Combat's Action Ouvrière (Workers' Action), who had been active in prewar labor conflicts.[20]

As the moment of fusion with Libération and Franc-Tireur approached, Combat had perhaps 70,000 or 75,000 people actively involved at some level of its organization.[21] Most significantly these militants were incorporated in a well-structured movement with a sophisticated specialization of functions then unparalleled in France's clandestine world. Frenay recalled that in December 1942, for the total of its services at the national level, Combat had 102 people living completely underground. "That is to say, we had, by that date, arrived at a true administration of the underground."[22] In comparison, Libération and Franc-Tireur were loosely organized and much smaller.[23]

Emmanuel d'Astier de la Vigerie, raised in a royalist milieu, had championed Maurras and the Action Française in his early years, but during the interwar years he had drifted steadily leftward. After seven years in the navy d'Astier resigned in 1926 to pursue a literary career. He was a fairly successful journalist with frequent commissions from various journals and reviews, and his support for the Popular Front and coverage of the Spanish Civil War and the Nuremburg rallies of 1938 had left him firmly antifascist. A charming and seductive conversationalist, his occasional inconsistency and refusal to adopt intran-

---

[20] *Témoignages* of Frenay and Bourdet, Archives, CHG; Bénouville, *Le Sacrifice du matin* (Paris: Robert Laffont, 1947) and Alban Vistel, *La Nuit* are excellent for explanations of the nonsectarian nature of the resisters' clandestine fraternity. Also Cerf-Ferrière, *Chemin clandestin*, pp. 178–80, who laments the loss of this brotherhood after the war.

[21] An evaluation of the numbers involved in any clandestine organization is a tricky business, and all conclusions can be only tentative. Leaders were always inclined to exaggerate strength in order to receive more aid from London or Algiers, and, as we have seen, even lied to members of their own movements in order to boost their recruitments. The circumstances evidently did not permit a careful accounting of membership, and even if rolls had been kept it would be difficult to decide how many adherents were in fact active militants. Henri Frenay, *témoignage*, Archives, CHG, suggests that Combat had 70 to 75,000 militants at the time of its fusion with Libération and Franc-Tireur. Granet and Michel, *Combat,* come to about the same conclusion, 70 to 100,000, based on evidence aside from Frenay's *témoignage*.

[22] *Témoignage* of Frenay, Archives, CHG.

[23] Henri Guillermin, Guillermin Papers, Archives, CHG, remembered joining Combat, because Franc-Tireur could not supply the material support he desired for sabotage, etc.

sigent positions encouraged some to suspect him of dilettantism, but others recognized instead the nonconformist nature of an intellectual.[24]

D'Astier's first attempt to counter the occupant and Vichy lasted barely two months before the police struck in January 1941. His early movement, La Dernière Colonne, was oriented toward direct military action, in hope of sabotaging the supply of Italian troops.[25] Tempered by misfortune, d'Astier set out to construct something more durable than La Dernière Colonne, which at the time of its destruction involved at most one hundred people.[26]

The most conspicuous characteristic of d'Astier's new movement, Libération, was its leftist political orientation. To many resisters opposition to Vichy's conservative National Revolution was by definition leftist, and d'Astier and his colleagues[27] made a conscious effort to attract a solid working-class base. In November 1941 a message from Léon Jouhaux, head of the CGT, appeared in Libération's clandestine journal, and in all the following issues a special section devoted to the workers witnessed the success of d'Astier's contacts with syndicalist leaders.[28] Libération also assured the clandestine production of *Le Populaire*, the Socialist newspaper. Thus the movement had links with the largest political parties and leading union organizations.

The CGT, the CFTC (the Catholic trade union), and the CAS (Comité d'Action Socialiste—the clandestine executive of the former Socialist party, SFIO) were all represented on Libération's directing committee. And secretary general of the CAS, Daniel Mayer, following directives from the imprisoned Léon Blum,[29] encouraged Socialist militants to join the resistance movements rather than attempt to

----

[24] *Témoignages* of Lévy, Frenay, Bourdet, Louis Terrenoire; Interview Pascal Copeau, 22 January 1970; Louis Martin-Chauffier, "Quand naissait 'Libération'," *Le Figaro littéraire*, no. 972 (3–9 December 1964), pp. 1, 19; Alban Vistel, *La Nuit*, pp. 70–74.

[25] *Témoignage* of Emmanuel d'Astier, Archives, CHG; others realized the practical limitations on military action, and the movement also produced a clandestine newspaper and several tracts for propaganda. See also *témoignages* of Georges Zerapha and Lucie Aubrac, Archives, CHG.

[26] *Témoignage* of d'Astier, Archives, CHG.

[27] The principal directors of Libération, aside from d'Astier, included Lucie and Raymond Aubrac, Roger Massip, Louis Martin-Chauffier, Jean Cavaillès, and later Pascal Copeau, Pierre Hervé, and Alban Vistel.

[28] *Libération* (November 1941); Alban Vistel, *La Nuit*, pp. 76–77.

[29] Daniel Mayer, *Les Socialistes dans la Résistance* (Paris: Presses Universitaires de France, 1968), passim, repeatedly notes that the CAS sought

Henri Frenay, head of the movement Combat. At the liberation he was the minister responsible for the return and relocation of prisoners and deportees.

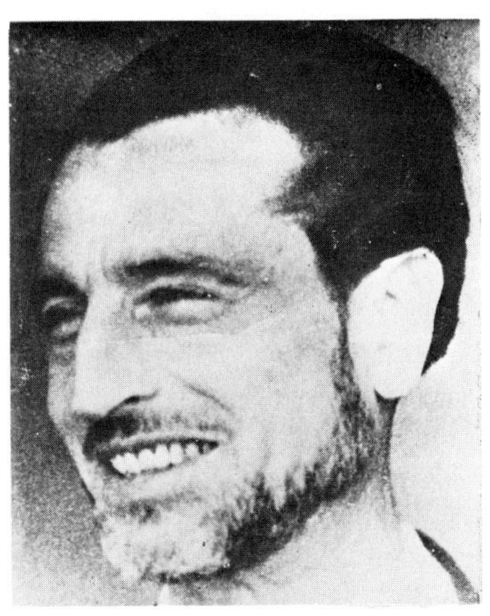

Emmanuel d'Astier de la Vigerie, head of the movement Libération. D'Astier was Minister of the Interior for a brief period during the liberation.

Jean Moulin, founder of the National Resistance Council (CNR), the man most responsible for unifying the Resistance in France. Arrested at Caluire, 21 June 1943, he was tortured to death by the Gestapo.

Jean-Pierre Lévy, head of the movement Franc-Tireur. Lévy was Franc-Tireur's first representative on the MUR's Directing Committee.

reconstruct the SFIO. As a result of this agreement, Socialist militants were probably the largest single group active in Libération,[30] and they were well represented in the other major movements of southern France.

Libération was not only the most consciously leftist southern movement, but also the first interior resistance movement to declare itself openly Gaullist in the May 1942 issue of its journal.[31] This commitment had been facilitated by the mission of Yvon Morandat, the first Gaullist agent sent into southern France. Morandat had arrived in the fall of 1941 with orders to contact syndicalist leaders to secure their support for de Gaulle. Departmental secretary of the CFTC in Savoie before the war, Morandat discovered Libération through his syndicalist friends and was so pleased with its political orientation that he went beyond his orders from London, joined the movement, and became an important member of its directing committee.[32] Morandat's influence, plus d'Astier's personal voyage to London in the spring of 1942, convinced the directors of Libération that they should endorse Charles de Gaulle as the symbol and leader of the Resistance.[33] Franc-Tireur and Combat made this same commitment later, but their early development, like that of Libération, was independent and unaided by de Gaulle's movement in London.

In contrast to Combat, Libération's range of activity was small. Certainly by the end of 1942 it had begun to expand; for example,

---

and followed Blum's advice on every decision faced by the clandestine party up to Blum's deportation. See Colton, *Léon Blum* (New York: Alfred A. Knopf, 1966), chaps. 14, 15, and 16, for Blum's wartime experiences.

[30] Noguères, *Histoire de la Résistance*, vol. 2 (Paris: Robert Laffont, 1966), says the Socialists provided 40 percent of Libération's membership. See also Colonel Passy (André Dewavrin), *10 Duke Street Londres* (Monte-Carlo: Éditions Raoul Solar, 1947), pp. 116, 258–61, and Colonel Passy (André Dewavrin), *Missions secrètes en France* (Paris: Librairie Plon, 1951).

[31] *Libération* (May 1942); Alban Vistel, *La Nuit*, p. 93; *témoignage* of Morandat, Archives, CHG.

[32] Alban Vistel, *La Nuit*, pp. 83–88; Michel, *Jean Moulin l'Unificateur* (Paris: Librairie Hachette, 1964), pp. 64–65; *témoignages* of Morandat, d'Astier, and Lévy. Lévy says that Morandat also helped Franc-Tireur, and at one point literally kept them from going under completely from lack of funds.

[33] Of course, Libération was by this time receiving direct financial assistance from London, as were the other movements, through de Gaulle's *délégué général* Jean Moulin.

Raymond Aubrac was organizing paramilitary groups consciously modeled after Combat's pattern.[34] But essentially Libération's major role was propaganda, its first concern the production of its clandestine journal.[35] In fact, this situation was not unique to Libération. For all of the resistance movements, especially those in southern France where political persuasion was more critical than in the occupied zone, the clandestine newspapers were extremely important. Before Laval instituted the forced labor draft, the underground papers were the movements' best recruiters.[36] Usually the most important leaders of the movement were the chief editors of the journal.[37] Even Combat with its multiple services and complex structure was for a long time primarily concerned with propaganda. The distribution of the journal depended on the organization of the AS's *sixaines* and *trentaines*. The Secret Army was for all practical purposes an unarmed and potential force until 1944. Claude Bourdet recalled:

> For most people, even those belonging to the organized Resistance, receiving packages and distributing journals long constituted the only material actions that they could perform. . . . Finally, the press was the only thing which gave to an individual in one part of the country the feeling that he was part of a national organization, [a fact] which was capital from the standpoint of morale.[38]

---

[34] *Témoignage* of Aubrac, Archives, CHG, admitted that he followed Combat's example when he established Libération's first AS groups, and added that Libération's military organization was "somewhat anarchic."

[35] Jacques Eschalier, *Étude de presse clandestine: Le Journal "Libération" zone sud, 1941–1944* (Faculté des Lettres et des Sciences Humaines de Paris, Année Scolaire 1961–1962, Diplôme d'Études Supérieures-Histoire Contemporaine), pp. 1–2.

[36] Cerf-Ferrière, *Chemin clandestin*, pp. 171–72.

[37] Eschalier, *Le Journal "Libération"*; for *Combat*, *témoignages* of Frenay, Bourdet and especially Jacqueline Bernard, Archives, CHG; also Jacqueline Bernard, "The Background of *The Plague*: Albert Camus' Experience in the French Resistance," *Kentucky Romance Quarterly* 14, no. 2 (1967): 165–73; and Cerf-Ferrière, *Chemin clandestin*, who was editor-in-chief of *Combat* until he left for Algiers in 1943; for Franc-Tireur, *témoignages* of Antoine Avinin and Lévy; in northern France, Christian Pineau, one founder of Libération-Nord, was alone responsible for the entire content of many of the original issues.

[38] *Témoignage* of Bourdet, Archives, CHG.

This statement should not suggest that the Resistance was primarily an intellectual game.[39] The distribution or even the reading of a clandestine journal was punishable by hard labor or sometimes death.[40] The men involved had to be intensively dedicated. For many the Resistance was the most meaningful and most dangerous experience of their lives. Referring to the patriotic self-sacrifice that inspired most of the first resisters to flirt with the dangers of a clandestine existence, one witness noted:

> Their first gesture had been to renounce bourgeois comforts, to leave their homes, their peaceful life and familiar habits and embrace a life full of discomfort and hazards, but necessary. "Do what one must, come what may," the slogan of Chivalry survived in the Resistance.
>
> For an intimate satisfaction, which was worth, it is true, any treasure, and for the hope of a regenerated France, men sacrificed their lives. No exaltation in this offering: no rank, nor medals, nor flags flapping in the breeze, nor marching music, not even uniforms; but an obscure combat, often poorly armed, a bullet in the neck at the corner of a street, solitary agony in a forest, mutilation in the torture chambers, an anonymous death the grandeur of which would remain unknown. . . .[41]

---

[39] Walter Lipgens, "European Federation in the Political Thought of Resistance Movements during World War II," *Central European History* 1, no. 1 (March 1968), implies that before 1945 the Resistance was for the most part strictly literary. But Lipgen's interpretation suffers from a failure to differentiate clearly between the various national resistances. His article also reveals the dangers of concentrating on the "ideas of the Resistance" without taking into account the close interrelationship of thought and action in the history of the Resistance. Certainly one completely misses the spirit of the Resistance in not understanding the primacy of action. See Michel, *Les Courants de pensée* (Paris: Presses Universitaires de France, 1962), p. 2. "The Resistance was first of all an action."

[40] See *Verordnungsblatt des Militärbefehlshabers in Frankreich* 2, nos. 51–84 (January 1942–February 1943): 462–63, for decrees to this effect by the German occupation authorities.

[41] Virieu, *Radio journal libre* (Paris-Lyon: Éditions Jean Cabut, 1947), p. 505. Pineau, *La Simple vérité* (Paris: Julliard, 1961), pp. 15–23, recounts some of the mental anguish, especially the fear of talking if arrested, that was constantly with the resisters, but adds (p. 92): "Curious fact, none of us imagined, despite the arrests and spectacular executions, that something could happen to us. This does not show our courage, but rather that unconsciousness which constitutes the morphine of adventure."

Certainly, there is much truth in this description, but at best it gives only a partial, rather romantic understanding of the Resistance. At first there were few *permanents*, and the average militant of Libération, Combat, or Franc-Tireur was not a full-time resister. Most resisters maintained their legal status as long as possible. Resistance work was done after hours, at least until the moment when news that the police were on his or her trail forced the conspirator to adopt a new identity.[42] Louis Martin-Chauffier, one of the editors for *Libération*, remembered: "One does not exactly have the sentiment of being underground when he continues to live at home and under his own name. In our house at Collonges, where we remained from May 1941 until May 1944, everyone was involved—parents, children, friends."[43] Despite the risks they ran, many resisters enjoyed lighter moments in their clandestine fraternity. Henri Frenay recalled that the necessary counterpoint to the austerity and dangers was "many happy hours, in an atmosphere of joyous exaltation . . . games with wild laughing, evenings full of gaiety in the apartment of Mlles. Buisson," even "pillow fights when the youthfulness of his comrades was unbridled."[44]

The third of the southern zone's major resistance movements, Franc-Tireur,[45] assumed its new name in December 1941, with the first printing of its clandestine journal, a "monthly in so far as possible and by the grace of the Marshal's police." After the occupation of southern France in November 1942, "and the Gestapo" was

---

[42] Françoise Bruneau, *Essai d'historique du mouvement né autour du journal clandestin "Résistance"* (Paris: S.E.D.E.S., 1951), p. 205, notes: "Its militants [the Resistance's troops] were overall, neither adventurers, nor extraordinary men, but rather good citizens. They acted at their jobs and within their family, against the military forces of the enemy, if they could, against the Nazi methods, if they had an occasion. . . . Without doubt they would have been happy to have done much more, but they were happy to have done something."

[43] "*Quand naissait 'Libération'*," pp. 1, 19.

[44] *Témoignage* of Frenay, Archives, CHG; in *Combat*, Marie Granet devotes Chapter 6, "L'Action: Clandestinité, arrestations . . . trahisons," to an excellent discussion of the vicissitudes of underground life. Also Farge, *Rebelles, soldats et citoyens* (Paris: Éditions Bernard Grasset, 1946), Bénouville, *Le Sacrifice*, and Pineau, *La Simple vérité* are particularly good for giving a sense of their clandestine existence.

[45] Sources for the early development of Franc-Tireur include the *témoignages* of Lévy, Avinin, Hervé Monjaret, Archives, CHG; Alban Vistel, La Nuit, and Noguères, *Histoire de la Résistance*, vol. 2; a scholar at the Comité d'histoire is now preparing a monographic study of the movement.

added to this comment that appeared under the title of each issue. The movement, centered at Lyon, grew out of several small groups that distributed tracts and a very small typewritten paper called *France-Liberté*. The leaders included former Radicals, members of La Jeune République, and two ex-Communists.[46] In contrast to Combat and Libération, Franc-Tireur's directors were usually men of some experience in politics, often with well-developed political philosophies. Thus it was natural that from its first issue *Le Franc-Tireur* adopted a definite political tone. Outspokenly democratic and republican, *Le Franc-Tireur*, unlike the journals of several of the early southern movements, never catered to those who put their faith in Marshal Pétain's double game.[47] In January 1942 *Le Franc-Tireur* claimed that Pétain's desire for personal power was the number one cause of defeat in 1940, and added:

> We know very well that in offering all this we are breaking with the current hypocrisy which claims that Laval, Darlan, Pucheu are the traitors and that the "Vieux Maréchal" can do nothing about it. . . . No, no, if Laval and the others have easily wallowed in treason, it is because Marshal Pétain . . . serves as chloroform to the French Resistance, covering with his name and his general's stars all of their acts, even the worst.[48]

Curiously, in this politicized movement, its *patron* was an exception, with no real political experience. Jean-Pierre Lévy, a Jewish technician, who before the war was commercial director of a firm in Alsace, was introduced into the brain trust of France-Liberté several months after its founding. The dynamic new recruit soon impressed the movement's founders. By the end of 1941 when the decision was made to produce a regular journal, Lévy was already one of the two most important chiefs of Franc-Tireur. When the other leader, Antoine Avinin, was arrested in March 1942, Lévy became unquestionably the movement's dominant personality.[49]

---

[46] The principal directors included Antoine Avinin, Eugène Claudius-Petit, Albert Bayet, Auguste Pinton, Noel Clavier, Élie Péju, and Jean Soudeille, as well as the *patron*, Jean-Pierre Lévy. Marc Bloch, the eminent medieval historian, and George Altman later joined the directory.

[47] *Témoignage* of Avinin, Archives, CHG.

[48] *Le Franc-Tireur*, no. 2 (January 1942).

[49] Avinin was released in June, then headed Franc-Tireur in Toulouse before moving on to very important responsibilities with the MUR on the national level.

Some of the original founders seasoned, as we have noted, in prewar politics and accustomed to normal democratic procedures were occasionally offended by their chief's tendency to make vital decisions without consulting the directing committee. One, Jean Jacques Soudeille, abandoned Franc-Tireur when Lévy, without consulting the other directors, met at Vichy with a high-ranking officer who had ambitions to leadership in the Resistance.[50]

Actually, Lévy's behavior as head of Franc-Tireur was not unique. Georges Zerapha, one of the founders of Libération and earlier the chief of La Dernière Colonne at Marseille, broke with d'Astier in 1942 because of a similar conflict. Zerapha later said: "He did not like the dictatorial procedures with which he [d'Astier] conducted the movement. He demanded explanations, wanted the committee to meet and be advised of the activities of the movement, while d'Astier did everything without saying anything and by his cleverness, managed to have it all accepted."[51]

These antagonisms illustrate two crucial aspects of relations between individuals in a clandestine environment. The chiefs were all-powerful in decision making, but all their troops were volunteers. All of the movements were similar in their conception of leadership. The conditions of clandestine life imposed on the resister a set of values that was different from those he had known previously. Union, discipline, and obedience appeared to be essential, and a certain mystique of the chief often emerged. The chiefs, who had personally recruited many of their followers and created their separate organizations, were very jealous of their prerogatives.[52] Leaders "took a stance on all problems, outlined strategy, formulated the policies and, like the true rebels that they were, thrown into a struggle from which they had little to hope for, never did they acknowledge any master."[53]

Essentially Frenay, d'Astier, and Lévy were dictators over their clandestine empires. When they consulted their directing committees it was by choice, not necessity, especially after formation of MUR, when

---

[50] *Témoignage* of Lévy, Archives, CHG; Noguères, *Histoire*, vol. 2, p. 627.

[51] *Témoignage* of Zerapha, Archives, CHG.

[52] See Granet and Michel, *Combat*, pp. 129–31, for the relationship between Frenay and the directing committee. This same relationship existed in most of the movements. See Cerf-Ferrière, *Chemin clandestin*, pp. 82–85, 89–90, for an expression of some qualification of the extent of the founder's power.

[53] Henri Michel and Mirkine-Guetzévitch, *Les Idées politiques et sociales de la Résistance* (Paris: Presses Universitaires de France, 1954), pp. 19–21.

the *patrons* or their seconds made all of the important decisions in meetings of the MUR's Directing Committee. After the fusion they felt that no reason remained for the existence of several directing committees, since the separate movements could not dispute the leaders' common decisions.[54]

However, every resister had volunteered, and his engagement signified faith in the leadership. If he lost faith the resister might simply withdraw his commitment. This peculiar bond of trust between the leader and led meant that the prudent chief would explain his actions whenever possible.[55] A note of instruction to the departmental Maquis heads of the MUR in October 1943 included this interesting order.

> Sort out implacably your *chefs de camp*. They must be leaders in every sense of the word. They will not be leaders because you have designated them as such, but only if they really know how to win and retain the confidence of their men. . . . The chiefs must understand that their men are not machines, but human beings like them, having their personalities, their pride, their qualities, and their faults. The *chefs de camp* must obtain discipline through their personal prestige and must make the effort to understand their men.[56]

Later, in the days just before the Allied invasion of France, when strict discipline was critical for the accomplishment of numerous sabotage missions, we find another interesting note of the military organization in Limoges from the MLN (Mouvement de la Libération Nationale—the enlarged MUR). "Principles of Action: (a) The chief is elected by the troops who place their confidence in him, and only after that, invested of an authority from higher up. . . ."[57]

Serge Asher-Ravanel, an MUR chief with national responsibilities, explains why in April 1944 he was forced to stay in Toulouse as

---

[54] Passy, *Missions secrètes en France*, p. 223. Also *témoignages* of Frenay and Bourdet, Archives, CHG.

[55] Capitaine Poitau, "Guerilla en Montagne," *Revue Historique de l'Armée* no. 3 (1968): 169–70, offers a good example of the *esprit de corps* developed by the conditions of clandestine life, when chiefs and troops shared the same discomforts and all common experiences.

[56] Note *Pour les responsables départementaux Maquis*, October 1943, p. 2, Papers of Alban Vistel, Archives, CHG.

[57] Abel Doysie, "*La Résistance dans la région de Limoges*" (a large mostly manuscript dossier, grouped by *départements, found in Bibliothèque*, CHG), p. 9.

regional chief of the FFI (Forces Françaises de l'Intérieur), although
he had been sent to install another officer. "In the course of discussions which lasted two days, I was obliged to acknowledge that our
comrades refused absolutely to accept this nomination. (We were
dealing with 'volunteers.' The notion of discipline necessitated convincing those interested and obtaining their accord.)"[58] Such a situation might easily lend itself to anarchy, and possibly many career
officers were hesitant to joint Maquis units for this very reason.[59] Most
often, though, especially when civilian leaders were involved, this fluid
relationship was satisfactory to both chiefs and followers.

Henry Ingrand, regional MUR chief for the Auvergne, remembered
that his troops were disciplined volunteers[60] who, having freely agreed
to their status, could be relied on to carry out his orders in the best
possible conditions of morale. There were no draftees in the Resistance. We shall see that these same relationships existed in the organization of the MUR, where mutual confidence at all stages of the
hierarchy meant considerable local initiative within the framework of
a theoretically centralized control.

When the Germans occupied southern France in November 1942,
the three movements that later formed the Mouvement Unis de la
Résistance were solidly implanted. By no means mass movements,[61]
Franc-Tireur, Libération, and Combat nevertheless had established
branches in all the regions of southern France and possessed seasoned
clandestine leadership ready to incorporate the flow of new adherents,
which increased steadily after the arrival of the Germans. Since the
movements had grown by a repeated process of absorbing smaller

---

[58] Serge Asher-Ravanel, "Le récit du colonel Ravanel," *l'Express* (26
March 1959): 7–9. Ravanel adds that similar nominations were treated in
the same fashion at Limoges and Montpellier. "They were not imposed on
the local resisters but made with their full accord."

[59] Michel, "The Psychology of the French Resister," *Journal of Contemporary History* 5, no. 3 (1970): 161–64; Paxton, *Parades and Politics at
Vichy*, pp. 3–38; and Colonel Costa de Beauregard, "Le Vercors," *L'Armée*
no. 6 (September 1960): 10–12.

[60] Interview Henry Ingrand, 11 March 1970.

[61] I have estimated Combat at about seventy-five thousand adherents in
January 1943. Franc-Tireur had perhaps thirty thousand at the same date,
according to the *témoignage* of Jean-Pierre Lévy and Henri Michel's
Histoire de la Résistance (Paris: Presses Universitaires de France, 1950),
p. 21. Libération undoubtedly had more followers than Franc-Tireur, but
numerically and structurally counted for less than Combat (Passy, *10 Duke
Street Londres*, and Passy, *Missions secrètes en France*).

local groups and uniting with larger forces, it seemed natural that the chiefs and militants would eventually pool their resources in one organization. Until superseded by more important positive elements, a combination of negative factors retarded their progress toward union. We need not trace in detail all of the steps leading to the creation of the MUR,[62] but shall consider some of the components that either inhibited or aided the process.

One primary ingredient was the barely concealed antipathy between d'Astier and Frenay.[63] Their differences in temperament and political outlook were compounded by an important disparity in the size of their movements. D'Astier declined to attend the November 1941 meeting in which Liberté and Vérités decided to join forces, in part at least because he feared Frenay's well-organized movement might dominate Libération.[64] But beyond the apprehensions about Combat's physical predominance, which Jean-Pierre Lévy also shared,[65] were reservations due to conflicting political stances. Both François de Menthon and Frenay had long refrained from attacking Marshal Pétain in their clandestine journals, and Frenay maintained some contacts with members of the Armistice Army at Vichy even after he resigned his position there.[66] The suspicions of Libération and Franc-Tireur members that Combat was a conservative or, as some claimed, reactionary movement, thus gained credence.[67]

Most damaging of all was a series of talks that Frenay had with

---

[62] This has been done very ably by Henri Michel in *Combat* and *Jean Moulin*; also useful are Passy, 2ᵉ *Bureau Londres* (Monte-Carlo: Éditions Raoul Solar, 1947) and *10 Duke Street Londres*; the *témoignages* of Frenay, d'Astier, and Lévy and their seconds Avinin, Bourdet and Copeau (interview, 23 January 1970), Jacques Soustelle, *Envers et contre tout*, vols. 1 and 2 (Paris: Robert Laffont, 1947 and 1950), and de Gaulle, *Mémoires*, vols. 1 and 2 (Paris: Librairie Plon, 1954 and 1956), especially documents appended to volume 2.

[63] *Témoignages* of d'Astier, Bourdet, Frenay, and Lévy, Archives, CHG.

[64] Alban Vistel, *La Nuit*, p. 78.

[65] *Témoignage* of Lévy, Archives, CHG.

[66] See issues of *Vérités* and first numbers of *Combat*. This position was not due to any special predilection for Pétain. Frenay claims he was strongly Gaullist long before he left Vichy (*témoignage* of Frenay), and de Menthon (*témoignage*, Archives, CHG) explained that they merely felt, given Pétain's vast popularity, that frontal attacks on the Marshal would damage their recruitment, so they preferred to stress his ministers' faults.

[67] Some even felt that Frenay had a fascist mentality. See *témoignage* of Monjaret, Archives, CHG.

Commandant Rollin, Directeur général de la sûreté nationale, and Pierre Pucheu, Vichy's minister of the interior, in February 1942. The talks were undertaken with the best possible intentions. Combat had been hurt by numerous arrests in January, and by agreeing to the interviews Frenay had secured the release of some of his captured comrades and hoped to buy enough time so that others, immediately threatened, could change addresses or identities. Combat had not agreed to any compromise with Vichy. The clearest result of the discussions had been that no understanding between Vichy and the Resistance was possible.[68]

But incontestably this *"affaire Frenay–Pucheu"* sowed serious discord among the resistance movements.[69] To the uninformed it seemed that when arrests were especially troubling to the Resistance, Combat was treating with the enemy. Had not Frenay received a safe-conduct pass from the heads of Vichy's police? D'Astier immediately broke off contact with Frenay, and all possibility of unification of the Resistance in southern France was delayed for several months. A further delay was occasioned by d'Astier's March 1942 trip to London, which irked Combat because Libération's chief claimed to have been mandated to speak for all southern resisters even though Combat, the largest movement, had given him no such authority.[70]

To problems of personalities and ideology was added the natural mistrust implicit in a clandestine situation. Despite heavy emphasis on security precautions,[71] arrests were frequent. Most were attributable to carelessness, but occasionally disaster resulted from the presence of a traitor within the ranks. Members of each movement questioned the security of the others and had confidence in only a few trusted com-

---

[68] See Granet and Michel, *Combat*, pp. 91–94, for a description of these talks; also *témoignages* of Frenay and Bourdet; letter of Rémy Roure quoted in Henri Frenay, *Méthodes d'un parti "alerte aux démocrates"* (Paris: Les Éditions Universelles, 1945); Michel, *Jean Moulin*, pp. 66–67, and Passy, *10 Duke Street, Londres*, pp. 99–102, 115–16.

[69] Noguères, *Histoire*, vol. 2, pp. 310–11, 339–46, and 550–51, points out that these tensions soon spread to the lower ranks as well; see also Cerf-Ferrière, *Chemin clandestin* for the observations of André Plaisantin.

[70] *Témoignage* of Bourdet, Archives, CHG and Passy, *10 Duke Street, Londres*, pp. 80–86 and 116.

[71] Warnings about security are very frequent in all of the clandestine newspapers. See *Combat*, *Franc-Tireur* and *Libération*, as well as the BIMUR (*Bulletin Intérieur des Mouvements Unis de la Résistance*), also *Consignes de sécurité*, Papers of Alban Vistel, Archives, CHG.

rades.[72] Even among militants of the same movement trust was often qualified. Yves Farge, a leading resister with friends in many movements, recalled: "There were few of us and we knew it well because, each time one of us disappeared, it was necessary to run across all of France to limit the damage. We liked one another, we admired one another, we were sure of one another, and yet the rules demanded that we consider every arrested comrade as likely to talk."[73]

An arrested resister, if released, often had trouble renewing contact with his friends,[74] particularly since the Gestapo or Vichy's police might be following such reunions with interest. Jean-Pierre Lévy, reflecting on the mutual suspicions among chiefs of the movements and their initial hesitation over unification, said: "The same distrust was found at every echelon, the secondary leaders balked, because everyone claimed to be sure of his chief, but not of his neighbor's. . . . We had in reality no guarantee on the choice that the chiefs made of their men."[75]

Given these internal problems among the movements, outside arbitration if not absolutely necessary for the proposed fusion was at least highly desirable. Mediation arrived in the person of Jean Moulin.[76]

---

[72] Distrust among resisters of the different zones was particularly strong. See Pineau, *La Simple vérité*, p. 93, and Bourdet, *témoignage*, Archives, CHG.

[73] Yves Farge, *Rebelles*, p. 19.

[74] See *témoignage* of François Cremieux, Archives, CHG, on the difficulty he had in contacting his former friends in the Resistance after his escape from prison.

[75] *Témoignage* of Lévy, Archives, CHG.

[76] Jean Moulin was one of the authentic heroes of the Resistance. Betrayed and arrested in June 1943 in circumstances never completely explained, he was savagely tortured and literally beaten to death by the Gestapo at Lyon. To the last questions from his torturers Moulin, an amateur painter, had replied by sketching a caricature of his brutal captor. His sister, Laure Moulin, recalled: "He had reached the limits of human suffering without betraying a single secret, he who knew them all. . . ." (Quoted in a speech by André Malraux at the Panthéon, 19 December 1964, when Moulin's ashes were deposited there in recognition of his service to France.) So large was his contribution that few books or testimonies on the Resistance are without some mention of Moulin. It would be impossible to list here all of the relevant material. Henri Michel's biography is excellent, and Laure Moulin's account adds complementary personal details. The other major sources for Moulin's actions will be cited below, especially in chap. 3, which will include a further discussion of his relations with the chiefs of the MUR and their attitude toward him.

Prefect at Chartres in May 1940, Moulin had been tortured by the Germans when he refused to sign a statement incriminating French soldiers in alleged atrocities, and later he was dismissed by Vichy for his resistance attitude. Moulin established residence in the unoccupied zone, made an independent survey of the resistance movements, and then overcame numerous obstacles to reach London, where he persuaded General de Gaulle of the need to bring the budding organizations under the Gaullist banner.[77]

When Moulin parachuted into France during the early hours of New Year's Day 1942, he returned as Charles de Gaulle's first full-fledged representative to the southern movements. In the year and a half before his second and fatal encounter with German torture chambers, Moulin accomplished a work unsurpassed in the annals of the Resistance. His most authoritative biographer wrote: ". . . before him [individual] resisters had risen up; at his death, they formed *The Resistance.*"[78] Combining skillful diplomacy with persistent determination, Moulin presided over the seemingly interminable negotiations that finally smoothed over all of the essential differences among the chiefs of Combat, Libération, and Franc-Tireur. Their official fusion into the Mouvements Unis de la Résistance was announced in January 1943, one year after Moulin's arrival. A large share of the credit for this unification belongs to Jean Moulin, but many factors beyond his exceptional personal ability aided de Gaulle's *délégué général.*

At his first meeting with Frenay in January 1942, Moulin gave Combat's chief 250,000 francs as the first of what were to become fairly regular subsidies from London to the movements.[79] Moulin, who enjoyed de Gaulle's full support, soon came to direct alone the flow within the interior of money, arms, radio transmitters, and personnel from de Gaulle to the movements. All communication with the French National Committee was sent through the *délégation*'s couriers. In short, Moulin controlled the lifeline of the resistance movements.[80] Such power added considerable weight to Moulin's effort at

---

[77] De Gaulle, *Mémoires*, vol. 1, pp. 233–35.

[78] Michel, *Jean Moulin*, p. 8.

[79] *Témoignage* of Henri Frenay, Archives, CHG; Laure Moulin, *Jean Moulin*, has appended Moulin's budgets to her account. Reports of Jacques Bingen, Archives, CHG, include the budgets for the later period.

[80] Michel, *Jean Moulin*, pp. 85–86.

persuasion. Frenay complained that his powers were "practically superior to those of General de Gaulle himself . . . really without any control."[81]

The movements' ties to de Gaulle went beyond the obvious material consideration. Although created without guidance from London, the movements had long felt close in spirit to de Gaulle, and by June 1942 Combat, Libération, and Franc-Tireur had each openly proclaimed the General their sole chief.[82] When Moulin's negotiations bogged down in France, he suggested in September that the three chiefs transfer their talks to London, where they could discuss the matter with de Gaulle and his associates.[83] The operation that was to have brought Moulin and Jean-Pierre Lévy to London failed, but Frenay and d'Astier arrived safely. By 22 October 1942, de Gaulle could write to Moulin that the two chiefs had agreed to a Coordinating Committee for the three principal movements of the unoccupied zone.[84] Moulin, assisted by the head of the Secret Army General Delestraint,[85] presided over this committee as the representative of the French National Committee. De Gaulle added:

> All Resistance organizations of any composition or political affiliation, other than the three principal groups associated with the Coordinating Committee, must be invited to attach their members to one of these groups and to merge their action units with units of the Secret Army now being formed. It is desirable to avoid the proliferation of numerous, small organizations which could hamper one another, arouse rivalries, and create confusion.[86]

---

[81] Letter of Frenay to Col. Passy, quoted in Passy, *Missions secrètes en France*, pp. 407–8.

[82] See *Combat*, *Franc-Tireur*, and *Libération* for May and June 1942.

[83] Passy, *10 Duke Street, Londres*, p. 246. These talks are described on pp. 246–48, 263–67, 271–78; De Gaulle, *Mémoires*, vol. 2, pp. 37–38, 376; Soustelle, *Envers et contre tout*, vol. 1, pp. 395–99; also *témoignages* of Frenay and d'Astier. All of these men were participants in the negotiations.

[84] De Gaulle, *Mémoires*, vol. 2, p. 376.

[85] Passy, *10 Duke Street, Londres*, pp. 271–72, and *témoignage* of Frenay, Archives, CHG. Frenay had suggested himself as head of the AS, but d'Astier refused absolutely, and Frenay suggested Delestraint. De Gaulle had served under Delestraint during the "drôle de guerre" and was happy to name him chief of the AS on 11 November. On 22 October 1942, he wrote Delestraint: "We will remake the French Army" (*Mémoires*, vol. 2, p. 376).

[86] De Gaulle, *Mémoires*, vol. 2, p. 376.

The movements agreed to a complete union of their paramilitary forces in the Secret Army, which was to be integrated into Allied strategic planning under the direct orders of General de Gaulle. The movements were to retain a certain political independence, however; in particular each would maintain control of its separate clandestine journal.

Months before establishment of the Coordinating Committee, changing circumstances—including pressure from militants at the base perhaps as much as from Moulin and de Gaulle at the top—had convinced the chiefs of the desirability of unification. Laval's institution of the *relève* and later the STO combined with the German occupation of southern France to send the movements a wave of new recruits, who usually joined the first groups they happened to find. Rarely did ideology play a major part in their selection, and the recruits had no predilection for any particular movement, especially since the ideological stances of the movements had become quite similar, stressing strong commitment to a future expanded role for labor and unqualified devotion to de Gaulle.[87]

In truth few other than the editors of the clandestine journals and heads of the movements had ever paid much attention to any fine points of political controversy.[88] Max Juvenal, a socialist who became one of the MUR's six regional heads, said: "We chose the journal *Combat* because we liked its name; I became chief of the AS for Aix-en-Provence and formed my *sixaines*."[89] Claude Bourdet traces the overlapping of movements to the very beginning.

> In fact, this separation of movements was rather illusory. Only a handful of Frenchmen were resisters. . . . And, in spite of our orders ("You must be a member of one organization and of one only"), we realized in arriving in a village

---

[87] Compare OSS Documents 19307 C (3–5 July 1942), 18997 S (12 June 1942), 18927 S (4 June 1942), and 24425 C (27 November 1942).

[88] Cerf-Ferrière, *Chemin clandestin*, pp. 76–78, reveals his early fears about Combat's political orientation but acknowledges that these fears were probably unjustified. "During my trips of the first quarter of 1942, I saw, most often, that our militants disregarded the articles in *Combat* dealing with politics. What interested them was what was written against the Germans, against the rotten press, against abusive requisitions, against Vichy's oppressive laws; what interested them was to distribute *Combat* and to recruit new members." Étienne Bauer (interview, 23 November 1969) agreed: "The militants at the base did not give a damn about politics!"

[89] *Témoignage* of Max Juvenal, Archives, CHG.

LE GENERAL DE GAULLE.

4, CARLTON GARDENS, S.W.I.
WHITEHALL 8444.

TRES SECRET

La présence simultanée à Londres de
Bernard et de Charvet a permis d'établir
l'entente entre leurs deux mouvements de
résistance, et de fixer les conditions de leur
activité sous l'autorité du Comité National.

J'ai vivement regretté votre absence
pendant cette mise au point. Je pense, cependant,
que les dispositions qui ont été arrêtées
faciliteront l'exécution de la mission qui vous
est confiée.

Vous aurez à assurer la présidence du
comité de coordination au sein duquel seront
représentés les trois principaux mouvements de
résistance: "COMBAT", "FRANC-TIREUR", "LIBÉRATION".
Vous continuerez d'autre part comme représentant
du Comité National en zone non-occupée, à prendre

Letter from de Gaulle to Jean Moulin, 22 October 1942, informing Moulin that he was to preside over a Coordinating Committee which would direct the resistance activities of Combat, Libération, and Franc-Tireur. Smaller resistance organizations were to be urged to merge with these three major movements. This order signaled the official birth of the Mouvements Unis de la Résistance. Bernard and Charvet were aliases for d'Astier and Frenay, the leaders of Libération and Combat.

that the same person might be the leader of Combat, of
Libération, of Franc-Tireur, and, in the bargain, of one or
two British or Gaullist networks. . . . I am exaggerating a

- 2 -

tous les contacts politiques que vous jugerez
opportuns. Vous pourrez y employer certains
de nos agents qui vous sont directement
subordonnés.

Toutes organisations de résistance,
quel que soit leur caractère, autres que les
trois grands mouvements groupés par le comité
de coordination, devront être invitées à affilier
leurs adhérents à l'un de ces mouvements et à
verser leurs groupes d'action dans les unités de
l'armée secrète en cours de constitution. Il
convient en effet d'éviter la prolifération de
multiples petites organisations qui risqueraient
de se gêner mutuellement, de susciter des
rivalités et de créer la confusion.

Je tiens à vous redire que vous avez
mon entière confiance et je vous adresse toutes
mes amitiés.

little, but not much. In any case, such a situation made
unification very desirable.[90]

Most new members, along with the majority of the rank-and-file
veterans, felt quite simply that strength lay in unity. A multiplicity

---

[90] Claude Bourdet, "Histoire de la Résistance française," *Après-Demain*,
nos. 30–33.

of small groups that duplicated one another's actions seemed a squandering of good intentions and a waste of effort. Moulin reported in August 1942 that almost all of the militants were spontaneously calling for fusion. The *délégué général* believed that agreement must first be reached at the top, but added: ". . . in a certain number of cities, in spite of us and the chiefs, coordination is, for all practical purposes, accomplished."[91]

This attitude at the base of the movements found several echoes in the leadership, especially among the second generation[92]—those who had joined the movement during 1942. We shall see that two of these men—Pascal Copeau, d'Astier's second in command for Libération, and Marcel Degliame, Combat's chief of the service Action Ouvrière, —soon rose to positions of great importance in both the MUR and the united, national organizations of the Resistance. Copeau recalled having no particular attachment to Libération as such. "I could have just as easily by chance stumbled upon Combat."[93] Therefore, he could see the advantages of unity without that mentality of a war veteran, which he felt hampered the original founders of the movements.[94] In these circumstances Copeau served rather as an intermediary among Moulin, d'Astier, and Frenay, repeatedly coaxing them toward compromise.[95]

Many of the original secondary leaders also were favorable to fusion and had long encouraged their chiefs in that direction.[96] And Jean-Pierre Lévy, whose movement expected to gain strength from the proposed fusion, had been from his first encounter with Jean Moulin a constant advocate of unification. His intercession with Frenay and d'Astier was a valuable asset for de Gaulle's often frustrated emissary.[97]

When d'Astier and Frenay returned to France, Lévy accepted with-

---

[91] Moulin's *Courrier* no. 9, quoted in Passy, *10 Duke Street, Londres,* p. 123.

[92] Noguères, *Histoire,* vol. 2, pp. 546–50.

[93] Copeau, quoted in Noguères, *Histoire,* vol. 2, p. 548; see also pp. 547–49.

[94] Noguères, *Histoire,* vol. 2.

[95] Noguères, *Histoire,* vol. 2. Indeed, Copeau described his actions as "plotting with Moulin to eliminate the founders"; also interview with Copeau, 23 January 1970.

[96] *Témoignage* of Bourdet, Archives, CHG.

[97] *Témoignage* of Hervé Monjaret, *témoignage* of Lévy, Archives, CHG. Compare Noguères, *Histoire,* vol. 2, pp. 448–50, "Les 'bons offices' de Franc-Tireur."

out hesitation the arrangements they had made with de Gaulle at London; and from coordination Combat, Libération, and Franc-Tireur rapidly moved to fusion. The discussions of the Coordinating Committee[98] led to the formal institution of the directory of the Mouvements Unis de la Résistance on 26 January 1943. Contrary to what might have been predicted in view of their earlier differences, the chiefs of the three movements, cooperating in a spirit of mutual loyalty, lost little time in giving concrete substance to the MUR. As he had in the Coordinating Committee, Moulin presided over meetings of the Directing Committee when he was at Lyon. In his absence one of the three founders chaired the sessions, and it was they rather than Moulin who actively administered the movements. The division of labor gave Frenay control over military policy, d'Astier political affairs, and Lévy responsibilities as Commissioner of Information, Security, and Material Resources.[99]

The MUR was organized according to a dual hierarchy of national services and regional directories. The services were modeled after those of Combat, whose superior organization everyone acknowledged. In fact, the creation of many MUR services was a simple procedure, involving the incorporation of a few elements of Libération or Franc-Tireur into the structure of the former Combat service.[100] The heads of most of the critical services—such as Noyautage des administrations Publiques (NAP),[101] Action Ouvrière (which included sabotage and direct action), Service Maquis, and Service des Renseignements (charged with gathering military intelligence for the Allies and with internal security for the movements), merely transferred their opera-

---

[98] The first session was held in Lyon, 27 November 1942. Following the initial meeting, the Coordinating Committee and later the Directing Committee of the MUR met as often as four times a week, but normally twice a week. (Bingen, "Rapport" of November 1943, Archives, CHG.) Passy, *10 Duke Street, Londres,* p. 17, says once a week, but Bingen, who attended many of the sessions, is probably correct.

[99] See C. D.–MUR (Comité directeur des Mouvements de Résistance Unis), 25 March 1943, Papers of Alban Vistel, Archives, CHG; and Granet and Michel, *Combat,* pp. 279–84.

[100] *Témoignage* of Bourdet, Archives, CHG.

[101] See above for the functions of this service. Under the MUR the NAP became a very important service with major responsibilities for the takeover of power. See "Chef régional à tous départements," 24 June 1943; Directives from "Turgot à toutes les régions," 17 May 1943; Papers of Alban Vistel, Archives, CHG.

tions from Combat to the MUR.[102] Whenever possible, these chiefs took on assistants from the other movements to facilitate cooperation. Faced with the initial predominance of Combat at the top in the national services, Libération and Franc-Tireur naturally attempted to balance its power at the regional and departmental levels.

The key provision in the Unity Manifesto[103] had provided for a single chief at each echelon in each of the six regions of southern France. The choice was to be made on the basis of merit, with no consideration to proportion among the three movements. Theoretically, the real executive power of the MUR was to be exercised through the regional directories. Instructions from the Directing Committee of the MUR stated explicitly:

> The *chef régional* has principal responsibility in all matters. He receives the regional budget and sees to its equitable distribution. He holds authority over the *chefs de service* and the *chefs départementaux*. He is accountable [for his actions] to the Directing Committee. He convokes the [regional] directory and is responsible for its regular meeting. In case of the absence of his assistants, he holds the power of decision.
>
> In emergencies, he has power of decision, even against the advice of his assistants. It is of course understood that, in this case, the issue will be brought before the National C. D., which may remove the *chef régional* from his functions if he has exceeded his authority.[104]

---

[102] Vistel, *La Nuit*, pp. 381–82, lists most of the key services and their directors. Also *témoignage* of Bourdet, Archives, CHG. We have seen that Combat clearly dominated the Secret Army as well.

[103] Its provisions are quoted in Passy, *Missions Secrètes en France*, pp. 308–9. The Manifesto was dated 26 January 1943.

[104] Le Comité Directeur, des Mouvements de Résistance Unis à tous les Directoires Régionaux," 14 May 1943, p. 1. Papers of Alban Vistel, Archives, CHG. Further directives included in the Papers with this fourteen-page document are: "Le C. D. des M. R. U. à tous services et toutes régions," 2–4 August 1943, five pages; "Le C. D. des M. R. U. à tous services, toutes régions," 18 August 1943, six pages; "C. D.–M. U. R.," 25 March 1943, two pages; and "C. D.–M. R. U. à tous les Chefs de Régions et tous les Services," 12 April 1943. This information is invaluable. It not only outlines precisely the structures of the MUR but also clearly reveals the difficulties met during the course of the unification, as well as the

Obviously the title of *chef régional* was a first-class prize, and understandably many of the old quarrels were revived as each movement claimed the laurels for its own members.[105]

Once again the disproportionate strength of Combat was a major problem. One of Libération's directors at Lyon admitted: "Incontestably it was probably the most powerful movement, at least by very far the best structured and the richest in valuable leadership."[106] Claude Bourdet complained that even when numerous concessions were granted to Libération d'Astier simply could not supply qualified men to fill the positions offered to his movement.[107]

Still, many things had changed since the first uncertain steps toward unity. All now accepted the principle of fusion, and discussions now involved the less basic question of application. Recruitment was no longer made in the name of the separate movements but, rather, under the banner of the Mouvements Unis de la Résistance.[108] Perhaps most important was the special concern of the Directing Committee to set an example of loyal cooperation. Directives from the center constantly demanded work in an *"esprit de discipline et de camaraderie,"*[109] and ordered the militants to "stop immediately the quarrels between persons and political factions,"[110] and to "put an end to the little disputes which are now inappropriate."[111] Further, the national chiefs established a Secrétariat Unique, which handled all corre-

---

national directors' attempts to overcome the problems, which they recognized with astonishing frankness and attacked with a refreshing unselfishness.

[105] See Granet and Michel, *Combat,* pp. 212–17; and especially Vistel, *La Nuit,* pp. 373–421, who recounts in detail the various problems at Lyon that accompanied the fusion. Also the *témoignages* of Bourdet, Michelet, Juvenal, and Ingrand, and interview Pascal Copeau, 23 January 1970, for conditions in other regions.

[106] Vistel, *Le Nuit,* p. 376.

[107] *Témoignage* of Bourdet, Archives, CHG.

[108] In R.6–Clermont Ferrand, Henry Ingrand remembered that he purposely started from zero and rebuilt the Resistance in his area in the name of the MUR (Interview, 11 March 1970).

[109] "C. D.–M. R. U. à tous les chefs de régions et tous les services," 12 April 1943, Papers of Alban Vistel, Archives, CHG. See also "Le Comité directeur . . . à tous les directoires régionaux," 14 May 1943, pp. 12–14, Papers of Alban Vistel, Archives, CHG.

[110] "Le C. D. des M. R. U. . . . toutes régions," 2–4 August 1943, p. 4.

[111] "Le C. D. des M. R. U. . . . toutes régions," 18 August 1943, p. 6. Papers of Alban Vistel, Archives, CHG.

spondence and liaison between the regions and the center.[112] The regional directories were not to address an individual member of the Directing Committee but were to correspond with the CD as a whole through its new secretariat.[113] A directive of 12 April 1943 granted:

> It is understood; in *absolutely exceptional instances*, the Chef de Région Unique and his two assistants can address, themselves directly to the members of the Directing Committee, heads of the three former movements. These personal letters will be sent under separate envelopes by the normal channels. They will pass, *without being opened*, to the Secretariat of the Directing Committee which will discuss them at their first meeting.
>
> This measure is taken in order not to cut the relations of confidence and friendship which exist between the men and chiefs of the former movements. But it will not be permitted that this communication envenom the existing difficulties, but on the contrary, that it smooth them out, because it is based on the total agreement existing between the members of the Directing Commitee.[114]

After the unification Frenay and d'Astier seemed mutually satisfied with their roles in the direction of the MUR. Instead of bickering with each other the former rivals were most often in agreement in concerting their opposition to the policies of Jean Moulin and the Gaullist délégation. Furthermore, d'Astier, Frenay, and Lévy left France by the summer of 1943 to assume positions with de Gaulle's CFLN (Comité Français de la Libération Nationale) as representatives of the interior Resistance.[115]

---

[112] "Le C. D. des M. R. U. . . . toutes régions," 18 August 1943, p. 6, and "C. D.–M. U. R.," 25 March 1943, Papers of Alban Vistel, Archives, CHG.

[113] "Le Comité Directeur . . . tous les directoires régionaux," 14 May 1943, p. 12, Papers of Alban Vistel, Archives, CHG. A note of 29 October 1943 defined in detail the role of the secrétariat général, "S. G. des M. U. R. à Office du Logement" (Logement was the code name for Region I or Lyon), Papers of Alban Vistel, Archives, CHG.

[114] "C. D.–M. R. U. à . . . tous les services," 12 April 1943, Papers of Alban Vistel, Archives, CHG.

[115] D'Astier, who was in London from May to July 1943, returned to France once more when the Directing Committee was transferred to Paris, but he remained only a short time before leaving to become minister of the interior at Algiers in the fall of 1943. After this time Pascal Copeau said

Thus control of the MUR fell to second-generation leaders, who, we have seen, worked together more easily than had the original *patrons*. For example, Raymond Aubrac of Libération reported that he and Combat's François Morin-Forestier had no trouble in installing the officers of the unified Secret Army within a month's time during January and February 1943. He and Forestier "got along well enough to forget the differences of doctrine and the rivalries of their founders, to place the best men in all positions. There was almost never a disagreement."[116] They simply chose the man who would be respected in a given local situation and traveled together to install the leader if his authority might be questioned.

Despite the prevailing spirit of loyal cooperation, several months passed before the unified movement became a reality. The spring and summer of 1943 was a particularly troubled time for the MUR. Political considerations often complicated the selection of the six regional heads , and since to be effective the nomination had to be accepted by all concerned, the decision could not be rushed. At Lyon, R.1., the situation was not clarified until August, when the choice of Alban Vistel received universal consent.[117] In two regions—R.5, Limoges, and R.2, Marseille—the naming of Edmond Michelet and Maurice Chevance-Bertin was accepted without incident. In these cases the Gestapo provided the stumbling block. Both men were arrested at the end of April. Thus new negotiations were necessary.[118]

Shortly thereafter another series of spectacular arrests plagued the Resistance. On 9 June General Delestraint, head of the AS, was taken at Paris, and on 21 June Jean Moulin and several important members of the MUR and the Secret Army were surprised by the Gestapo at Caluire near Lyon.[119] These tragedies were followed by raids in July on important MUR headquarters locations at Lyon. In these circumstances, on the suggestion of Claude Serreules, a Gaullist representative, the Directing Committee decided to move to Paris, which offered

---

contacts with the original *patrons* were very irregular and undependable. The *patrons* were clearly removed from any direct control over the operations of the MUR (Interview, Pascal Copeau, 23 January 1970.)

[116] *Témoignage* of Raymond Aubrac, Archives, CHG.

[117] *Témoignage* of Bourdet, Archives, CHG; Vistel, *La Nuit*, pp. 373–431.

[118] *Témoignages* of Bourdet and Michelet, Archives, CHG; Granet and Michel, *Combat*, pp. 212–17.

[119] Laure Moulin, *Jean Moulin*, pp. 437–51, and Michel, *Jean Moulin*, pp. 173–94. See chap. 3 for the further implications of this tragedy.

safer hideouts for the resisters.[120] The suppression of the demarcation line after the total occupation meant that operations could be directed as easily from Paris as they had been earlier from Lyon.

The absence of the founders, delays in firmly establishing the regional directories, and severe repression in the spring and summer of 1943 in several regions led to serious crises, which were aggravated further by conflicts between the separate hierarchies of services and regional directories. In theory the regional head was the supreme authority in every realm of the MUR's activity. The local and regional chiefs of the national services were required to discuss any important decision with the *chef régional* and to keep him regularly informed of their actions.[121] In reality the situation varied from region to region.

The crucial factor was always the personality of the regional head.[122] The region designated R.6—Clermont-Ferrand almost never had a problem. All respected Henry Ingrand, the *chef régional*, and no major decision in either the political or the military sphere was made without his knowledge and consent.[123] In other areas the regional directory was more of a team effort, with no one dominant voice. This situation, especially during a period of instability after arrests of recognized leaders, permitted individual chiefs of the various services to assert a large measure of independence. In particular the Groupes Francs and Maquis often acted as autonomous bodies.[124] Some resisters feared that Michel Brault (Jerome) was attempting to set up his personal resistance fief by separating Maquis bands from the MUR.[125] Claude

---

[120] "Rapport de Sophie (i.e., Serreules)," 16 August 1943, Papers of Oudard, Archives, CHG.

[121] "Le Comité Directeur . . . tous les Directoires Régionaux," 14 May 1943, Papers of Alban Vistel, Archives, CHG; and other directives cited above (n. 104).

[122] *Témoignage* of Bourdet, Archives, CHG; Bourdet remarked that the regional directories "included a representative of each of the three movements, one having a veto over the other two, and thereby holding the role of *chef régional.* However, according to the authority and quality of the *chef de région,* the Directory was either consultative, or a true directory, the members of which were practically equals."

[123] *Témoignages* of Bourdet, Frenay, and Ingrand, Archives, CHG, interview Henry Ingrand, 11 March 1970.

[124] *Témoignages* of Bourdet and Frenay, Archives, CHG. Madeleine Baudoin, *Histoire des Groupes Francs (M.U.R.) des Bouches-du-Rhône* (Paris: Presses Universitaires de France, 1962), passim, unconsciously reveals the elitist mentality of the Groupes Francs' militants.

[125] *Témoignages* of Bourdet and Juvenal, Archives, CHG. See also "Rapport Bingen," end of November 1943, Papers of Oudard, Archives, CHG.

Bourdet attested: "The conflict was quasi-permanent between the *chefs de région* and the regional *responsables* of the services. The *chefs de région* tended to command in too strict a manner, while the regional *responsables* were inclined to act independently."[126]

When incidents occurred, chiefs of services and regions were responsible before the *Directing Committee*. The schematically rigid organization of the MUR was, in fact, quite flexible. Whenever a *chef régional* failed in his duty, a regional chief of a particular service might —indeed was encouraged to—take up the slack. In a directive to all regions, 2 August 1943, the Directing Committee reaffirmed the pre-eminence of the *chefs régionaux* but observed:

> In fact, in a praiseworthy desire for efficacity, the chiefs of the national services have frequently been led to exceed their rights and to establish on their own authority, units made necessary by the decisions of the C. D. The *Chefs régionaux* are right to rise up against this state of affairs. But only on the condition that they themselves are not at fault. They cannot, in effect, complain that their authority is not respected and, at the same time, rely on the delegates from the center to do their work. It is obvious that if the work is not done normally in the regions according to the given directives, the delegates of the national services cannot be blamed for having acted in the place of the defaulting regional authorities. However, everything created by the delegates of the national services must be immediately turned over to the *chefs régionaux* and the *chefs départementaux*.[127]

The major concern of the MUR directors was that the job be done. Orders from the top were subject to local interpretation. Considerable local initiative was both permitted and desired.[128] For the critical operations anticipated during the liberation period, it was assumed that liaison between the Directing Committee and the regions would be precarious, and even the lines between regions and their subordinate departments might be cut.[129] Therefore great emphasis was placed on

---

126 *Témoignage* of Bourdet, Archives, CHG.

127 "Le C. D. des M. R. U. . . . toutes régions," 2–4 August 1943, p. 2, Papers of Alban Vistel, Archives, CHG.

128 Interview, Henry Ingrand (11 March 1970), and interview, Max Juvenal (8 June 1970).

129 "Le C. D. des M. R. U. . . . toutes régions," 18 August 1943, p. 1. Papers of Alban Vistel, Archives, CHG.

building up solid departmental organizations with effective leadership, if necessary, at the cost of all theoretical diagrams on chain of command. And finally the desired result was obtained.

It was no small tribute to the solid foundation erected by the original *founders* of the Resistance in southern France that after their departure the movement they had created weathered this tumultuous spring and summer admirably and overcame several dramatic crises with astonishing speed. By the fall of 1943 the MUR had substantially regrouped its forces and had become truly one movement. A Gaullist agent noted that the plural Mouvement[s] Uni[s] de la Résistance remained something of an anomaly.[130] To be sure, clashes of personalities, conflicts between services and regions, and some conflicts caused by memories of the three separate movements reappeared from time to time.[131] But one participant in retrospect surmised: "These appeared as no more than waves which could not hide the depths." If occasional disturbances arose, he continued, they were easily explained. "We were not angels, we did not inhabit a peaceful empyrean, we were torn, tormented, passionate men."[132]

No drastic alterations in the movement occurred after the Directing Committee moved to Paris. On 8 February 1944 three small northern movements, Défense de la France, Résistance, and Lorraine, joined the original movements to form the Mouvement de la Libération Nationale (MLN). However, all five major movements of the northern zone refused the MUR's invitation for a vast union of all the Resistance in a Union Nationale de la Résistance Francaise (UNR). The formation of the MLN served mainly to give these smaller movements the representation they had lacked in the national resistance organizations.[133] Although Défense de la France had one of the most widely circulated clandestine journals, its actions, like those of the other two movements, were largely restricted to propaganda. Thus the additions effected no significant changes in the MUR structure or directing personnel.[134]

---

[130] "Rapport Bingen," November 1943, Papers of Oudard, Archives, CHG.

[131] A few years after the liberation, the movements formed their separate *amicales,* indicating that the differences were never completely surmounted. This situation, though, was concerned more with postliberation politics than with clandestine divisions. See chap. 5.

[132] Vistel, *La Nuit,* p. 383.

[133] *Témoignage* of Antoine Avinin, Archives, CHG.

[134] For the formation of the MLN see Marie Granet, *Défense de la*

By and large during 1944 the MUR turned from the more complicated task of creating an organization to the simpler if no less serious
problem of replacing its dead. As the liberation approached, increasing
sympathy and cooperation from the population encouraged the resisters, but unfortunately repression, too, was on the rise. "Friend, if
you fall, a friend will step from the shadows to take your place," said
the *Chant des Partisans,* the semiofficial theme song of the French
Resistance. Many persons fell in the months before the liberation as
the Milice waged a campaign of official terror in an attempt to exterminate the resisters.[135] No sooner were local liberation committees established than arrests or executions destroyed the patient work of
weeks, and all had to begin once more.[136] In a letter of 24 April 1944
to Emmanuel d'Astier, Yvon Morandat described the climate within
France. "I must tell you that this is a reign of terror, and that when
one leaves a comrade, he feels more like saying '*adieu*' than '*au
revoir*'."[137] Of course, arrests and death had always been an unpre-
dictable element in clandestine life. Perhaps they just seemed more
tragic at a time when victory appeared so close.[138]

In April the Directing Committee of the MLN appointed Pascal
Copeau and Marcel Degliame to make an inspection tour as a sort of
roving executive with full powers over the southern zone. Antoine
Avinin and Robert Lacoste were left to represent the MUR at Paris.
Copeau for civilian affairs and Degliame for military problems had

---

France, "Histoire d'un Mouvement de Résistance (1940–1944)" (Paris:
Presses Universitaires de France, 1960), pp. 148–58; also BIMUR, 18 January 1944 and 22 February 1944. Also various reports of Bingen, Serreules,
and Morandat, who follow the progress of the negotiations, Archives, CHG,
and a letter of Natalis Dumez, founder of one of the smaller northern
movements, la Voix du Nord, including information on the MLN in
northern France. The letter dated 16 November 1970 was transmitted to
the author by M. Omer Mercier, whose father, the addressee, solicited the
information on behalf of the author.

[135] OSS Documents 62365 R, 15 March 1944; letter of Yvon Morandat in
Papers of Serreules, Archives, CHG; reports of Closon, January and February 1944, Archives, CHG; *témoignage* of Antoine Avinin, Archives, CHG,
recalled that of the ten departmental leaders for the region around Toulouse,
none appointed during the summer of 1943 was left by the spring of 1944.

[136] "Rapport de Fouché" (Closon), no. 4, arrived London, 1 April 1944,
Archives, CHG.

[137] Papers of Serreules, Archives, CHG.

[138] See the appeal of Albert Camus for the Allies to speed up their invasion of France. "D'un résistant intellectuel," Papers of Oudard, Archives,
CHG.

the authority to appoint or replace any local chief, and their decisions were without appeal. In addition every member of the Directing Committee was empowered to act alone, carrying the full authority of the total Committee in any situation that required his intervention wherever he might be.[139] The purpose of Copeau's and Degliame's inspection was to end any local disputes and to assure the presence of effective leadership for the decisive events of the liberation. In fact, as its leaders had long realized, the effectiveness of the MLN ultimately depended on the quality of its regional and departmental chiefs. The MLN structure left wide initiative to these men and was an expression of the confidence placed in them. Soon the final struggle for liberation would determine whether or not this confidence was warranted.

In his November 1943 report the Gaullist Délégué Général for southern France attested to the strength of the MUR. "Except in the region of Marseille, where arrests have decapitated the organization so as to require a reorganization, there exists a hierarchy which functions very well; from the *arrondissement* [city administrative division] to the department, to the region, and up to the C. D. of the M. U. R. there is an active correspondence and a very *solid* bond of cooperation."[140] Numerous observers were unanimous in favorably contrasting the organization of the MUR with that of the northern movements.[141] At the end of 1943 the MUR was unquestionably the best structured, most highly diversified resistance movement in France.[142] Consequently it played a large role in the evolution of the national resistance organizations that began to take shape in the fall of 1943. In particular many of the commissions of the CNR (Conseil National de la Résistance) were simple extensions of the MUR's services to a national scale and often involved the same personnel.[143]

---

[139] Interview Pascal Copeau (23 January 1970) and "S. G. du M. L. N. à toutes régions," 29 April 1944, Papers of Alban Vistel, Archives, CHG.

[140] Bingen, "Rapport" of November 1943, pp. 13–14 (see also pp. 15–17), Archives, CHG.

[141] Various reports of Bingen, Serreules, Brossolette, Closon and Morandat, Archives, CHG. All of these men were Gaullist *délégués*. Also Michel Debré, *Un Grand mouvement préfectoral*, extract of the review, *Les Cahiers politiques*, February–March 1946 (Paris: Imprimierie Curial-Archereau, 1946).

[142] See the budgets allotted to the various movements as recorded in reports of Bingen, Archives, CHG, as some indication of the importance of the MUR. No other movement received comparable support from London.

[143] René Hostache, *Le Conseil National de la Résistance* (Paris: Presses Universitaires de France, 1958), pp. 126–27.

The northern movements, long inclined to think of the Resistance in purely military terms, were reluctant to cooperate with the politicized southern movements, and they left to MUR initiative the organization of such important commissions as the NAP.[144] Louis Closon, the Gaullist representative charged with establishing Departmental Liberation Committees (CDL) to organize civil powers at the liberation, reported that when he approached them about these Committees the northern resisters who were preoccupied with military affairs, made him feel he was "asking them to leave their work."[145] In contrast, Closon noted that the MUR had early grasped the importance of political considerations so that the creation of the Departmental Liberation Committees was proceding smoothly in the South.[146]

As we shall see, several chiefs of the MUR, including Antoine Avinin, Marcel Degliame, Claude Bourdet, and Pascal Copeau, held critical posts in the hierarchy of the National Resistance. Much of their attention until the liberation was devoted to cooperation with the Gaullist representatives in order to give life to the proposals of the Conseil National de la Résistance and de Gaulle's CFLN, especially those concerning the establishment of Departmental Liberation Committees and a united military force, the FFI (Forces Françaises de l'Intérieur).

---

[144] Closon, "Rapport" no. 3, 11 November 1943, Archives, CHG, and *témoignage* of Bourdet, Archives, CHG.

[145] Closon, "Rapport" no. 3, 11 November 1943, p. 2.

[146] Closon, "Rapport" no. 3, 11 November 1943, Archives, CHG, p. 2.

CHAPTER 3

The Movements
and de Gaulle

ACCORDING TO Henri Frenay:

> Between the Resistance in France and Fighting France
> [the exterior Resistance under de Gaulle], from the begin-
> ning, whether voluntarily or not, an immense misunder-
> standing took shape. . . . The Resistance, the true Resistance,
> that of the men of the first hour, never felt it owed its exis-
> tence to the call of June 18. . . . For our mission was derived
> from our conscience alone and from our will. Our attach-
> ment to [de Gaulle] was spontaneous and voluntary. . . . Be-
> cause we were not *"chargés de mission,"* but free men,
> accepting freely his authority, we brought him the support of
> a captive but struggling France.[1]

The relations between the Mouvements Unis de la Résistance and
the exterior Resistance were seldom harmonious. Recurrent friction
accompanied every stage of their collaboration. How could it have

---

[1] *Témoignage* of Henri Frenay, Archives, CHG, p. 65, and beginning with
"For"; Henri Frenay, "De Gaulle et la Résistance," *Preuves* no. 70 (December 1956), p. 84.

been otherwise with two groups equally confident that they alone were the actual expression of the vital soul of the *real* France?[2] Still, occasional petty quarrels between individuals and arguments over the practical implementation of policies should not be allowed to obscure a fundamental unity of principle and common goals. Once committed to de Gaulle, at least until after the total liberation of France, the unwavering loyalty of the interior Resistance to the distant symbol of their struggle was incontestable.

Few of the men who built the interior movements had heard de Gaulle's historic appeal of 18 June 1940, and certainly most of them would have acted no differently had there been no General Charles de Gaulle.[3] Clearly the General's call for resistance did not create the interior Resistance. Nevertheless numerous people did hear the BBC broadcast on 18 June, and more heard it repeated in the weeks that followed. De Gaulle's frequent broadcasts on the British radio were followed by an ever increasing number of Frenchmen and undoubtedly boosted the recruitment in the interior movements.[4] We have seen that one of the first questions new recruits often asked was "Are you in contact with London?"

Even though they may not have heard de Gaulle on 18 June, the initial reaction of many leading resisters to the armistice was to try to

---

[2] Henri Michel, *Les Courants de pensée de la Résistance* (Paris: Presses Universitaires de France, 1962), chap. 14, pp. 426–43. "Esprit et Mission de la Résistance" describes the interior resisters' conception that "La Résistance c'est la France"; in contrast to chap. 4, "Mission de la France Libre," pp. 51–70, which evokes the exterior resisters' idea that "La France Combattante, c'est la France." M. Étienne Bauer, interview, 5 January 1970, recalled: "We had the impression that we were France, all of France."

[3] *Témoignages* of Frenay, Bourdet, Michelet, and many others, Archives, CHG. Also Claude Bourdet's interesting article, "Une Médiation," in *Le Monde*, 13 November 1970. (One of several commentaries of former resisters that appeared in *Le Monde* following de Gaulle's death.)

[4] Particularly in the early days of the Resistance the BBC reached a larger audience than the small circulation of the clandestine newspapers could attract. Georges Bidault, *D'une Résistance à l'autre* (Paris: Les Presses du Siècle, 1965), p. 36, claims: "The BBC literally made de Gaulle." See Nicholas Wahl, *De Gaulle and the Resistance* (Ph.D. diss., Harvard University, 1956), pp. 179–80, for a description of the tests of public opinion carried out by the Gaullists who would call for hours of silence during national holidays, etc. The texts of most of the BBC French broadcasts during the war are found in De Gaulle, *Discours et Messages*, vol. 1, "Pendant la Guerre" (Paris: Librairie Plon, 1970), and Maurice Schumann, *Honneur et patrie* (Paris: Éditions du Livre Français, 1946).

reach London.[5] Only when they failed in this attempt had they helped organize the Resistance within France. Long before they agreed to accept direct orders from London or Algiers, most resisters were properly termed Gaullists in the sense of a spiritual kinship; de Gaulle was the symbol of all they were fighting to secure. Pierre Brossolette, a socialist resister, described de Gaulle as:

> . . . that sort of genius, so rare in our epoch, to be a man of great refusals, a refusal to capitulate, a refusal to bow himself or to let France bow before any summons or maneuver, a refusal to compromise under the pretext of safeguard, a refusal of anything base, hypocritical or petty. It is by all these refusals that he had saved France's existence. . . .[6]

Before this sentimental attachment to de Gaulle the symbol could be transformed into obedience to de Gaulle the undisputable commander, the resisters demanded evidence of the General's republicanism. The left-oriented movements, from milieus traditionally suspicious of military men, had no intention of enthroning a new Bonaparte after the Germans were defeated. Brossolette, a most outspoken Gaullist, envisioned the thrilling day of victory: "When at the head of the tanks of the army of deliverance . . . he [de Gaulle] will be carried all along the Champs-Élysées, surrounded by the choked murmur of the women's great sobs of joy, the unending stacatto of your acclamations. . ."; but he added that all Frenchmen knew ". . . It is not for a man that we fight, but for a cause. . . ."[7]

Even after acknowledging his leadership, the movements cautioned de Gaulle that they would "rise against him, as against any dictator, if he came to wish in his turn to institute a personal government."[8] Despite their evident sympathy for de Gaulle, the interior resisters knew very little about the General's convictions. His statements, not

---

[5] Jacques Debu-Bridel, *Les Partis contre de Gaulle* (Paris: Aimery Somogy, 1948), preface; Bénouville, *Le Sacrifice du matin* (Paris: Robert Laffont, 1947), in the first chapter describes his and other resisters' attempts to join de Gaulle; also *témoignage* of Bourdet, Archives, CHG, and interview Copeau, 23 January 1970, who both tried to join de Gaulle before acting in France.

[6] Françoise Bruneau, *Essai d'historique, du movement né autour du journal clandestin "Résistance"* (Paris: S.E.D.E.S., 1951), p. 17.

[7] René Ozouf, *Pierre Brossolette* (Paris: Librairie Gedalge, 1946), pp. 38–39.

[8] *Combat*, no. 50, 1 November 1943.

unlike their own clandestine journals, were much clearer in their attacks on Vichy and on the failures of the former Third Republic than in the presentation of specific political alternatives.[9] Consequently, in March 1942, resistance chiefs from both zones delegated Christian Pineau, a founder of the northern movement Libération-Nord, to visit de Gaulle in London and request clarification of the General's political viewpoint.[10]

Undoubtedly much happy celebration greeted Pineau on his return, for his mission had yielded extraordinary results. De Gaulle sent him back to France with a straightforward declaration of war aims, which Combat, Libération, Franc-Tireur, and several northern journals published in June.

True, liberation of the national territory and full restoration of French sovereignty over the empire were the immediate concern.[11] But once the enemy was chased out of France, "All of our men and women will elect the National Assembly which will decide in full sovereignty the destinies of the country."[12] Enemy war criminals and French collaborators must be punished, and the totalitarian regimes and coalitions of private interest that had aided them against the national interest were to be overthrown for good. In addition to national security, the French people were to have social security, "practical guarantees which will assure to everyone liberty and dignity in his work and his existence."[13] In short, de Gaulle promised the practical realization of "the French secular ideal of *liberté, égalité, fraternité.*"[14]

Internationally the issues were no less clear-cut. The conflict, according to de Gaulle, was one of democracy versus "the mechanical organization of human masses which the enemy had achieved in disregard

---

[9] See De Gaulle, *Discours et messages*, vol. 1, passim, for this evolution.

[10] Pineau, *La Simple vérité* (Paris: Julliard, 1961), p. 131, recalled the spontaneous approval of men in the southern zone, such as André Philip, Emmanuel d'Astier, and Henri Frenay who "gave or sent me recommendations, insisting on the necessity to explain to General de Gaulle the need to take political stands, to pronounce himself firmly for Democracy, to give Frenchmen prospects for a future opposed to that of Vichy." Pineau, pp. 152–91, describes his negotiations with the Gaullists in London.

[11] Pineau, *La Simple vérité*, pp. 607–9; de Gaulle, *Discours et messages*, vol. 1, pp. 205–6.

[12] De Gaulle, *Discours et messages*, vol. 1, p. 206. Women had never voted in France before this time.

[13] De Gaulle, *Discours et messages*, vol. 1.

[14] De Gaulle, *Discours et messages*, vol. 1.

of all religions, all morality, all charity."[15] The victory that Frenchmen
and all democratic peoples desired was for "liberty, justice, and the
right of men to rule themselves" in a peaceful community of international cooperation.[16] The interior movements could not have hoped
for a more satisfying response to their questions.[17] Clearly de Gaulle
had sided with the angels—a move that stood him in good stead when
the Allies, and United States President Franklin D. Roosevelt in particular, were about to "walk with the devil"[18] in North Africa.

The Anglo-American invasion of North Africa in November 1942
was planned and executed without reference to General de Gaulle
and the Fighting French.[19] When the Allied forces landed on 7 November 1942, French troops vigorously opposed them in several
sectors. The Americans had hoped to land without opposition, but a
plot by several anti-German, pro-Vichy conspirators failed conspicuously to neutralize Vichy's North African military forces. The conspiracy's figurehead, General Henri Honoré Giraud, arrived late (he
was at sea on a submarine during the landings) and lacked enough
prestige to have his cease-fire orders obeyed. Hence the American
commander, General Mark Clark, was forced to bargain with Admiral Darlan, commander-in-chief of Vichy's land and sea forces.
In fact, General Dwight D. Eisenhower, overall commander for

---

[15] De Gaulle, *Discours et messages*, vol. 1.

[16] De Gaulle, *Discours et messages*, vol. 1, p. 207.

[17] After the appearance of his declaration, issues of *Combat* and the other
journals commented extensively on de Gaulle's stand. For example, *Combat*,
no. 33, August 1942, saluted de Gaulle as the "First Resister of France" who
had been chosen chief and symbol of the Resistance largely because of his
adherence to Republican ideals.

[18] Winston Churchill, *The Hinge of Fate* (vol. 4 of *The Second World
War* [Boston: Houghton Mifflin Co., 1950]. Edition used here is the paperback [New York: Bantam Books, 1962]), p. 552, "President Roosevelt to
Prime Minister, 20 November 1942." In reference to the "temporary ex-
pedient" of an agreement with Admiral Darlan in North Africa, FDR noted
that he had quoted to the press an Orthodox Church proverb used in the
Balkans: "My children, it is permitted you in time of grave danger to walk
with the devil until you have crossed the bridge."

[19] OSS Document 21488 S, A Summary of Documents Covering Conversations between representatives of OSS and the Fighting French in London, 3–10 September 1942, expresses the Americans' skepticism about the
strength of the Gaullist movement. Especially in North Africa they felt that
the Gaullists could give no real military aid and that the Americans would
find more help among "favorably disposed elements in the French army
and the underground para-military organizations not definitely aligned with
de Gaulle."

Operation Torch, held supreme authority over North Africa after the cease-fire,[20] but the Americans named Darlan (and after his assassination, 25 December 1942, Giraud), repository of all French civil and military authority in North Africa.[21]

These developments shocked and appalled the resisters in France. To them Darlan, head of the Vichy government from February 1941 until Laval's return in April 1942, incarnated the policy of collaboration. In May 1941 he had negotiated the Paris Protocols, which granted the Germans use of French bases in Syria and proposed Vichy's suppression of the Gaullist dissidence in Africa at the recognized and accepted risk of open war against the British.[22] Although they might understand the temporary use of "this coward and traitor

[20] Churchill, *The Hinge of Fate*, p. 548, and *The Papers of Dwight D. Eisenhower* (Baltimore, Md.: Johns Hopkins University Press, 1970), vols. 1 and 2, documents concerning Operation Torch make it very clear that in the last resort Eisenhower retained dictatorial powers over North Africa. Also, *Foreign Relations of the United States, Diplomatic Papers: 1943*, vol. 2 (Washington, 1964), p. 23, a telegram from FDR to Churchill on 1 January 1943 stated: "I feel very strongly that we have a military occupation in North Africa and as such our Commanding General has complete charge of all matters civil as well as military."

[21] The events in North Africa, which can be given only in barest outline here, are amply documented. Sources for this paragraph and the following brief discussion of the complicated situation at Algiers include: De Gaulle, *Mémoires de guerre* (Paris: Librairie Plon, 1954); Soustelle, *Envers et contre tout*, 2 vols. (Paris: Robert Laffont, 1947 and 1950); Albert Kammerer, *Du débarquement africain au meutre de Darlan* (Paris: Flammarion, 1949); Crusoé (Jacques Lemaigre-Debreuil), *Vicissitudes d'une victoire* (Paris: Les Éditions de l'Ame Française, 1946); Churchill, *Hinge of Fate* and *Closing the Ring*; Eisenhower, *Papers*, vols. 2 and 3; Eisenhower, *Crusade in Europe* (Garden City, N.Y.: Doubleday and Co., 1948); *Foreign Relations of the United States, Diplomatic Papers: 1943*, vol. 2: *Europe* (Washington, 1964); Mark W. Clark, *Calculated Risk* (New York: Harper, 1950); Duff Cooper, *Old Men Forget* (London: Hart-Davis, 1954); Robert Murphy, *Diplomat among Warriors* (Garden City, N.Y.: Doubleday and Co., 1964); Harry C. Butcher, *My Three Years with Eisenhower* (New York: Simon and Schuster, 1946); Yves Maxime Danan, *La Vie politique à Alger de 1940 à 1944* (Paris: Librairie générale de droit et de jurisprudence, 1963); Henri Giraud, *Un seul but la Victoire* (Paris: René Julliard, 1949); Henri Michel, *Les Courants de pensée de la résistance*, part 3, "Le Giraudisme," pp. 445–76; and Funk, *Charles de Gaulle: The Crucial Years, 1943–1944* (Norman: University of Oklahoma Press, 1959).

[22] Text of these Protocols, signed 27 and 28 May 1941 by Darlan, Abetz, and Warlimont, found in Captured German Documents, T-77, roll 829, frames 5566675–697; also in English translation in *Documents on German Foreign Policy*, series D, 12 (Washington, D.C.: U.S. Government Printing Office, 1962), no. 559, pp. 892–900.

Darlan"[23] to save lives and end the shooting, the resisters could not believe that the Americans would allow Darlan to rule North Africa in Pétain's name. In December 1942 *Combat* declared: "In no case will the Resistance tolerate the sinister plot to turn over to Vichy through Darlan the fruits of the Allied victory in North Africa."[24] And the editors of the journal *Résistance* added:

> To recognize the accords of Algiers would mean above all to diminish the morale of the country; France should not be, under any title, the France of treason. A Darlan cannot, in whatever fashion, represent the country. We have protested, in the name of legality and morality, against the duperies and lies of a Hitler and a Mussolini; this was not in order to accept the machiavellianism of certain men of Vichy.[25]

After the Christmas Day assassination of Darlan,[26] the resisters', disappointment in the Americans was increased by the appointment of General Giraud as his replacement and by Roosevelt's continued hostility to de Gaulle. Giraud, whose hatred of the Germans was beyond question, had been hailed in the clandestine journals after his dramatic escape from captivity in Germany.[27] But a meeting with several leading resisters soon revealed that Giraud had no understanding of political and ideological complications beyond the military conflict.[28] When Laval pressured him to return to prison in Germany as a gesture of collaboration, the general agreed only to send a declaration of loyalty to Pétain.[29] Even though this statement was obviously extorted from Giraud, its effect was to lower his standing

---

[23] *Combat* no. 40, December 1942.

[24] *Combat* no. 38, December 1942; *Le Franc-Tireur*, 15 August 1943, in an "Open Letter to President Roosevelt" warned that he was being misled by advisers such as Admiral Leahy and Camille Chautemps. Vichy could not represent France.

[25] Bruneau, *Essai d'historique*, p. 14, quotes third issue of *Résistance*.

[26] President Roosevelt pronounced this act "cold blooded murder," but to the Gaullists it was a patriotic act. See Soustelle, *Envers et contre tout*, vol. 2, pp. 82–83, 91.

[27] *Combat*, May 1942. Giraud described his escape from the castle of Königstein in *Mes Évasions* (Paris: Julliard, 1946).

[28] *Témoignages* of Bourdet and de Menthon, Archives, CHG.

[29] See Geoffrey Warner, *Pierre Laval and the Eclipse of France* (New York: Macmillan Co., 1968), pp. 297–99, and Jäckel, *Frankreich in Hitlers Europa* (Stuttgart: Verlags Amstalt, 1966), pp. 221–22, for the repercussions of Giraud's escape on German–Vichy relations.

with the resisters. More damaging were indications that he was in fact not unsympathetic to Vichy and the National Revolution.

Despite Darlan's removal, North Africa continued to be governed under the old Vichy system. Officials still loyal to Pétain's regime remained in their posts, the anti-Semitic legislation remained in effect, and political prisoners, especially Communist and Gaullist resisters, were still detained in concentration camps. Only after the Americans became worried about public opinion and sent Jean Monnet to coach Giraud in civil affairs did he announce on 14 March 1943 that eventually the Republic must be restored and that Vichy's legislation would be null and void.[30]

Possibly Giraud did not realize the significance of his new democratic pose. The general was probably quite sincere in his repeated assertions that he only made war and was not interested in politics. At Algiers Giraud seemed totally wrapped up in his projects for rearming the French army and his fantasies of commanding the Allied forces that would invade France at the liberation.[31] Friends and foes acknowledged Giraud's political ineptitude.[32] As the Americans had feared, once de Gaulle and Giraud were face to face it was child's play for the Fighting French leader to efface their appointee. On 3 June 1943 a Comité Français de la Libération Nationale (CFLN) was established, and the two generals became co-chairmen, flanked theoretically by an equal number of their supporters.[33] In fact, all of de Gaulle's nominees to the CFLN were partisan politicians who knew what they wanted; Giraud's were generally moderates who felt no strong sense of loyalty to Giraud.[34] By 6 November de Gaulle had maneuvered Giraud into signing a decree that declared Charles de Gaulle elected president of the CFLN with a mandate to ensure: "the

---

[30] Funk, *De Gaulle*, pp. 105–10.

[31] Giraud had accepted the plans of the conspirators on the understanding that an invasion would also strike France and that he would command it. Perhaps Giraud fancied himself World War II's Marshal Foch. See Crusoé, *Vicissitudes* and Eisenhower, *Papers*, vols. 1 and 2, especially vol. 2, no. 586.

[32] Crusoé, *Vicissitudes*. Giraud, *Un seul but*, willingly acknowledged his political ineptitude.

[33] De Gaulle, *Mémoires*, vol. 2, pp. 488–93.

[34] For example, Jean Monnet, whom Roosevelt actually sent to aid Giraud, told Robert Murphy, FDR's special representative in North Africa, that "he had come to Algiers not so much to serve Giraud as to seek a solution which would create unity among all French factions." Murphy, *Diplomat*, p. 179.

complete separation of the Government and the Military Command, as well as the latter's [Giraud's] subordination to the former."[35]

The political significance of his actions may have eluded Giraud, but certainly not the interior resisters. Announcing Giraud's escape from Königstein, *Combat* declared: "We do not know whether Giraud is republican, royalist, democrat, or if he dreams of autocracy, and that matters little today."[36] When the Allies landed in North Africa the same journal proclaimed: "A great war leader, General Giraud, has retaken his place in the battle."[37] But when Giraud avoided contact with de Gaulle, the resisters became alarmed. "General Giraud, France is waiting! . . . Men associated with treason are not qualified to lead the fight of honor. . . ."[38] In February a "Letter to General Giraud" urged him to escape a third time—not from the Germans this time but from his Vichy entourage. "Your place is with us—escape!"[39] Finally in April Henri Frenay's *Combat* editorial, *"The people have chosen,"* stated that Giraud might still be entrusted with military duties, but because of his association with Pétain's sympathizers he could not presume to act as spokesman for France. Only de Gaulle could fill that role.

> He [de Gaulle] speaks the language of France. . . . He has never wavered. . . . Between de Gaulle and Giraud the people have chosen de Gaulle. Such is its will. . . . The choice is not just between two men but between the values they represent . . . the ideal which they incarnate.[40]

---

[35] De Gaulle, *Mémoires*, vol. 2, p. 537.

[36] *Combat*, second number for May 1942.

[37] Special supplement to *Combat*, November 1942.

[38] *Combat* no. 39, January 1943.

[39] *Combat* no. 41, February 1943.

[40] *Combat* no. 43, 15 April 1943. For the resisters' attitudes toward Giraud and de Gaulle see OSS Documents 30321 S, 39014 C, 67783 S, 61207 S, and 31330 C. The OSS reports that describe shifts in public opinion and in the attitudes of resistance groups are of uneven quality; some observers appear to have been very well informed, but others seem to have based their opinions on conjecture or on advice from an extremely limited range of contacts. One report evaluates support for the Gaullists at 5 percent; another, dated the same month, suggests 95 percent. But taken overall the report reflects a definite shift away from Vichy toward de Gaulle. By 1944 most of the reports indicate widespread sympathy for de Gaulle in France. For Giraud the reports almost unanimously indicate no support at all among the resistance movements.

To the resisters, intentionally or not Giraud had become inextricably associated with Vichy's antirepublicanism.[41]

The resisters' convictions were reinforced as numerous former Vichy adherents made their way to Algiers to offer their services to the Resistance—Giraud style. After all, what was Giraud doing if not acting out the Marshal's secret desire, carrying out the other half of Pétain's double game? In France Giraudist Sympathizers included remnants of the Armistice Army; the ORA (Organisation de Résistance de l'Armée), that began to form Maquis units, whose officers often seemed more concerned about restoring order at the liberation or preventing a Communist takeover than fighting Germans.[42] As the shifting winds of war began to favor the Allies, many opportunists, especially conservatives shocked by the revolutionary de Gaulle, abandoned the sinking ship of Vichy to join Giraud. Unquestionably some had sincerely believed in Pétain. Now, disenchanted by the Marshal's failure to oppose the total occupation of France, these men went to North Africa hoping to actively fight the Germans.[43] But after two years of cat-and-mouse with Vichy's police, the resisters could not be expected to distinguish between conviction and credulity. Giraud's administration of North Africa appeared to the resistance movements "an *ersatz,* and even a poor *ersatz* of Vichy. . . ."[44]

The resisters thought they were being betrayed or hoaxed by the Allies' support of Giraud. Their natural reaction was an even more

---

[41] The MUR's position was stated formally in a note from the Comité Directeur on 16 April 1943, "Fouché à Toutes Régions," pp. 1–3. "I Position des Mouvements de Résistance Unis à l'égard de General Giraud." Papers of Alban Vistel, Archives, CHG. " 'All united against the *Boche*' is an excellent formula on the condition that one knows who commands and who they will put in the place of the *Boche*. Those who say 'I do not play politics' are naive. . . . See also "Diderot à Tous Services Toutes Régions: Conflit de Gaulle–Giraud," 12 July 1943, five pages, Papers of Alban Vistel. Document communicated to the author by M. Vistel.

[42] Passy, *Missions Secrètes en France* (Paris: Librairie Plon, 1951), pp. 5–14. Some of Giraud's followers saw the problem of the liberation as one of maintaining order "with several battalions of Senegalese sharp-shooters" (p. 13). The most blatant exposition of this point of view is found in Colonel du Jonchay, *La Résistance et les communistes* (Paris: Éditions France-Empire, 1968).

[43] For example, General de Lattre de Tassigny, the only high-ranking officer to try to oppose the German invasion of the unoccupied zone in November 1942, escaped after his arrest by Vichy authorities and became the head of the First French Army under de Gaulle.

[44] Passy, *Missions secrètes en France*, pp. 5–6.

emphatic commitment to de Gaulle.[45] Shortly after the Allied landings, the Coordinating Committee of the MUR and representatives of the trade unions and political parties, including the Socialists, Radicals, Popular Democrats, and the Fédération Républicaine, sent congratulations to the Allied governments and saluted General Giraud. They insisted, though: "In no circumstances will we agree that the rallying of those responsible for political or military treachery be considered as an excuse for past crimes. We ask that the new destiny of liberated North Africa be placed in General de Gaulle's hands immediately."[46] On the eve of the meeting of de Gaulle and Giraud in May 1943, the position of the Conseil National de la Résistance was stated unequivocally.

> All the movements and parties of the Resistance declare formally: . . . 2) That the people of France will never accept the subordination of General de Gaulle to General Giraud, and request the rapid installation at Algiers of a provisional government, under the presidency of General de Gaulle; General Giraud would become the military chief. 3) That General de Gaulle will remain the only chief of the French Resistance, whatever is the result of the negotiations.[47]

Eventually, of course, the Gaullist resisters had their way, but the bitterness engendered by this "quarrel of the two generals" left a residue of bad memories. After a final argument over the fusion of the Gaullist and Giraudist intelligence services—a move Giraud opposed[48]—General de Gaulle assigned Giraud to the position of inspector general of the Armies, probably knowing that Giraud would refuse to remain at Algiers as a powerless figurehead.[49] At first Giraud refused to accept the new appointment or to resign, but he was unable to find any further support from the Allies and was forced to retire on 12 April 1944.[50]

---

[45] Henri Michel, *Les Idées politiques et sociales de la Résistance* (Paris: Presses Universitaires de France, 1954), p. 26.

[46] De Gaulle, *Mémoires*, vol. 2, p. 475. Also a copy in English translation in OSS Document 28241 S.

[47] De Gaulle, *Mémoires*, vol. 2, p. 475.

[48] Soustelle, *Envers et contre tout*, vol. 2, p. 327, and passim.

[49] Funk, *De Gaulle*, pp. 233–35; and De Gaulle, *Mémoires*, vol. 2, pp. 570–71.

[50] Soustelle, *Envers et contre tout*, vol. 2, p. 349, and Funk, *De Gaulle*, pp. 233–36.

Even after Giraud's removal the Giraudist ORA within France, not unlike the Communist FTP (Francs-Tireurs et Partisans), occasionally remained a separate band apart from Gaullist control even though it was theoretically an integral part of the FFI. Still, these squabbles were small and isolated flareups that were ultimately of little consequence.

The significance of the Giraud–de Gaulle conflict did not lie in a power struggle between two Frenchmen; Giraud never had any meaningful support inside France. And it was not simply Gaullist progressive democratic ideology versus Giraudist conservatism, though the contrast was an essential one. The fundamental issue was Allied, particularly American, intrusion into what the resisters considered strictly French affairs; Giraud's authority was derived solely from the dictates of President Roosevelt. Long after Giraud's ouster, in spite of impressive evidence that de Gaulle enjoyed considerable support in France, Roosevelt adamantly refused to acknowledge the CFLN and de Gaulle as the legitimate Provisional Government of France.[51]

Despite their basic sympathy for the American people and the traditional friendship of the two countries, the resisters could not excuse the Americans for their earlier dealings with Vichy and for sustaining Giraud against de Gaulle. An open "letter to the Americans" in *Combat*, February 1943, asked: "You often cite Washington and Lafayette. Ask yourself: What would they think of all this?"[52]

As the liberation became more imminent and proposals for an Allied Military Government (AMGOT) were considered, irritation

---

[51] Funk, *De Gaulle*, especially pp. 3–4, 270–76, 295, 297–99, 301–3, and 316–18, provides an excellent and fairminded summary of relations between de Gaulle and Roosevelt. Funk states: "By October, 1943, there was good evidence that de Gaulle, not Giraud was the man to work with; by December this evidence was conclusive; and by January, 1944, virtually every responsible officer in the North African theater and in Washington, including Eisenhower, Murphy, Wilson, McCloy, Stimson, and even Hull, had become convinced that closer relations with the FCNL were imperative. The responsibility for denying the Committee falls squarely on the shoulders of the President, who, for month after month—from January to July, 1944—stubbornly refused to submit" (p. 301). *Foreign Relations of the United States, Diplomatic Papers: 1943*, vol. 2: *Europe*, pp. 11–112, 145–47, 155–57, 194–97, reveal Roosevelt's attitude toward de Gaulle.

[52] This rebuke was in contrast to earlier editions of *Combat*, for example, no. 2, December 1941, when the U.S. had just entered the war. America was hailed as the savior of France whose vast industrial potential made victory certain.

and verbal rebukes threatened to become outright hostility. The weekly *Bulletin Intérieur des Mouvements Unis de la Résistance* (BIMUR) criticized the Allied imposition of Marshal Badoglio, a former Mussolini lieutenant, on the Italian people,[53] repeatedly complained about General de Gaulle's absence from important Allied conferences, and expressed the resisters' apparently sincere fears of American collusion with Vichy to prevent the Gaullist Resistance from seizing power. The bulletin also voiced suspicions of negotiations between Rommel and the Americans to overthrow Hitler and later join in a German, Anglo-Saxon, anti-Bolshevik crusade against the Soviet Union.[54] In his analysis of the underground journals, a surprised OSS agent commented on the "extraordinary rumors" about American policy. "Frankly, America does not have a very high standing among the editors and writers of these French clandestine papers."[55]

Le Franc-Tireur of 1 March 1944 warned that de Gaulle must be recognized as head of the French government and that France would not allow anything similar to the foisting of Marshal Badoglio on the Italians. None of the resistance movements could understand British and American failure to endorse de Gaulle before the liberation, and they vehemently protested the idea that the American president might attempt to contest the destiny of France. On 14 July 1944 *Le Franc-Tireur* exclaimed proudly: "France . . . does not concede . . . that French policy can be dictated by concern to please, or not to displease, the Americans."[56]

The resisters' reaction was by no means limited to words. Their plans for a national insurrection were based on the assumption that

---

[53] On the Italian situation, see *Bulletin Intérieur de l'A. S. de la Région de Toulouse* (an MUR journal), no. 5, 20 August 1943.

[54] The BIMUR was not so widely distributed as the regular clandestine newspapers but was sent to all of the cadres—the leaders at every echelon of the MUR. Almost every issue from December 1943 through the Allied invasion expressed this deep-seated suspicion of American policy. A few examples include the issues of 14 and 21 December 1943; 4 January, 8 February, 2 and 16 March, and 5 and 20 April 1944. The same attitudes are reflected in varying degrees in the separate journals, *Combat*, *Libération* and *Le Franc-Tireur*, which was especially sharp in its denunciation of American policy. For example, 1 March, 30 June, and 14 July 1944.

[55] OSS Document 53747 R, dated 13 January 1944, sent from Switzerland, where the agent undoubtedly had access to all of the MUR journals.

[56] *Le Franc-Tireur*, 14 July 1944.

the Americans might indeed try to administer France under an AMGOT. Their instructions for the seizure of radio facilities illustrated the resisters' concern.

> We must affirm the existence of a nationwide French radio. It is necessary for liberated Frenchmen to speak as rapidly as possible from national soil to those who are not yet [liberated]. It is possible—if not probable—that the liberating authorities may oppose this design. All means of persuasion, all arguments must be put forward with firmness to overcome this opposition. It will be necessary, of course, to submit to the imperatives of military and diplomatic censors, but we must neglect nothing which will give the broadcasts a national character. And while cooperation with the Liberation armies is imposed like a duty, there is no reason to submit blindly [to them]. We have a national position to defend toe to toe. . . .[57]

Directives for the insurrection from the Directing Committee of the MUR to its militants consistently stressed the importance of installing an effective pro-Gaullist administration in every locality *before* the arrival of Allied troops in order to place the Anglo-Americans before a fait accompli.[58]

In general the interior resisters were less critical of the British than of the Americans. True, the BIMUR of 16 March 1944 regretted "the singular predilection of the British government for every 'established' form of government."[59] But Winston Churchill had backed de Gaulle from the first and stood by him even after many acrimonious disputes. Further, the resisters in France had far more direct contact with

---

[57] *Cahier Bleu: Directives élaborées par la Résistance Métropolitaine, promulguées à Alger en 1944, puis à Paris lors de la libération de la France* (Numéro spécial hors série de L'Echo de la Presse et da la Publicité), p. 12.

[58] "Le Comité Directeur des Mouvements de Résistance Unis à tous les directoires régionaux," 14 May 1943, p. 4; Circulaire of 5 November 1943, "Référence Insurrection," pp. 1–2. "Note du Comité Central des M. U. R. sur les comités de Libération et les commissaires de la république," October 1943; "S. G. du M. L. N. à . . . toutes régions," 24 June 1944, passing on decisions of the CNR; and "L'Exécutif Zone Sud du M. L. N. à Tous Directoires régionaux départementaux" (no date, but probably May 1944, from internal evidence), pp. 1 and 5, Papers of Alban Vistel, Archives, CHG.

[59] BIMUR, 16 March 1944.

British agents than with Americans,[60] and until 1944 the matériel and armaments that the movements received came almost exclusively from London.

The operations of the British SOE (Special Operations Executive),[61] however, were frequently a source of friction. Regional heads of the MUR often complained that British officers set up independent operations in their territories. Since British planes carried all of the parachute drops, SOE agents usually received priority[62] and often tempted militants away from the movements with an offer of arms that the MUR chiefs could not match. Occasionally the SOE's French recruits pretended to be General de Gaulle's agents in order to secure the help of the movements.[63] Naturally the movements' founders objected to such procedures and ordered that every overture of agents of the SOE or any other foreign service be immediately reported to the chiefs. Failure to report a contact could result in a militant's exclusion from the movement.[64] Exasperated by the efforts of certain British agents in France to appropriate members of his movement, Henri Frenay informed Major Sir Collin Gubbins, head of the SOE operations, that if such behavior was not stopped "he would order them [the British agents] shot in preference to hirelings of the Gestapo."[65]

Predictably the incidents involving British agents, like American policy, rebounded in de Gaulle's favor. Every bit as sensitive as de Gaulle to considerations of national honor, the interior resisters deeply resented the Allies' treatment of France as a lesser power.[66] Each expression of de Gaulle's haughtiness and refusal to compromise

---

[60] Norman Kogan, "American Policies toward European Resistance Movements," *Deuxième Conférence Internationale d'Histoire de la Résistance* (Milano, 1961), pp. 8–14.

[61] M. R. D. Foot, *SOE in France* (London: Her Majesty's Stationery Office, 1966) is the semiofficial history of the Special Operations Executive.

[62] Henri Raymond, "Experiences of an SOE Agent in France," p. 120.

[63] *Témoignages* of Bourdet and Frenay; Bénouville, *Le Sacrifice;* and "Rapport sur l'Activité du Service K," 12 November 1943, Papers of Alban Vistel, Archives, CHG.

[64] See "Exécutif A. S. du M. L. N. à toutes régions, tous départements—Objet: Contacts avec les agents de l'I. S. du WAR OFFICE, et tous représentants des services Étrangers," 20 June 1944; and "R. S. G./A. à Pascal—Raoul," 20 July 1944, both in Papers of Alban Vistel, Archives, CHG.

[65] *Témoignage* of Frenay, Archives, CHG.

[66] BIMUR, numerous issues in late 1943 and until the liberation.

delighted the resisters as much as it infuriated Roosevelt and irritated Churchill.[67] Their agreement in May 1943 to create the Conseil National de la Résistance (CNR) for that specific purpose indicated that the resistance movements had clearly mandated Charles de Gaulle to speak for France in international affairs.[68] But even though they were attached to de Gaulle as the symbol of their struggle and leader of the revolution they hoped to achieve, the interior resisters, proud of the movements they had raised on their own, were less willing to see the General alone holding the reins within France. And they were even less ready to turn over their troops to mere agents of de Gaulle on missions from London or Algiers.

We have seen that Jean Moulin, de Gaulle's first full-fledged emissary to the interior resistance movements in southern France, had considerable difficulty in consumating the union of the MUR. His attempt to bring the resisters under effective control by the Fighting French ran into serious problems that went beyond the personal rivalries of the resistance chiefs. A fundamental and apparently irreconcilable difference in their conceptions of the movements' role plagued relations between de Gaulle and the MUR from beginning to end. Charles de Gaulle was no ordinary soldier, but his military background significantly colored his ideas. At London with the Comité National Français (CNF—the French National Committee) and later at Algiers before the CFLN, he was accustomed to a situation in which: "Everyone gives his opinion and General de Gaulle, like Louis XIV in the Council of State, resolves and decides."[69]

In de Gaulle's design for the Resistance, the movements were but one part of a coordinated, hierarchical organization with a definite chain of command. Viewed from London the interior Resistance ap-

---

[67] The urging of Henri Frenay and General Catroux that de Gaulle assume a more flexible policy was exceptional.

[68] See René Hostache, *Le Conseil National de la Résistance* (Paris: Presses Universitaires de France, 1958).

[69] Michel and Guetzévitch, *Les Idées*, p. 19; see also Passy, *Missions secrètes en France*, pp. 176–77; Michel, *Les Courants de Pensée*, "Pre-éminence du Chef," pp. 31–33. Soustelle, *Envers et contre tout*, vol. 1, pp. 286–87, says most decisions were unanimous, though there were often vigorous debates. On particularly serious questions each of the national commissioners had his say; but as de Gaulle recalled, *Mémoires*, vol. 1, 224–25, despite occasional disagreements: "In the last resort . . . it was always, finally, *le pauvre moi* who was accountable for all." See de Gaulle, *Mémoires*, vol. 2, pp. 175–76, for comments to the same effect about the CFLN at Algiers.

peared to be: ". . . an abundance of desires to do good, of courageous thoughts, exalted imaginations expressed through disorderly acts without real effectiveness."[70] Only if unified and integrated into the ranks of the Fighting French could the resistance movements play a constructive part in the liberation and renovation of France.[71] In the words of Jacques Soustelle, one of de Gaulle's most fervent apostles in London and Algiers:

> We wanted these efforts and sacrifices [of the interior resisters] to be credited to France in the same manner as the battles and casualties of the Free French Forces [F. F. L. —Forces Françaises Libres]. Therefore, we never admitted that one could trace any line of demarcation within the Resistance: for us, the Resistance was the whole formed by the F. F. L., the liberated overseas territories, and those who, in the territory not yet liberated, took part in the struggle against the enemy. . . . The initial stand of General de Gaulle was sometimes to lead us into trouble with certain Resistance leaders, other times into difficulties and conflicts with our allies. But it derived from our very nature, and we could not have changed it any more than a leopard can change its spots.[72]

Thus the natural tendency of the exterior Resistance was to attempt to subjugate the interior movements to strict control,[73] a process that frequently meant curtailing the authority of the interior leadership.

The chiefs of the MUR did not contest de Gaulle's ultimate authority, but they felt fully competent to direct their own organizations. Henri Frenay saw his position as analogous to a governmental minister, responsible before the premier, de Gaulle, but supreme over his own department.[74] The movements rejected the idea that an outsider might hold executive discretion over their actions in France. Leaders of the movements felt that the Gaullist Délégation Générale in France should serve primarily as a liaison between them and General de Gaulle—a sort of technical secretariat to channel material and

---

[70] Passy, *10 Duke Street Londres*, pp. 104–5.
[71] De Gaulle, *Mémoires*, vol. 1, pp. 225–38.
[72] Soustelle, *Envers et contre tout*, vol. 1, p. 184.
[73] Michel, *Les Courants de pensée*, pp. 65–66.
[74] Passy, *Missions secrète en France*, pp. 218–19, and Soustelle, *Envers et contre tout*, vol. 2, pp. 163–68, quoting reports of Jean Moulin.

information to the resisters. During the negotiations with de Gaulle that preceded the fusion of their movements, Frenay and d'Astier demanded suppression of the position of délégué général in southern France. With the creation of the MUR, they argued, Moulin's presence was no longer necessary, "the Resistance no longer needed a legal guardian."[75]

Moulin's courage, ability, and incontestable familiarity with the rules of clandestine life won him the unanimous if sometimes grudging respect of the resisters. Many of the envoys from London, however, showed little understanding of interior conditions and less respect for the interior resisters. The resentment produced by the imposing manner of some agents sent by General de Gaulle and the BCRA is evident in the words of Guillain de Bénouville, a member of the MUR's Directing Committee.

> . . . from the moment they arrived they obstinately wished to take command of our formations, although, in agreement with our militants, we considered them as liaison officers attached to our formations which were Gaullist beyond question; but it is equally true that the fashion in which they were formed on the one hand and on the other, the separation from the government, conferred upon them a sort of autonomy which could not be contested without implying that the government lacked confidence in the Resistance.[76]

Yves Farge, head of the Comité d'Action contre la Déportation (CAD) suggested: "In the eyes of the Chiefs of Staff, we were 'agents'; they intended to play with us in the same fashion that Conan Doyle manipulated his characters. The *deuxième bureau* [BCRA] method too often bruised our sensitivities."[77]

The Gaullist officers sometimes brought orders from London that reflected a serious incomprehension of underground life in France. Jean Moulin's first mission included the task of separating the movements' paramilitary formations from their political activities. According to Colonel Passy (André Dewavrin), chief of the BCRA, it was de Gaulle's particular concern that the two realms be kept separate.[78] In view of the organization of the Mouvements Unis de la

---

[75] Passy, *10 Duke Street Londres*, p. 247.
[76] Bénouville, *Le Sacrifice*, p. 481.
[77] Farge, *Rebelles soldats et citoyens*, p. 43.
[78] Passy, *2e Bureau Londres*, p. 225.

Résistance, particularly in the early stages when everyone did a little bit of everything, it is not surprising that such proposals troubled the movements. A similar directive in the fall of 1943 ordered the decentralization of the Resistance into autonomous groups controlled by regional military delegates in direct radio contact with London.[79] Essentially such instructions revealed a total disregard of the existing structure of the MUR and a determination to impose organization from the outside; in practice they proved inapplicable.

All of the original MUR leaders objected to Moulin's effort to divorce the Secret Army from the movements.[80] In the revolutionary struggle they were waging, distinctions between civilian and military affairs were meaningless. Although not primarily concerned with politics, most resisters desired a renovated political regime for France at the liberation and while opposing the Germans they were working toward that end. Thus motivated, the local sectors of the MUR formed a solid base for military and political action. All of the resisters thought of themselves as soldiers but at the same time recognized the principle of civilian control. When the new injunctions were handed down, a departmental leader in Region I—Lyon complained:

> . . . We have been opposed from the first to the separation of the so-called unified movements into A. P. (Political Action) and A. M. (Military Action). . . .
>
> All of my efforts until now have been towards a strong organization of sectors, *realized principally around the administrative or political chef de secteur.* This person is always a militant whose commitment dates from the early days of the occupation, one who, in addition, commands the esteem and confidence of the troops of the Resistance. . . .[81]

To reverse this development would be a mistake, concluded the report, indicating that "the insurrectional spirit of the troops of the Resistance is either not understood or *deliberately ignored.*"[82]

Eventually the exterior services were forced to acknowledge their mistake. On 5 November 1943, Pierre Brossolette, Colonel Passy's

---

[79] Soustelle, *Envers et contre tout,* vol. 2, pp. 308–10.

[80] Vistel, *La Nuit,* p. 425ff.

[81] Chef Départmental Rigaud à Socrate," 11 December 1943, three pages, papers of Alban Vistel, Archives, CHG.

[82] Ibid.

Members of a maquis *band at Vachère-en-Quint (Drôme) pose for a photograph in their forest campsite. Note the German spiked helmet (Pickelhaube) sported by the* maquisard *standing at the right.*

closest associate and one of the staunchest Gaullists, reported considerable confusion in France.

> . . . the heavy fault lies, *as you and I said in July*, in the stupid illusion that decentralization can come about by decree of the Holy Ghost, and that after having decreed it, it suffices to send in regional officers for everything to fall into place. All of that, dressed in theoretical schemes and insane *kriegspiels*, is a simple folly. In the southern zone, it is possible that the situation is ripe enough for the regional officer to land with some chance of success in their areas. But in the Z. N. it is "unthinkable." In order to have decentralization, there must be a very strong regional and departmental organization. . . .[83]

Brossolette concluded that the problem was neither the reestablishment of centralization under zonal officers nor a question of whether

---

[83] "Lettre personnelle de Pedro [Brossolette] à Arquebuse [Passy]." Begun 5 November, ended 8 November 1943; in Reports of Brossolette, Archives, CHG.

the BCRA officers would be commanded from London or the interior. They simply must discover:

> . . . how each one in his region, subdivisions, or departments was going to enter into contact with the [existing] elements, sometimes coordinated, but often not. First of all, they must make contact with the chiefs of the movements at Paris, because they remain, for their regional subordinates, the *grands patrons. . . . The only great problem, as you have seen, is* the coordination of the civilian and the military aspects. . . . That is precisely what the ingenious combinations erected by your services have rendered *systematically impossible.*[84]

Several interrelated considerations may explain de Gaulle's determination to organize the movements' military forces into a Secret Army directly tied to him. From the first the exterior resisters had looked somewhat askance at the southern zone's predilection for political action. If the movements wanted to distribute a few propaganda leaflets, that was all right and might have a beneficial effect on public opinion; but might not their passionate political stands work to the detriment of common action?[85] After all, the serious business of the Resistance, its "profound reality,"[86] was its paramilitary aspect.

What counted for the exterior was the gathering of military intelligence and the formation of disciplined guerrilla bands to act on orders from London in coordination with Allied strategy, especially for sabotage during the invasion of France. Extensive guerrilla action before the invasion threatened not only senseless reprisals on the civilian population but also the possible reinforcement of the occupation forces before the Allied landings. Such activities should be restricted to the minimum necessary for training under the guidance of qualified military cadres designated by de Gaulle. The liberation itself should be as orderly as possible, and the irregular troops of the Resistance should be incorporated into the regular French army as soon as possible. Under the careful scrutiny of the Allied powers, France

---

[84] "Lettre personnelle de Pedro à Arquebuse," 5–8 November 1943.

[85] De Gaulle, *Mémoires,* vol. 1, p. 230. "Lettre Personnelle de Pedro à Arquebuse," 5–8 November 1943, p. 4: "Excuse me for having insisted extensively on the military question. But you know that for me it is that which counts before all," and "Compte-Rendu de Mission," 10 November 1943, Reports of Brossolette, Archives, CHG.

[86] "Rapport de Brumaire [Brossolette] en date du 18 Octobre." Archives, CHG.

could not afford the appearance of chaos in the wake of the liberating armies. Would not the existence of relatively autonomous bands of resisters represent a serious threat to de Gaulle's plans for restoration of French grandeur—perhaps even pose the question of civil war?[87]

The interior resisters saw the situation in an entirely different light. The movements agreed with de Gaulle that most of their adherents were much more interested in fighting Germans than concerned with hypothetical programs of postwar reforms.[88] Nevertheless, the Secret Army that they had created was no traditional auxiliary for regular operations, and its objectives were not simply military alone. Henri Frenay pictured a Secret Army that was:

> . . . an instrument both military and revolutionary. . . . Liberation and Revolution are two aspects of the same problem, indivisibly linked. . . . Discipline in the A. S. is a result of confidence and friendship; no subordination exists in the military sense of the word. . . . A revolutionary army names its chiefs, they are not imposed. . . . It is not an army that we have forged, not a hierarchical, organized mass, but bands of partisans, who wish to fight even more for their interior liberties than against the invader.[89]

To maintain the morale of these voluntary combatants, immediate action was essential. Groups that cautiously waited for the invasion were the most apt to fall prey to the Gestapo or Milice without ever having fought.[90]

The resisters seized on and incessantly repeated de Gaulle's phrase, "The National Liberation is inseparable from the National Insurrection,"[91] and so did not share the exterior's fear of disorder at the

---

[87] De Gaulle's fears of this nature are evident in his *Mémoires*, passim. Despite a few words of praise for the resisters' uncommon courage, suspicion of their intentions remained a pervasive element in de Gaulle's calculations.

[88] Compare de Gaulle, *Mémoires*, vol. 1, p. 230, to Cerf-Ferrière, *Chemin clandestin*, pp. 76–79, Michel, *Les Courants de pensée*, pp. 2–3, and *Les Idées*, pp. 9 and 15, Hostache, *Le Conseil National de la Résistance*, pp. 176–77, all of whom stress the primary consideration of *action* for the resisters.

[89] Passy, *Missions secrètes en France*, p. 417.

[90] "S. G. du M. L. N. à toutes régions: Lettre de Service pour l'E. M. des C. F. L.," Papers of Alban Vistel, Archives, CHG, 11 April 1944, noted: "There is no greater danger than inaction."

[91] *Action*, no. 2, December 1943: "Comité central des mouvements de Résistance à tous chefs de régions et services," 8 December 1943, notes:

liberation. The directives for action at D-Day circulated 5 November 1943 to all the regions and services of the MUR included detailed instructions for the NAP's technical seizure of power. "A N. A. P. chief must never consider his work completed before having assured entirely the takeover *from the interior* of the administration in question and reduced the role of supporting elements to protection against exterior attack. . . ."[92]

Every effort was to be exerted toward a smooth transfer of powers to the Provisional Government. But even if the Vichy regime were to dissolve spontaneously, and no opposition whatsoever was encountered to the installation of CFLN authorities: "it would be absurd and in any case outrageous for the French people to expect the absence of any mass demonstrations animated by a just desire for punishment."[93] On the contrary: "An eventual passivity of the masses, contenting itself with cheerful demonstrations and triumphal arches at the arrival of the liberators would bode no good for the future independence of our country."[94] In their carefully prepared plans for the insurrection, the Liberation Committees should "neither neglect nor fear the force of the popular masses, but instead should use them."[95] An enthusiastic insurrection was the only way to ensure France's independence and a political future of its choice. In conclusion:

> It would be singularly dangerous to have absolute confidence in foreign military chiefs of staff, in foreign political envoys, or in officers of a French army of the colonial type to institute a Republic and permit the French people to express itself.
>
> In order to succeed, the Insurrection must be a powerful

"The hour has come to harden our militants in immediate action, because the National Insurrection is our surest hope for liberation and independence. Thus will be tempered immediately in action the troops of the French Resistance who will be called on to cooperate with the Allies in case of a debarkation." Papers of Alban Vistel, Archives, CHG. The Communist movements, the Front National in particular, were especially insistent in tying their appeals for more direct action to de Gaulle's words. See especially the issues of the *Bulletin d'Information du Front National*.

[92] "Circulaire du 5 Novembre, 1943," Papers of Alban Vistel, Archives, CHG, p. 5.

[93] Ibid., pp. 5–6.

[94] "Circulaire du 5 Novembre, 1943," Papers of Alban Vistel, Archives, CHG, p. 6.

[95] Ibid.

popular uprising, an uprising of all French patriots against the enemy and the traitors in his service.[96]

To the interior resisters, the exterior leadership's more conservative conceptions represented a disturbing "hostility to any popular action, fear of 'troubles', etc. . . . ,"[97] which overlooked an essential fact that: *"The War is the affair of all of the French People."*[98]

Given such underlying conceptual divergences, frequent disputes over the actual control of the Resistance's forces were probably unavoidable. The MUR directors feuded with Jean Moulin about command of the Secret Army, the reception of direct aid from the Americans in Switzerland, and the establishment of a National Resistance Council. Henri Frenay, who had played the major role in the development of the Secret Army, was prevented from assuming leadership of the Resistance's paramilitary troops because of rivalries among the movements. Nevertheless, after personally suggesting the appointment of General Charles Delestraint to head the AS, Combat's chief conspired to retain effective control despite the official designations.

Frenay argued that Delestraint's lack of clandestine experience endangered the AS's security,[99] and he rejected the general's attitude that the troops should be held inactive until D-Day. Then he proposed that as the MUR's military chief he act as a sort of war minister charged with supervision of the recruitment, training, and employment of the AS forces, and merely submit progress reports to Delestraint. The general realized that this plan would render his position ornamental, and he insisted that General de Gaulle's nomination carried no subordination to any kind of committee. Several meetings

---

[96] Ibid.

[97] "Fouché, délégué général F. F. I., zone sud," 1 June 1944, p. 5. Papers of Alban Vistel, Archives, CHG.

[98] "Fouché, délégué général." See also "Rapport sur la situation de R. 1," 1 July 1944, p. 2; and "L'Exécutif zone sud du M. L. N. à tous directories régionaux et départementaux," no date, probably May 1944, from internal evidence, p. 4. Papers of Alban Vistel, Archives, CHG.

[99] Unfortunately, as Moulin freely admitted (Passy, *Missions secrètes en France*, pp. 138–42), Frenay was right about Delestraint's unfamiliarity with the rules of underground life. On 9 July 1943, the unlucky general was arrested in Paris, where he had registered in a hotel under his real name. Delestraint was deported and then murdered at Buchenwald shortly before the arrival of the Allied armies.

of Delestraint, Moulin, and Frenay erupted into violent arguments, with Frenay, according to Moulin, cursing the general in "inadmissable language."[100]

Finding themselves close to an open rupture, the other directors of the MUR were willing to compromise. On 6 May 1943 the Directing Committee agreed that Delestraint held final authority in military matters and was responsible for the reception and distribution of all weapons. Nevertheless, the movements retained control of the Maquis and the Groupes Francs for immediate guerrilla action against enemy targets, which General de Gaulle would specify through Delestraint.[101] An "*Instruction personnelle et secrète du général de Gaulle au général Delestraint, commandant l'armée de l'intérier*" on 21 May settled the issue by admitting the "necessity of immediate action" and leaving the movements great initiative in that realm. However, the directive granted Delestraint the power to name regional and subregional commanders. It concluded that from the time of the Allied embarkation: "He will exercise effectively the command of all formations constituting the Army of the Interior and all independent military units."[102]

During the months when Moulin and the MUR were at odds over the Secret Army, Henri Frenay was in contact with representatives of the American Office of Strategic Services in Switzerland. In return for the transmission of all the military intelligence the movements collected, the Americans offered Frenay large sums of money, which could be used to subsidize Maquis groups organized by the MUR. Frenay negotiated with the Americans on his own, but the Directing Committee backed his initiative and voted to establish a permanent delegation in Switzerland in the name of the MUR. Moulin was incensed to learn of this new development, which he felt was an American attempt to undermine the Gaullist Resistance.[103] A major contribution of the Gaullist services to the Allies was the critical mili-

---

[100] Passy, *Missions secrètes en France*, pp. 364–65. For the whole controversy over the Secret Army, see also pp. 19–23, 138–142, 193–201, and 364–69. Also Soustelle, *Envers et contre tout*, vol. 2, pp. 142–44, 162–70. Compare Henri Michel, *Jean Moulin*, pp. 126–35. *Témoignages* of Frenay and Bourdet, Archives CHG.

[101] Passy, *Missions secrètes en France*, pp. 364–65.

[102] De Gaulle, *Mémoires*, vol. 2, pp. 477–78.

[103] Passy, *Missions secrètes en France*, pp. 211–14, and Soustelle, *Envers et contre tout*, vol. 2, pp. 165–66.

tary information that the movements transmitted to the BCRA in London. If the Americans received this information directly, they would have no need to ask the help of Charles de Gaulle.

In behalf of the MUR Frenay replied that no political commitment was involved. The MUR delegation would send all information in packages labeled with a Gaullist insignia, and the Americans understood fully that the MUR was loyal to de Gaulle. The arrangements made with the Americans would allow swifter transmission of information from France to London. Further, de Gaulle's own representative at Geneva had been informed about the negotiations and looked with favor on them. Finally, the Americans were offering to provide the money and supplies that the Maquis and the movements critically needed at a time when money from London was hopelessly inadequate.[104]

Indeed, Moulin acknowledged the justice of Frenay's argument that the proffered American aid was enormous compared to what he could dispense, and he appealed to General de Gaulle to increase his support immediately, at least enough to match the American offer. "The day when we can say that it is you and not the Allies, who finance the struggle against deportation, it is certain that the position of Gaullism in France will be greatly reinforced."[105] Still Moulin persisted in his opposition to any support not channeled through the French Committee. On 7 May 1943 Moulin reported to de Gaulle that he had agreed only to the retention of a MUR delegation in Switzerland, where the movements would be:

> . . . free to have . . . relations with the Americans or British, in so far as the relations had the goal of informing our Allies about the morale of the French Resistance and that they were exclusive of all military questions, which must rest in your hands and in those of your accredited representatives in France. I have personally given my accord for exchanges of information, in liaison with your representative in Switzerland, permitting notably the movements to send reports

---

[104] Passy, *Missions secrètes en France*, pp. 212–14; Soustelle, *Envers et contre tout*, vol. 2, pp. 165–66; *témoignages* of Frenay and Bourdet, Archives, CHG; Bénouville, *Le Sacrifice*, pp. 311–12, 326, 358–64. Compare Granet and Michel, *Combat*, pp. 196–201.

[105] Passy, *Missions secrètes en France*, pp. 212–14.

on the interior situation in France and articles destined for American or British newspapers.[106]

In the end the MUR yielded to Moulin's insistence that all military information be submitted directly to the BCRA. Just as in the dispute over the Secret Army, the movements reconciled themselves to Moulin's position in order to present a united front behind de Gaulle in face of the challenge presented by U.S. support for General Giraud. It was precisely this motive that provided the major justification for the creation of the National Resistance Council (CNR).

Contrasting experiences, attitudes, and organization of the Resistance in northern France precluded facile cooperation between the northern movements and the MUR. Resisters in neither zone were anxious to entrust executive authority over their troops to the leaders of movements from other regions. The movements were even less willing to permit representatives of political parties to share in their direction of the Resistance. In the spring of 1943 General de Gaulle commissioned Jean Moulin to unite all of the interior Resistance in a common organization that would include movements, parties, and syndicates. The movements unanimously opposed the project.[107] Frenay conceded that evidence of support for de Gaulle from the Republic's former political parties was important in the eyes of Churchill and Roosevelt, but he asked: "Why not simply solicit letters from men such as Blum, Herriot, Jeanneney, and Louis Marin?" Would not their word in the name of their parties serve as ample bond for Allied consumption?[108] The movements accepted the idea of the

---

[106] Soustelle, *Envers et contre tout*, vol. 2, p. 166.

[107] Michel, *Jean Moulin*, pp. 106–16 and 166–68, and Hostache, *Le Conseil*, pp. 116–18.

[108] *Témoignage* of Frenay, Archives, CHG, and Frenay, "De Gaulle et la Résistance," pp. 81–82. De Gaulle in fact sent an agent with this specific mission, and the rewards were generally gratifying. Letters of confidence came from Marin, Jeanneney, Herriot, Mandel, and others, including a particularly fruitful correspondence with Léon Blum. De Gaulle then used these letters in an attempt to convince President Roosevelt of his democratic intentions. See *Foreign Relations of the United States, Diplomatic Papers: 1942*, vol. 2: *Europe*, pp. 541–44, for indications that the Americans were not convinced by de Gaulle's arguments. Frenay continued to believe that the CNR was de Gaulle's worst mistake and ended all chances of a genuine renovation of French political life. He refused to sit on the Council, and Bourdet represented Combat.

CNR only after the Gaullist delegates granted that the parties represented on the council would not be the old parties of the Third Republic as such (resisters felt those parties had been conspicuously absent from the active Resistance) but, rather, "sectors of opinion."[109]

At the first session of the CNR in Paris at 48 Rue du Four, 27 May 1943, Moulin cited general de Gaulle's statements.

> . . . [I]f democracy presupposed organized parties, the presence in the midst of the Council of representatives of former political parties must not be considered as officially sanctioning the reconstruction of the said parties, as they had existed before the Armistice.
>
> On the contrary, General de Gaulle had made the intellectual and disciplinary effort necessary to construct large ideological bodies capable of insuring the solidity and stability of French public life.[110]

The five largest movements of the northern zone,[111] grouped in a Committee of Coordination, absolutely refused, as had the MUR, to permit the CNR to act as an executive committee that could control the activities of the individual movements.[112] The head of the Gaullist BCRA, Colonel Passy, expressed very well the attitude of the movements toward the new creation:

> . . . the chiefs considered then, almost unanimously, that the C. N. R. would be a phantom organization, whose sole interest resided in the fact that its existence would give General de Gaulle an extra card in his discussions with the Allies. All realized that this National Resistance Council could meet

---

[109] Passy, *Missions secrètes en France*, pp. 183–84.

[110] Soustelle, *Envers et contre tout*, vol. 2, p. 172.

[111] These movements were Ceux de la Libération, Ceux de la Résistance, Organisation Civil et Militaire (OCM), Libération-Nord, and the Front National. The coordination of the northern zone, patterned after Moulin's achievement with the MUR, was the handiwork of Colonel Passy and Pierre Brossolette. (See Passy, *Missions secrètes en France*, for an account of their mission "Brumaire-Arquebuse.") When Moulin arrived at Paris and, on 3 April 1943, met with the committee, over which de Gaulle had named him president, he had only to put his stamp of approval on the work of Passy and Brossolette.

[112] Passy, *Missions secrètes en France*, p. 174.

only very rarely, and that its role, so long as the enemy occupied the territory, would be, if not nil, at least very modest.[113]

The day after the Council's first meeting, in order to coordinate their actions and to ensure this minimal role for the CNR, the northern movements joined the MUR in establishing a Comité Central de la Résistance (CC), which included no representatives of the parties or syndicates.[114]

The creation of the Central Committee was at least in part a gesture of desperation as the movements were confronted with the accumulation of power in the hands of one man, de Gaulle's *délégué général*. As president of the coordinating committees of both zones, head of the Gaullist Délégation, and now president of the CNR, Moulin's potential influence over the interior Resistance was enormous. He had been sent to the resisters as the representative of de Gaulle's CNF; yet now theoretically he was becoming the movements' chief spokesman to de Gaulle. The resisters naturally were convinced that in every situation Moulin would adopt the viewpoint of the exterior Resistance in preference to that of the interior.[115] In the opinion of Henri Frenay: "General de Gaulle decided alone, without taking the advice of any of us, without listening to our observations or criticisms, to give a single man entire responsibility for liaison with the Resistance and in fact for its direction."[116]

Undoubtedly de Gaulle would have been happy to see Moulin, who always enjoyed the General's complete confidence, take effective command of the interior Resistance. But the tragedy at Caluire removed Moulin from the scene before the CNR had progressed beyond the symbolic gesture of declaring its complete loyalty to General de

---

[113] Passy, *Missions secrètes en France,* p. 184.

[114] Bénouville, *Le Sacrifice,* p. 358.

[115] Passy, *Missions secrètes en France,* p. 408, quoting a letter of Frenay to Passy. Michel, *Jean Moulin,* chapter 16, "La Crise de Croissance de la Résistance," particularly pp. 106–17, 135–38.

[116] Passy, *Missions secrètes en France,* pp. 391–92, letter of Frenay to Passy. Michel, *Jean Moulin,* p. 138, points out that Frenay was wrong in part. Despite Moulin's great powers he was acting merely as de Gaulle's deputy, carrying out specific orders from London. Of course, it was natural that Moulin in France rather than de Gaulle in London would be blamed for any unpopular measures.

Gaulle. In one of his final reports to de Gaulle, Moulin, all too prophetically had written:

> I am now hunted at the same time by Vichy and the *Gestapo* who . . . are not unaware of my identity, nor my activities. My task is becoming more and more delicate, while the difficulties increase constantly. I am determined to hold on as long as possible, but if I should disappear, I should not have had the time to familiarize my successors [with the necessary information].[117]

According to de Gaulle and his deputies in London and Algiers, the arrest of Jean Moulin at Caluire, 21 June 1943, was a disaster and was directly responsible for the tragic estrangement of the interior Resistance from the exterior.[118] Seduced by diabolical intrigues of the Communist party, the CNR soon elected a new president, appointed an executive bureau, and set off on an apparently independent course, seeking to establish a dual authority in competition with de Gaulle's CFLN. In fact, if clandestine life easily lends itself to the language of conspiracy, a description of the movements' actions after Moulin's arrest in such terms is far too simplistic to be completely satisfactory.[119] Unquestionably, Moulin's disappearance set off some serious repercussions for relations between the interior and de Gaulle, but a challenge to the CFLN was not one of them.

After Moulin's arrest a new atmosphere surrounded relations between the movements and the *Délégation*. One reason for this change was suggested by Emmanuel d'Astier's comment: "Rex [Moulin] would have replacements, but no equals."[120] Claude Bourdet agreed that Claude Bouchinet-Serreules and Jacques Bingen, who took charge of the Délégation for the interim in anticipation of a permanent replacement for Moulin, were "men of lesser stature" than their predecessor.[121] Both were new to clandestine life. Serreules arrived in France to second Moulin in northern France just five days before the

---

[117] Passy, *Missions secrètes en France*, pp. 237–38.

[118] De Gaulle, *Mémoires*, vol. 2, pp. 163–67; Passy, *Missions secrètes en France*, pp. 258–60; and Soustelle, *Envers et contre tout*, vol. 2, pp. 306–9.

[119] René Hostache's excellent study, *Le Conseil National de la Résistance*, offers a comprehensive account of the CNR from its inception through the liberation, which helps to correct such "devil theories."

[120] D'Astier, *De la Chute*, p. 92.

[121] Bourdet, "Histoire de la Résistance française."

arrests at Caluire, and Bingen, who was sent to oversee the Délégation in southern France, arrived on 16 August 1943. Hence they were willing to accept advice from the more experienced resisters. Undeniably, they lacked the requisite prestige and self-confidence to dominate the movements as Moulin had.[122] Moreover, Serreules and Bingen seemed to conceive of their role in a fundamentally different manner. Colonel Passy noted "the rod of iron under which Rex held the movements"[123]; in contrast, his successors tended to work with rather than over the movements.

Some, encouraged by a proposal from two of the northern movements, felt that Moulin should not be replaced and that the Délégation should be reduced in power and completely separated from the movements.[124] However, Serreules reported on 7 October 1943: "My task has been made easier by the fact that most of the chiefs of the movements were reasonable in not following those who wished to steer them in this path. They understood that our role was not at all to curb their independence, but only to help them develop and coordinate their efforts."[125] Describing his contacts with the movements, Serreules continued: "These relations have always been friendly and confident, and we have consistently worked together in a spirit of very frank cordiality. . . . I do not think that any serious conflict has arisen between us in three months. . . . It is for us a particular honor to consider the chiefs of the various movements as true friends."[126]

Serreules and Bingen frequently approached the movements for assistance and readily gave them credit for services rendered. Bingen, praising the solid organization forged by the Directing Committee of the MUR wrote:

> It is with them that I work constantly and through their channels that I act . . . it is to Poncarral [General de Jussieu, chief of the AS] that the regional officers [sent from London] owe gratitude for the smoothing out of many ticklish ques-

---

[122] Yvon Morandat reported to London several times that he was continually trying to bolster Bingen's self-confidence.

[123] Passy, *Missions secrètes en France*, p. 17.

[124] Claude Serreules, "Rapport d'activités" June 1943–March 1944, Papers of Serreules, Archives, CHG (*Délégation Général*).

[125] Serreules, "Rapport" of 7 October 1943, p. 3, Archives, CHG. One wonders how pleased General de Gaulle might have been with this attitude, which was certainly not his own.

[126] Serreules, "Rapport" of 7 October 1943, p. 3.

> tions, it is to Dormoy [Degliame] that we owe a coordina-
> tion of immediate action, [he has created] a complete
> organization which allows a large economy of means and
> transmissions [of messages and matériel] to sensitive points,
> Jerome [Brault, chief of the MUR's *Service Maquis*] deserves
> the credit for having coordinated all action dealing with the
> *Maquis*.[127]

Since he was charged with the Délégation's operations in southern France, Bingen had the most direct contact with the MUR. His attitude toward the movements' leaders closely resembled the sentiments Serreules expressed earlier. Referring to Pascal Copeau, the MUR's representative on the bureau of the CNR, Bingen noted "his immense qualities of good sense, dissimulated finesse, and tenacity," and added: "Furthermore, he has become a very dear personal friend of mine."[128]

The movements' directors also facilitated this detente in relations between the Délégation and the interior Resistance. Shortly before Moulin's arrest, when d'Astier and Frenay left France to represent the interior resisters on the CFLN, control of the Mouvements Unis de la Résistance passed into the hands of a second generation of leaders—men who were perhaps less jealous of their personal prerogatives than the original founders of the MUR had been. Coincidentally, the Délégation's second generation passed through a baptism by fire similar to what the MUR experienced during the summer of 1943, when a disastrous series of arrests forced the Directing Committee to move from Lyon to Paris. In September the Gestapo raided one of the Délégation's central offices, necessitating a thorough overhaul of its system of liaison. This reorganization was impeded by the intervention of the BCRA chief Colonel Passy, who suspected that Bingen and Serreules were under police surveillance and ordered all his agents to avoid any contact with them.[129] The resentment this action engen-

---

[127] Bingen, "Rapport" of November 1943, pp. 13–14, Archives, CHG.

[128] Bingen, "Rapport" of February 1944, pp. 15–16, Archives, CHG.

[129] This affair was very complicated and it is difficult to say where the truth lies. Brossolette and British agent Yeo Thomas both insist that Serreules' carelessness was responsible for the raid and that the numerous documents seized—several giving real rather than code names—posed a great danger to the whole Resistance. But Surreules and Bingen rejoined that they were the best judges of their own security, which the BCRA was only further threatening by its intervention. Eventually CFLN Commis-

dered induced the *délégués* to share at least in part the movements' animosity for the BCRA, which the resisters had long suspected of reactionary politics and hostility to the movements' revolutionary goals.[130]

Another circumstance that fostered closer cooperation between the Délégation and the movements was de Gaulle's curiously extended neglect of his agents in France. Perhaps because of the complicated situation at Algiers where at the time he was jousting with Giraud for control of the CFLN, de Gaulle left the Délégation without instructions and his agents without official confirmation of their authority for several months after Moulin's arrest.[131] Both Serreules and Bingen complained time and again about the almost total absence of guidance from the CFLN.[132] Consequently, the Délégation members were forced to resort to their own imaginations and resources. In the process they often took measures in accord with the movement chiefs, and not surprisingly adopted to some degree the mentality of the interior resisters.

Immediately after Caluire Serreules cabled London to say that he

---

sioner of the Interior E. d'Astier ordered Bingen to yield to the BCRA's demand that Serreules return to London. But the *délégués*, who had acted immediately to warn everyone incriminated in the captured material, continued to argue that no serious arrests could be traced to the lost documents. For documentation see the reports of Brossolette; Bingen and Serreules' numerous telegrams and their reports; all in Archives, CHG. Bruce Marshall, *The White Rabbit* (London, 1952), written with the help of Yeo Thomas, is manifestly unfair to Serreules and Bingen.

[130] Interviews with Étienne Bauer, 5 January 1970, and Pascal Copeau, 23 January 1970; *témoignage* of J.-P. Lévy; Vistel, *La Nuit*, pp. 329–31; Passy, *10 Duke Street Londres*, pp. 256–57; and Jean Pierre-Bloch, *Mes Jours heureux* (Paris: Éditions du Bateau, 1946), pp. 282–83.

[131] This was de Gaulle's explanation in the *Mémoires*, vol. 2, pp. 163–66. It is also possible that de Gaulle simply underestimated the importance of the situation inside of France. The large space devoted to external affairs (international affairs, the exterior armed forces, the Empire, etc.) in his *Mémoires*, compared to that on the interior Resistance, provides some measure of the significance he attached to them.

[132] Numerous cables and reports of Bingen and Serreules, Archives, CHG, all expressing sentiments similar to Bingen's *Rapport* of April 1944: "... since the departure of Sophie (Serreules), 300 cables constituting more than 100 messages have been sent by us on the most diverse questions. A large number of these posing precise questions already brought up and studied here, and to which most often concrete propositions were joined to the questions posed. But we have had practically no response to our questions." See also "Rapports" of Closon, Archives, CHG, and Bidault, *D'une Résistance*, pp. 43–46.

would mind the store until Moulin's replacement was named. At the same time and in frequent messages during the following weeks, Serreules proposed that Georges Bidault be designated *délégué général* and president of the CNR.[133] A former member of the directing committees of both Combat and the Front National in southern France, a Christian Democrat, and one of Moulin's closest associates,[134] Bidault had friends among all elements of the Resistance and was familiar with the operation of the Délégation. With no appointment forthcoming from de Gaulle, the movements decided to choose their own president for the CNR, a step that Serreules felt the circumstances justified. If the CNR was to be a true expression of the interior Resistance, Serreules felt that the resisters should freely elect the Council's president.[135] Furthermore, as he related in his report of 23 August 1943, he was attempting to orient their choice and asserted: "I have reasons to believe they will decide on the name of Rousseau [Bidault]."[136] Indeed, the method of election helped guarantee that Serreules's preferred candidate would win. Serreules contacted CNR members individually, telling them that most of the others had settled on Georges Bidault and asking if they agreed.[137] Not surprisingly, Bidault received thirteen votes against only one opposing ballot.[138]

Since considerations of security discouraged plenary sessions of the CNR—only three were held before the liberation—a five-man bureau was designated in September by mutual accord of the other members

---

[133] Telegram received 6 July 1943 from Sophie (Serreules), sent during a meeting of the CD of the MUR; *Courrier* du 27 Juillet 1943, "Rapport d'activités," June 1943–March 1944. All in Archives, CHG.

[134] When Moulin established the *Bureau d'Information et de Presse* (BIP) in 1942 to provide the Resistance movements with a central press service and to supply London with propaganda about the interior Resistance, Bidault had been chosen director because of his prewar experience as editor of *l'Aube*.

[135] "Rapport d'activités," June 1943–March 1944, pp. 3–4, Archives, CHG.

[136] Ibid.

[137] Daniel Mayer, *Les Socialistes dans la Résistance*, pp. 71–72, recalled that he and André Le Troquer changed the Socialist party's vote from Louis Saillant to Bidault when approached in this manner.

[138] E. d'Astier was the only opponent, though one member cast a blank ballot and Bidault himself voted for Frenay. See *Rapport* of Serreules, Archives, CHG, and Bidault, *D'une Résistance*, pp. 46–48.

to direct the Council's work.[139] A member of the Délégation also participated in the bureau's deliberations, which normally took place twice a week. Earlier the interior leaders had flatly rejected Jean Moulin's orders from de Gaulle to set up such a permanent bureau for the CNR because they feared that such a group would allow the representatives of political parties to influence the internal activities of their movements. They had established instead a Central Committee to coordinate their actions. This organization continued to exist for a while. It met infrequently, and Serreules or Bingen presided over the sessions. It was soon evident, however, that the movements could effectively exercise control of their formations through the CNR, and the Central Committee was dissolved in March 1944, eliminating its unnecessary duplication of efforts with the CNR.[140]

The CNR bureau formed various commissions to direct the many aspects of the Resistance. A member of the Délégation was usually included on these commissions, to act as technical adviser or serve as arbitrator where necessary. On most of the commissions the Délégation and the movements approached their common tasks in a most loyal and fraternal manner, as was evident in their preparations for the civil administration of France at the liberation.[141]

In the fall of 1943 Francis Closon, who had arrived in France with Bingen, began the organization of the Comités Départementaux de Libération (CDL). These committees had been envisioned in the summer of 1943 in discussion between officials at London and representatives of the MUR, in particular Henri Frenay and Emmanuel d'Astier. They imagined the committees as miniature resistance councils, modeled after the CNR, that would demonstrate on the local level the widespread support for de Gaulle and the CFLN within France.[142] Originally projected as consultative bodies that after the liberation would advise the prefects appointed by the CFLN,[143] in

---

[139] Pascal Copeau represented the MUR. The other members were Bidault, Louis Saillant (CGT), Pierre Ginsburger "Villon" (Front National), and Maxime Blocq-Mascart (Organisation Civile et Militaire).

[140] Serreules, "Rapport d'activités," June 1943–March 1944, pp. 2–3. Hostache, *Le Conseil*, pp. 218–19, and Bénouville, *Le Sacrifice*, p. 486.

[141] Hostache, *Le Conseil*, chaps. 4, 5, 8, 9, and 10.

[142] Hostache, *Le Conseil*, pp. 288–89.

[143] Michel and Guetzévitch, *Les Idées politiques et sociales de la résistance*, "Texte de l'Ordonnance sur l'Organization des Pouvoirs Publics en France Après la Libération," 21 April 1944, pp. 269–74.

practice the CDL assumed a much larger role. In fact they became active agents, their small bureaus or *noyaux actifs* responsible for coordinating the insurrection and seizing power. Serreules reported: "From their original statute as consultative organs, entering into function *only after* the liberation for a purely civil and political role, the C. L. [CDL] have become little by little active committees in the fight *for* the liberation."[144]

Closon, reflecting the attitude of the CFLN, nonetheless felt that the Departmental Liberation Committees should be subordinate to the *préfets* and the *commissaires de la république*, whom de Gaulle charged with all executive power during the period preceding the establishment of a regular administration. Otherwise, Closon feared that the Committees, if not firmly controlled, might attempt to act as independent "soviets"; and perhaps, where dominated by the Communist party, the CDL might even be used to challenge the Provisional Government's authority.[145]

This suggestion ran counter to the plans of the movements. A note emanating from the MUR and relayed to London, 17 October 1943, stated that the "project of London" seemed to conceive of the insurrection as "a prefectorial movement."[146] There appeared to be some question of whether or not they really wanted an insurrection, but: "In any case, whether they wish it or not, there will be one in the regions organized by the M.U.R. To be sure, this insurrection will be carried out by the men of the resistance movements and not the prefects. . . ."[147] As the exterior Resistance presented it, the project for the CDL had some aspects of "a concession to the Resistance, to which they give an honorific consultative role."[148] In reality, argued the resisters, the interior leaders would be more likely to have the necessary prestige to control the situation. Therefore:

> It is thus perfectly legitimate and politically necessary that, at least for a certain time, the authority of the government be delegated at every echelon to the same men who

---

144 "Source Corot [Serreules]," received March 1944, Papers of Serreules, Archives, CHG.

145 Closon, "Rapport" (10 November 1943); *témoignage* of Closon, pp. 8–9; and "Rapport" no. 4 (Closon) of 1 April 1944, pp. 8–9. All in Archives, CHG.

146 Papers of Serreules, Archives, CHG.

147 Ibid.

148 Ibid.

will direct the insurrection, that is, the current leaders of the Resistance. This is the only way to spare the Provisional Government immediate political difficulties, because, in the southern zone, only the M.U.R. are capable of coordinating the action of all the political forces including the Communist Party without provoking protest.[149]

In addition, if the prefects and commissioners were to have extensive executive powers, they should, of course, be drawn from the ranks of the MUR. It should be noted that this pretention to control the insurrection was limited strictly to the immediate insurrectionary period. The MUR made no claim to install these men permanently. Indeed, they said that many of their regional heads were not local men and would want to return to their homes as soon as conditions were normalized.[150]

Even if Closon disagreed with the MUR's conception of the insurrection, he acknowledged that the *commissaires de la république* "must be chosen with the accord of the resistance movements whose forces they will utilize,"[151] just as the president of the CDL would have to be chosen by the resisters if he hoped to exercise effective authority. Furthermore, Closon repeatedly affirmed that the excellent organization of the MUR as well as its critical understanding of political problems had considerably aided his work in southern France, where formation of the CDL had advanced much more rapidly than in the North.[152] In April 1944 he reported: "I am constantly in liaison with the C.D.–M. U. R. which offers my assistant and me a very precious assistance. The divergences of views of our first contacts have long disappeared and we work together in the most perfect agreement."[153] Closon anticipated no serious problems in southern France aside from the disarray caused by arrests, a danger that continually hung over all of the Resistance.

Paralleling Closon's mission was that of a three-man commission charged with the designation of the administrators, in particular the

---

[149] Papers of Serreules, Archives, CHG. For the original reaction of Claude Bourdet to the idea of the CDLs, see also Closon, "Rapport" of 10 September 1943, p. 2, Archives, CHG.

[150] Ibid. "Note," Papers of Serreules, Archives, CHG.

[151] Closon, "Rapport" 10 October 1943, pp. 1–2, Archives, CHG.

[152] "Rapports" of October, November 1943, February and April 1944, Archives, CHG.

[153] "Rapport" no. 4 of 1 April 1944, Archives, CHG.

prefects and *commissaires de la république*, who would administer France during the insurrection and until the Provisional Government was solidly implanted. Michel Debré presided over the *Commission de Désignations*, which included Émile Laffon and the acting *délégué général* Émile Bollaert (later replaced by Alexandre Parodi).[154] It was understood that the men appointed as prefects and commissioners would be primarily representatives of the central authority, the CFLN,[155] but Debré stated that everyone agreed "to the necessity as well to choose these representatives, whether commissioners or prefects, among the members of the Resistance or, where that was not possible, at least with the approval of the Resistance."[156]

In October a first list of over one hundred prefects had been established, but by the spring of 1944 severe police repression had reduced the number of nominees to hardly forty-five, and the work had to be redone.[157] Debré recalled:

> The first artisans of this new work were once again the resistance movements. It was to them that I first addressed the inquiries, the search for new candidates, the notification of nominations. For the southern zone, Anzot [Antoine Avinin] . . . had acquired a sort of monopoly. During almost a year we began meeting one Wednesday per month, then two Wednesdays, finally in the last days each week . . . thus it was that, region by region, department by department, whispering together in chairs at the Kléber or the Malakoff [two *cafés* on the Place Trocadéro in Paris], we went through

---

[154] See Closon, "Rapport" 10 September 1943; and Morandat, "Rapports," Archives, CHG.

[155] De Gaulle knew that all three members of the commission were strong Gaullists, and he counted on them to suggest commissioners and prefects whose loyalty to de Gaulle was certain. Alfred Rieber, *Stalin and the French Communist Party 1941–1947* (New York: Columbia University Press, 1962), p. 64, says: "In making their selection they adhered to the unwritten rule that there would be neither a Communist *Commissaire* nor a Communist *Préfet* in a maritime or border region or department."

[156] Michel Debré, *Un Grand mouvement préfectoral* (Extrait de la Revue *Les Cahiers politiques* [February–March, 1946], Paris: Imprimerie Curial-Archereau, 1946), p. 9; see p. 15, Debré adds that he and Laffon were allowed great liberty by the C. F. L. N. in choosing the *commissaires*, but "It was however necessary to choose the candidates with care, and to prudently discuss them with the movements."

[157] Debré, *Un Grand mouvement préfectoral*, p. 15.

all the prefectures of the southern zone, from Mende to Chateauroux, from Tarbes to Annecy.[158]

Conferences with other leaders of the southern zone were unnecessary because the Directing Committee of the MUR had given Avinin full powers in this realm.[159]

The active partnership between the MUR and members of the Gaullist Délégation in the establishment of the CDL and naming of administrators helps to explain the growth of a feeling of solidarity shared by all of those inside France whose contacts with the exterior Resistance were at time tenuous. Often during the fall of 1943 and the first months of 1944, the opinions of the Délégation were closer to those expressed by the movements than to the conceptions of the distant CFLN. Concerned about the absence of communication, in November Bingen pleaded to the CFLN: "I beg you in the future to be so kind as to let us know the points of view of the Central Power which are not identical to those of the delegates of the Resistance."[160] In January he observed: "By a strange phenomenon, it seems that every man who leaves France to remain outside excludes himself psychologically from the French community."[161]

Even resisters who had been leaders of the interior Resistance, when absorbed in a new role at Algiers, seemed to forget the revolutionary viewpoints they once held as representatives of the Resistance. Everyone inside France, asserted Bingen, felt that de Gaulle and the CFLN were more concerned with international relations and the future than with the really urgent problems of the interior Resistance in the present.[162]

In contrast to the Moulin period, the Délégation was rarely at odds with the movements. Moulin had denounced Frenay's contacts with the Americans; Bingen encouraged the CFLN to work through the MUR's delegation in Switzerland as the most logical and efficient

---

[158] Debré, *Un Grand mouvement préfectoral*, p. 12.

[159] Debré, *Un Grand mouvement*, pp. 3, 13, and *témoignage* of Avinin, Archives, CHG.

[160] Bingen, "Rapport Grenat," end of November 1943, p. 1. Archives, CHG.

[161] Bingen, "Rapport" of January 1944, pp. 5–6. The same sentiment was expressed in Bingen's later "Rapports" of February 1944, p. 17, and April 1944, pp. 17–18. All in Archives, CHG.

[162] Bingen, "Rapport" of January 1944, pp. 5–6.

outlet for financing the Resistance.[163] On numerous occasions the *délégués* championed the viewpoint of the interior resisters. They constantly cried for more arms, demanded that the Communist party be represented on the CFLN, and insisted that Pierre Pucheu, Vichy's ex-minister of the interior, be executed.[164] Most notably, the Délégation made common cause with the movements in its relations with Colonel Passy's BCRA.

The BCRA alleged that after Moulin's arrest Communist infiltration, in particular domination of the CNR's Commission d'Action Militaire (COMAC), posed a serious threat to Gaullist control of military operations at the liberation. The Bureau concluded: "The only remedy was to underpin the whole organization by supplying each region, then each department and every important *maquis* unit, with officers parachuted from London or Algiers and instructed in clandestine and military techniques; [they would] control parachute supply and radio communications."[165] In its attempt to decentralize the Resistance and control it directly from London, the BCRA was not only by-passing the resistance movements but was also ignoring the Gaullist Délégation.[166]

Agitated by this situation, the Comité Régional de la Libération of Clermont-Ferrand protested at length against "the attitude of defiance that the chiefs of staff of the F. F. I. [in London and Algiers] seem to have adopted towards the French Resistance."[167] The committee's resolution of 10 February 1944 explained:

> Two high-level officers, saying they were mandated by the Chiefs of Staff at Algiers, were parachuted into the region of Vichy last month. By chance running across the departmental head of the M. U. R., these two officers said they had come to accomplish a technical job (command of the mili-

---

[163] Bingen, "Rapports" of November 1943, pp. 12–13; January 1944, p. 12; February 1944, pp. 10–11; and April 1944, pp. 9–10. All in Archives, CHG.

[164] Bingen, "Rapport" of February 1944, pp. 5–7; also several *rapports* of Serreules and Morandat to the same effect. All in Archives, CHG.

[165] Soustelle, *Envers et contre tout*, vol. 2, p. 308; see also pp. 301–10, 361–62 for the BCRA point of view.

[166] Henri Michel, *Jean Moulin*, p. 195; in describing this period wrote: "Everything happened as if, during a short time, the *Délégation* had been practically suppressed."

[167] "Une Resolution du comité régional de la libération de Clermont-Ferrand," reprinted in BUMUR, 7 March 1944.

tary region of Vichy) for which moreover, they solicited the aid of our men. They had judged it useless to enter into contact with the regional organization of the M. U. R. or to involve them in any sort of consultation, intending, according to their orders, to act independent of the organized Resistance and the *chefs d'action* belonging to it. . . . The *Comité de la Libération* unanimously demands that the C. F. L. N. immediately fix clearly its position in this case.[168]

The Délégation did not object to the principle of decentralization, nor did the movements; the *délégués* simply argued that effective control could be established only by working through the movements.[169] Since they were on good terms with the interior leadership, the *délégués'* contacts should be utilized to the fullest in coordinating the activities of military officers sent from London or Algiers as well as officers of the *Centre des Opérations de Parachutage et d'Atterrissages* (COPA) or *Section d'atterrissages et de parachutages* (SAP.) These groups, charged with the reception of parachuted arms and supplies, pretended to receive orders only from the BCRA. According to the *délégués*, these officers, whose hoarding of weapons was bitterly resented by the movements, had to be subordinated to the délégation and ordered to distribute the supplies they had received from the exterior.[170]

In essence the members of the Délégation were trying to tell General de Gaulle: "You can operate most successfully in France through the resistance movements. Trust them!" It was perhaps because the exterior leadership reproached him for this outspoken conciliatory relationship with the movements that Jacques Bingen, who ran the Délégation for six months, was never officially named the *délégué général*.[171] Instead, in March 1944 de Gaulle appointed Alexandre Parodi, who had served previously in a minor role in the cabinet as

---

[168] Ibid.

[169] "Rapports" of Bingen, end of April 1944, p. 13. Archives, CHG; recall that the MUR was geared to autonomous action at the departmental level during the liberation. We have seen that Brossolette, Passy's closest friend, admitted that they had to work with the movements if they hoped to achieve satisfactory results.

[170] "Rapports" of Bingen and Serreules, Archives, CHG. The resisters agreed with the *délégués* on this point. See especially Maurice Kriegel-Valrimont, *La Libération: Les archives du COMAC (Mai-Août 1944)*, (Paris: Les Éditions de Minuit, 1964).

[171] Hostache, *Le Conseil*, p. 192–94.

maître de requêtes and in the Ministry of Labor as director general. Parodi was active in the underground Comité général d'Études (CGE), an advisory body of "experts" that Jean Moulin created to study constitutional questions for the future government. The group was responsible for drawing up proposals for the purge and reconstruction of the administration in France.[172]

Undoubtedly fearful of Communist influence over the Resistance, de Gaulle wanted assurance that if conflict arose his followers in critical positions would be more loyal to him than to the movements. In a personal letter on 31 July 1944 de Gaulle urged Parodi "always to speak very loud and very clear in the name of the State." While the "multiple formations and action of our admirable interior resistance are the means by which the nation is struggling for its salvation," nevertheless, insisted de Gaulle, "The State is above all these formations and actions." Therefore: "You are the representative of the Government. That is to say that in the last resort your orders must be imposed."[173]

No convincing evidence has been produced to support the contention that the interior movements ever intended to use their forces in any way against de Gaulle. Virtually every directive the MUR chiefs issued included a declaration of their allegiance to the CFLN; none challenged de Gaulle's preeminent authority.[174] We have seen that at every turn in his volatile relations with the Allies, de Gaulle could rely on the support of the interior Resistance. When the honor and *grandeur* of France were at issue, the resisters and de Gaulle were as one.

---

[172] Hostache, *Le Conseil*, chaps. 5, 7, passim.

[173] Soustelle, *Envers et contre tout*, vol. 2, pp. 420–21. Parodi indeed evidenced a somewhat greater independence from the movements. For example, he overruled Pascal Copeau's choice of a Communist for Bingen's replacement as *délégué* in the southern zone. However, he cooperated fully with the CNR. Bidault recalled that their relations with Parodi were always excellent. (Interview, 25 March 1970, and *D'une Résistance*, p. 49.)

[174] Obviously I have not seen every directive issued by the Comité Directeur of the MUR. Some of them must have been destroyed and will never be brought to light. But based on the very extensive numbers of documents that do exist, especially those contributed to the CHG by Alban Vistel, it is safe to assert that any instructions suggesting direct opposition to de Gaulle could not have been in line with the established and often confirmed policies of the MUR. The absence of any MUR-sanctioned actions to the contrary during the liberation provided a final confirmation of the movement's complete loyalty to de Gaulle.

This unwavering support was confirmed repeatedly by actions the movements considered wrongheaded and even against their best interests. They had not wanted a national resistance council, which would grant the political parties and syndicates a voice in their affairs. They had rejected desperately needed aid from the Americans because it was not being channeled through Gaullist headquarters. Time and again, the resisters made concessions to men in London and Algiers who in turn seemed to ignore the realities of clandestine existence. To be sure, the resisters rather resented these men who sent orders but did not share the unrelenting dangers of those within France. But even the Gaullist *délégués* to the interior shared this prejudice, so natural to the clandestine fraternity of the Resistance. The resisters were occasionally disappointed by their contacts with de Gaulle, but they were never disloyal to the man that they, and destiny, had chosen to lead France toward a brighter future.

Yet it is certain that the exterior resisters never fully trusted the interior Resistance. De Gaulle clearly misinterpreted the natural desire of the movements, *in his name and in the name of the CFLN,* to control their own troops in operations on French soil. The most obvious, though incomplete, explanation of de Gaulle's regrettable suspicion of those who had served him so well at the cost of incalculable sacrifices was the influence that the Communist party had exerted on the Resistance. Were the Communists, as de Gaulle believed, in fact dominating the Resistance in general, and the MUR in particular?

CHAPTER 4

The Movements and the Communists

IN THE FALL of 1941, in his reflection on several curious pirouettes of political tactics executed by the Communists during the thirties, Léon Blum termed the French Communist party "a foreign nationalist party . . . a sect foreign to the nation."[1] The imprisoned Socialist leader remarked that their "idolatrous submission to Stalin"[2] had once again thrown the French Communists into harmony with French patriotism, but he suggested that for the Communist party to be truly assimilated into the national community "a radical change must occur, either in the nature of the bond which ties it to Soviet Russia, or in the nature of the relations which will unite Soviet Russia to the European community."[3]

The leaders of the Mouvements Unis de la Résistance were among those who shared Blum's hope that the common struggle against the occupant might permanently convert the Communists to patriotism. In its negotiations with the Communist party the MUR offered loyal

---

[1] *L'Oeuvre de Léon Blum (1940–1945): À l'Échèlle Humaine*, vol. 5 of *L'Oeuvre* (Paris: Éditions Albin Michel, 1955), p. 457, "un parti nationaliste étranger," and p. 459, "une secte étrangère à la nation."

[2] *L'Oeuvre de Léon Blum*, p. 458.

[3] *L'Oeuvre de Léon Blum*, p. 459.

cooperation in good faith, granting the Communists every opportunity to prove the sincerity of their avowed convictions. In counterpoint the party's actions during the Occupation gave the movements grounds for both encouragement and suspicion.

For several years the most bellicose of French anti-Fascists and champions of national defense, the Communists were forced into an embarrassing about-face when the Soviet Union signed a nonaggression pact with Germany in August 1939.[4] When Hitler attacked Poland and the Soviet Union moved in to take its share of the spoils in eastern Poland, the Communists, who had been the most willing to "die for Danzig," suddenly realized the conflict was an imperialist war for which French and British capitalist governments shared responsibility with the Germans.[5] It really had nothing to do with "the people."

In the months that followed, the logic of this position required that the party first, agitate for a "popular" French government that would seek an immediate peace with Germany; second, engage in defeatism by means of antiwar propaganda and industrial sabotage; and finally, when the Germans occupied Paris, urge open fraternization with the enemy troops. The *Humanité* of 4 July 1940 commented: "It is particularly reassuring in these unhappy times to see numerous Parisian workers conversing amicably with the German soldiers, either in the street or at the corner *bistro*. . . . Bravo, comrades, continue, even if it displeases certain bourgeois, who are as stupid as they are pernicious."[6]

---

[4] See Auguste Lecoeur, *Le Parti communiste français et la Résistance août 1939–juin 1941* (Paris: Librairie Plon, 1968); and several works by Angelo Tasca (A. Rossi), *Les Cahiers du bolchevisme pendant la campagne 1939–1940* (Paris: D. Wapler, 1951); *Les Communistes français pendant la drôle de guerre* (Paris: Les Iles d'Or, 1954); and *Physiologie du parti communiste français* (Paris: Éditions Self, 1948).

[5] After the invasion of France, *l'Humanité* was much more explicit in its denunciation of French and British "imperialism" than in its casual references to Hitler's aggression. On 15 May 1940, no. 46 of the party's paper stated: "When two gangsters fight among themselves, honest men should not aid one of them, under the pretext that the other has given him an 'irregular' blow. They attempt instead to profit from the occasion to put both of them out of the possibility to harm [others]." In other words, *l'Humanité* explained, the French people should work against their own government, as would the German people, in order to establish a "Government of peace," which in collaboration with the Soviet Union would assure a general peace.

[6] Quoted in Rossi, *Les Communistes . . . la drôle de guerre*, p. 330. Similarly, *l'Humanité*, no. 61, 13 July 1940, quoted in Lecoeur, *Le Parti com-

A misplaced confidence that the Nazi–Soviet Pact would secure them German indulgence led the Communists to request permission for the legal production of *l'Humanité* at the beginning of the occupation.[7] Also, the party ordered militants who had been hiding from the French police since the Chamber of Deputies outlawed the party in 1939 to speak out publicly and to distribute propaganda in the open. This puzzling step of an organization that later flattered itself on its excellent clandestine security only facilitated the task of the police, who arrested the militants as soon as they emerged from the underground.[8] The Germans did not respond favorably to either the party's directives for fraternization or its pleas that arrested Communists be released because they alone had opposed the war.[9]

Actually the Communists' flirtation with the occupant was quite brief as the one-sidedness of the affair became readily apparent. The party had never completely dropped its antinazism, and early made the distinction between the German people and their Nazi rulers. Fraternization with German soldiers was one thing; collaboration to facilitate Hitler's exploitation of France was something else. From the first the Communists criticized Vichy's continual surrenders to Germany's exorbitant demands. Before June 1941 the party's clandestine journals mixed scathing denunciations of Pétain's government with more restrained but increasingly frequent attacks on Hitler's regime.

The main thrust of Communist propaganda, though, was in favor of peace rather than active opposition to Germany.[10] The party's call in May 1941 for a *Front National* to struggle for the independence of

---

muniste, p. 89, and in *Histoire du parti communiste français* (Paris: Éditions Unir, 1962), II (written by anonymous party members), p. 33; this issue denounces active resistance. "The people of France want peace. They demand energetic measures against those who, by the order of imperialist England, would bring the French back into the war."

[7] Charles Tillon, *Les F. T. P.* (Paris: René Julliard, 1962), p. 63; Annie Kriegel, *Les communistes français: essai d'ethnographie politique* (Paris: Éditions du Seuil, 1968), p. 82; Lecoeur, *Le Parti communiste,* pp. 85–95.

[8] Lecoeur, *Le Parti communiste,* pp. 85–95.

[9] Turning to Vichy, the Communist deputies offered to testify at Riom to emphasize their opposition to the war by placing the blame on Daladier, Blum, and others, but they also accused several members of Pétain's government.

[10] No completely satisfactory history of the Communist party during the occupation exists. Henri Michel, in Part 5 of his *Les Courants de pensée,* pp. 551–721, has done an excellent job of unraveling the enigma of Communist policy during the occupation. For an extremely fair interpretation of the sometimes ambiguous party line, Michel's chapters are invaluable.

France was not a battle cry against the Germans but, rather, a demand for peace. The Communists feared Darlan's negotiations with the Nazis might force France out of its neutrality between the two imperialist blocs.[11] Despite the party's numerous postwar versions of its primacy in the Resistance, no convincing evidence exists to show that the official Communist line prior to 22 June 1941 included active opposition to Germany.[12] Indeed, those who were engaged in such resistance were condemned as lackeys of British imperialism.[13]

By clinging stubbornly to a position passed along from Moscow, the Communists had practically isolated themselves from the rest of the French nation. The severe repression of the Communist party in the months after its endorsement of the Nazi-Soviet Pact reflected widespread public disapproval, which was by no means limited to the party's traditional enemies. Almost a third of the Communist deputies left the party, and countless dismayed militants simply suspended their activities.[14] Ironically, by the virulence of its reaction the government might have saved the party from the self-destruction that its unpopular position might well have entailed.[15] If unwilling to support the party's sudden shift to pacifism, many Communists would nevertheless rally to the defense of their party, threatened with annihilation by the excessive harassment of a hostile government. The first OS (Organisation Speciale) groups formed by the Communists

---

[11] Michel, *Les Courants de pensée,* p. 563, and Lecoeur, *Le Parti communiste.* The Captured German Documents, T-77, Roll 829, frames 5566675–697, a copy of the Paris Protocols, which were signed by Darlan, Abetz, and Warlimont, 27 and 28 May 1941, shows that the Communists' fears were not unjustified in that Darlan was willing to risk war against the English with France fighting beside Germany. An English translation, "Protocols Signed at Paris on May 27 and May 28, 1941," is found in *Documents on German Foreign Policy 1918–1945,* Series D, 12 (Washington, D.C.: U.S. Government Printing Office, 1962), no. 559, pp. 892–900.

[12] The ingenious revisionist arguments of Henri Noguères in *Histoire de la résistance en France,* vol. 1 (Paris: Laffont, 1967), which suggest a contrary opinion, are rather polemically, but convincingly, demolished by Lecoeur, *Le Parti communiste,* passim.

[13] See the early issues of *l'Université Libre; l'Humanité,* no. 58, 1 July 1940, reproduced in Rossi, *Les Communistes . . . la drole de guerre,* pp. 336–37, called de Gaulle an "agent of English finance"; also Michel, *Les Courants de pensée,* pp. 569–72.

[14] Rossi, *Les Communistes,* passim, Lecoeur, *Le Partisan* (Paris: Flammarion, 1963), pp. 106–7.

[15] Kriegel, *Les communistes,* p. 81; and Rossi, *Les Communistes,* pp. 25–26, and passim.

in October 1940 were created for the party's own defense rather than for offensive actions against German troops.[16]

Conversely, several more or less autonomous groups of French Communists either ignored or acted contrary to the official party line immediately following the German occupation of France.[17] Many Communists as individuals joined the ranks of the budding resistance movements. Others actually worked through or took over their local party machinery, regrouping and organizing the militants for underground opposition. The central party apparatus condemned such actions, and those who led this initial Resistance were termed renegades and provocateurs, and occasionally were marked for elimination. Georges Guingouin, a Communist who had organized armed resistance bands in the Limousin at the beginning of 1941 and later was the regional FFI commander, escaped execution at the party's orders by taking exceptional security measures. He agreed to reestablish contact with the party's direction only at the end of 1942, after he received an apology for their earlier attitude and numerous guarantees for the future.[18]

It is impossible to determine precisely how many Communists were actually involved in the Resistance at this early date, or how many energetically supported the official line. One knowledgeable authority warns against forcing

> ... an antagonism which is more one of thoughts than acts, which must be understood in a context of extreme weakness. For the truth is that the Party was then a phantom of a Party, and coexistence of two political orientations, was, basically, a coexistence of feeble desires whose vague contours are divined only through barely outlined gestures, frustrated projects, uncertain texts.[19]

---

[16] Lecoeur, *Le Parti communiste*, pp. 80–84, criticizes Noguères' "complaisance" in writing (*Histoire*, vol. 1, p. 58) that these groups were created to "engage in direct action against the occupant."

[17] Kriegel, *Les communistes*, pp. 81–83.

[18] Lecoeur, *Le Parti communiste*, pp. 36–37. Lecoeur cites (p. 36) the example of a Communist resister in the northern zone who was executed by a groupe OS, but suggests that such cases were in fact exceptional. Baudoin, *Histoire des groupes francs (MUR) des Bouches-du Rhône* (Paris: Presses Universitaires de France, 1962), "Epilogue: L'affaire Lévis," pp. 173–201, gives another example of militants of the Party who were purged for having resisted too early.

[19] Kriegel, *Les communistes*, p. 82.

Probably the recurrent controversy over the date of the Communist party's official entry into the active anti-German resistance has had more interest for French political polemicists than actual significance in the history of the Resistance. After all, what were the other, theoretically more national, parties doing before June 1941? The debacle of 1940 had divided and shattered every organization, social group, and political party in France. Most were very slow to recover from the shambles. Certainly no political party was quickly reorganized, as such, for clandestine resistance to the occupant. Even the underground movements that had opposed the Germans from the first were only at the beginnings of effective organization by June 1941; and some of them clearly lagged behind the Communists in denouncing the Vichy regime.[20] Before any group could carry out an effective opposition, it had to locate and coordinate its forces. Actions that the Communist party later tried to label Resistance were perhaps little more than its attempts to reform its scattered ranks and reestablish a functioning liaison between the center and the regions.

Still, if only in self-defense, the Communist party was at least active long before 22 June 1941. When the Germans attacked the Soviet Union—the clandestine *Université Libre*, a party paper, termed it "the greatest felony known in the history of civilized nations"[21]—the Communists were ready to throw their full weight into the balance against Germany. Many militants who had supported begrudgingly the earlier party line undoubtedly breathed a great sigh of relief to see the party return to its identification with French patriotism. From that moment until the liberation, there were nowhere any more vociferous, courageous, or dedicated patriots than the French Communists.[22]

---

[20] See Lecoeur's statement (*Le Parti communiste français*, pp. 53–54) of "... this fundamental truth, that the P. C. F. entered the Resistance against Vichy before everyone, but entered the struggle against the occupant only from June, 1941," should be qualified by one question that naturally comes to mind. Would a government opposed to collaboration and headed by Blum, Daladier, or Reynaud (all of whom were violently denounced as war *provocateurs* and allies of the "200 families" in *l'Humanité*) have found any greater sympathy from the PC than the Pétain government before June 1941?

[21] *l'Université Libre*, numéro spécial, 25 June 1941.

[22] See for example, *Les Lettres françaises*, no. 3, November 1942, calling for the celebration of the anniversary of Valmy and of 11 November: "We do not forget the great dates of our history." Throughout the occupation *l'Université Libre*, *l'Humanité*, and all of the FN's publications were very

Once committed unequivocally to the Resistance, the Communists were, among all the resisters, the most outspoken champions of unity of action.[23] Specifically, they urged all patriots of whatever political persuasion to join them in a Front National (FN) to fight for the liberation of France. The range of adherents extended from the far right to the far left, and until the liberation the FN carefully cultivated a nonpolitical image. Pierre Villon, a Communist member of the Front's directing committee, was requested to reassure those militants who might be disquieted by charges that the FN was simply a branch of the Communist party. In the FN's *Bulletin d'information,* Number 5, he asserted:

> . . . the F. N. is not the organization of a party, not even a party such as the Communist Party, which has given nevertheless ample proof of its patriotism. . . .
>
> The *Front National* is the great organization of all patriots for liberation. Every Frenchman, whether he be former P. S. F., Radical or Socialist, whether he be without-party or Communist, whether he be a believer or atheist, has in it not only his place as a rank and file member, but further, if he proves himself worthy by his action and devotion, as a director at any echelon. If there are Communist comrades who have not understood this, I can tell them in the name of my party, that they are wrong, *for what counts for my party is not to hold the top posts of an organization such as the F.N., but to reach the goal which must be attained in the interest of the life, happiness, and future of our people.* Now this goal which matters today is clear: we must force out the invader.[24]

In fact during the last months of the Occupation when the FN welcomed into its ranks many ex-Vichyites who had suddenly seen the light, the directors of the MUR sometimes felt that the FN was too open in its recruitment.[25] Similarly in the quarrel between de

---

careful to highlight every national holiday, drawing heavily on the history of the Revolution.

[23] Michel, *Les Courants de pensée,* p. 606.

[24] The *Bulletin d'Information,* no. 7, April 1944, includes statements to the same effect.

[25] Interviews with Étienne Bauer, 5 January 1970, and Pascal Copeau, 23 January 1970, both of whom recalled the PC's surprising nominations of many conservative personalities for various clandestine posts. Also, Claude

Gaulle and Giraud the Communists had remained neutral, while virtually every other movement and party had backed General de Gaulle.[26]

As further evidence of the nonsectarian character of the Front National, the Communists could point to the non-Communist members of their executive organs. For example, Georges Bidault, while a director of Combat, was also a member of the Front's directing committee in southern France. Also, in theory the Communist party delegated only 10 percent of its effectives for work with the Front National,[27] and the large majority of the FN's troops were not Communist party members. Nevertheless, from the first its Communist elements undoubtedly dominated the FN. Two Communists, Pierre Villon (Ginsburger), the Front's representative on the CNR's executive *bureau*, and Charles Tillon, commander of the Francs-Tireurs et Partisans Français (FTP), the Front's military expression, were the FN's most dynamic and influential leaders. Essentially the policies and tactics that the Front National and the Communist party advocated during the Occupation were identical.[28] Certainly the MUR considered their relations with the FN and the Communist party to be integrally related.[29]

The resistance movements in southern France had no official contact with the Communist party before the summer of 1941. Because of the Communists' ambiguous stance before Hitler's invasion of the Soviet Union, many of the early resisters were supicious of the party's first attempts to establish friendly relations. Henri Frenay's reaction to the establishment of the Front National was frankly hostile. He advised patriotic Frenchmen never to join the FN. "Frenchmen!

Bourdet, "La politique intérieure de la résistance," *Les Temps Modernes,* no. 112–13, 1955, p. 1849.

[26] René Hostache, *Le Conseil National de la Résistance* (Paris: Presses Universitaires de France, 1958), p. 143. The Communists sent an ambassador to both de Gaulle and Giraud at Algiers, and their contact with Giraud appeared fruitful when FN militants armed by Giraud took over all of the prefectures when Corsica was liberated. The PC always referred to this as an example to be followed by the national insurrection in France.

[27] This percentage of 1941 was later doubled according to a note "Sur la Necéssité de la fusion de l'A. S. et des F. T. P.," joined to the text of an "Accord d'action commune entre les F. T. P. et l'A. S.," 29 December 1943, Papers of Alban Vistel, Archives, CHG.

[28] Michel, *Les Courants de pensée*, part 5, passim.

[29] *Témoignages* of Frenay, Bourdet, Avinin and others, Archives, CHG.

Beware! . . . Anti-German Frenchmen should take care—they risk being odiously tricked."[30] Referring to the FN's recruitment manifesto, which called for an anti-Hitlerian crusade, Frenay declared:

> It is we authentic Frenchmen, equally opposed to Hitlerism and Stalinism, who are leading this crusade. The anti-German front that Moscow wishes to constitute, we have in fact achieved. It will be revealed in due time. In our ranks are found men from all the former parties, men for whom the defeat was the occasion for a sincere examination of conscience. There are those who come from the Communist Party and others from the *Action Française:* between the two runs the full gamut of opinion. They are united because they consider that there is no longer room for partisan divisions in face of the invader. More sincerely than the Communist Party, they aspire to profound social reforms necessary to remove the opposition between classes and to obtain a substantial amelioration of the condition of life of the workers.[31]

Despite this initial wariness, the movements were soon impressed by the exemplary courage and activism of the Communist resisters. The Communist doctrine of guerrilla warfare, calling for widespread immediate action, spectacular sabotage, and attacks on the occupation troops, was particularly attractive to most resisters who desired above all to fight the Germans. The tendency of Vichy and the German authorities to refer to all captured resisters, regardless of their origins, as Communists and terrorists lent credence to the popular impression that the Communists were the most active resisters.[32] Also, Vichy's virulent anti-Communism, apparent in its selection of Communists rather than "good Frenchmen" to be shot as hostages, won additional sympathy for the party.[33] Finally, the Red Army's tenacious resistance to the German invasion and the success of its offensives in later months rebounded to the credit of the Soviet Union's greatest booster

---

[30] *Vérités* no. 12, 25 September 1941.

[31] Ibid.

[32] Bingen, "Rapport" of November 1943, *Beige,* pp. 4–5. Throughout the Captured German Documents resistance activity, particularly of a violent nature, is often referred to simply as Communist activity.

[33] Noguères, *Histoire,* vol. 2, pp. 79–83, 150–53, Annex I, p. 677, and Annex V, p. 687.

within France. Indeed, during the final stages of the Occupation many Frenchmen began to contrast the tremendous sacrifices of the Russian people to the long-awaited Anglo-American second front, which never seemed to materialize except in sometimes careless bombing raids that took a serious toll in French lives.[34]

The undeniable sacrifices and heroism of the Communists, which eventually effaced the original suspicions of many resisters, fostered cooperation between the movements and the Communist party. An understanding was furthered in September 1942, when the Soviet Union recognized the Comité National Français (CNF) under de Gaulle as the "Directing organ of Fighting France, alone qualified to organize the participation of citizens of France and its territories in the war and to represent, before the Government of the U.S.S.R., French interests, insofar as they are affected by the conduct of the war."[35] Shortly thereafter, Fernand Grenier went to London to serve as the Communist party's representative to the CNF.[36]

The first evidence of common action by the movements and the party came on 16 October 1942 when a tract opposing the forced labor draft (STO) was distributed in factories throughout the southern zone over the signatures of Combat, Libération, Franc-Tireur, the Communist party, and the Front National. "Not a man in Germany. ... You will not leave! You will not work for the enemy. You will not abandon your children, your work, your home, your country. . . ."[37] The response to this first appeal led to rather widespread strikes and forced the Vichy government to withdraw temporarily the lists of workers destined for Germany. However, the subsequent occupation of southern France after the Allied landings in North Africa greatly increased the dangers and difficulty of opposition to the STO. Never-

---

[34] OSS Document OB-8838, a report on the opinion in France, 15–25 October 1943, concludes that Russia was gaining the sympathy that the Anglo-Americans were losing. Another OSS report, Document 31330 C, dated 1 April 1943, related the workers' attitudes, especially after American tactics in North Africa, which had resulted in a growing sympathy for the Soviets and a mistrust of the Americans.

[35] De Gaulle, *Mémoires,* vol. 2, p. 371.

[36] Fernand Grenier, *C'était ainsi* (Paris: Éditions Sociales, 1959), passim, recounts his experiences in London.

[37] Passy, *Missions secrètes en France,* pp. 3, 300–304. According to Michel, *Combat,* p. 100, the initiative for this joint action suggested by the FN came from militants at the base, since d'Astier and Frenay were in London at the time.

theless, the desirability of cooperation, especially when workers were involved, had been demonstrated.

Early in 1943 the Mouvements Unis de la Résistance entered into the first of several arrangements with the Communist party related to their unity of action in the Resistance. A circular, dated 16 April 1943, explained to the regions:

> In practice, action coordinated with the Communist Party will result from a permanent contact at the national echelon, and by the designation at the regional level of a *responsable* for the Communist Party and a *responsable* of the *Mouvements de Résistance Unis,* who will determine together common action. This contact will be established in the regions during a forthcoming visit by the national delegates of the Communists and M.R.U.[38]

A month later instructions for the organization of the regional MUR directories included the designation of a representative specially charged with relations with the regional delegate of the Communist party. Thus, as of that date, 14 May, the accord realized had not yet been effected.[39]

Shortly thereafter, with the formation of the Conseil National de la Résistance (CNR) and the Comité Central de la Résistance (CC), official contacts between the movements and the PC were extended. Also, the transfer of the MUR headquarters to Paris in the summer of 1943 facilitated communications at the higher echelon. All of the major resistance movements in both zones agreed that the Communists deserved representation on these central resistance organizations, but on 26 November 1943, the MUR went beyond some of the others in offering the Front National an integral fusion of their movements in southern France.[40]

A month later an *"Accord d'action commune entre les F. T. P. et l'A. S.,"* dated 29 December 1943, was circulated to the regions along

---

[38] *Comité Directeur des Mouvements de Résistance Unis: Fouché à Toutes Régions,* 16 April 1943, p. 3. Papers of Alban Vistel, Archives, CHG.

[39] "Le Comité Directeur des Mouvements de Résistance Unis à tous les Directoires Régionaux," 14 May 1943, p. 9, Papers of Alban Vistel, Archives, CHG.

[40] *C. D. M. U. R. au C. D. du F. N. Z. S.,* 26 November 1943, Papers of Alban Vistel, Archives, CHG.

with the MUR's note revealing the motivations behind the projected fusion of their military command with that of the Communist FTP. Aside from the evident desirability of unity of command for an effective military action, there remained the political problem presented by the FTP. Observing that the Communists often provided only the cadres for these largely non-communist groups, the MUR circular noted:

> In fact several F. T. P. are at present very far from being Communist, and in many places, the P. C. is having trouble keeping its troops in order.
>
> Nevertheless, when we address ourselves to the F. T. P., we see the Communist Party behind its staff. Therefore, there can be no question of acting without reflection, and we must ponder the full significance of our gesture.[41]

In essence the MUR viewed its policy of cooperation with the Communists as the natural complement of de Gaulle's foreign policy, including a major goal of alliance with Russia. Such an alliance would be fruitful "only if within the country the P. C. shares in some fashion the responsibilities of power, otherwise it will be no more effective than that signed by Laval in 1935."[42]

What of the possibility that the Communists might maneuver disloyally against their partners as they had occasionally in the past? After studying the clandestine literature of the PC, including some addressed exclusively to party members, MUR leaders concluded:

> . . . it seems to us that the patriotism preached by the Party's Central Committee is not destined for propaganda alone, but is a real sentiment that the Communists intend to incorporate in their doctrine and their program. This desire on the part of the leadership is not always understood at the intermediary echelon, which often shows itself still strongly sectarian. It could be then that we will have more difficulty at this level than at the national level. The national directors, aware of the future role of their Party, seem definitely cured of "blanquisme," that is to say, of little con-

---

[41] "Sur la Necéssité de la fusion de l'A. S. et des F. T. P.," Papers of Alban Vistel, Archives, CHG.

[42] "Sur la Necéssité," p. 2.

spiracies crowned by a riot. The departmental *responsables* are not yet there, so we must be patient with them.

All the same, to ask if an eventual ally is sincere is to misunderstand the problems. Positions are not taken once and for all, they can evolve during the collaboration. The important thing is that no partner be passive and that each one bring in propositions logically acceptable to all.[43]

From the beginning of 1944 until the liberation, the two major organizational problems the Resistance faced were the constitution of the FFI (Forces Françaises de l'Interieur) through the fusion of the Secret Army, the FTP, and the former Armistice Army's ORA; and the establishment of liberation committees in all the departments. In order to coordinate their efforts for these major tasks and to regulate practical questions about the direction of immediate action against the Germans, representatives of the MUR, PC, FN, and the CGT met in monthly work sessions.[44] As the liberation approached, Pascal Copeau and Marcel Degliame, representing the MLN Directing Committee, left Paris for southern France to handle on location all questions of cooperation, especially between the FTP, FN, and MUR.[45] Soon after D-Day the Directing Committee of the FN for southern France and the *exécutif zone sud* of the MLN distributed a resolution urging the immediate end to any rivalries that might separate their two organizations and proclaiming their "perfect identity of views."[46]

On the surface all of the preceding examples indicate from the beginning of the MUR that the southern movements were willing to work closely with the Communists. In fact, from the first both parties

---

[43] "Sur la Necéssité," p. 2.

[44] A letter dated 15 April 1944, "La Comité Directeur du Mouvement de la Libération Nationale au Comité Exécutif du Parti Socialiste," Papers of Alban Vistel, Archives, CHG, states that these meetings had been held for three or four months at the request of the PC. So they presumably began around January 1944.

[45] Interview Pascal Copeau, 23 January 1970. Degliame was especially charged with military relations and Copeau with civil affairs. According to Copeau, one of their major concerns was to keep the peace and strengthen the unity between Communist and non-Communist groups.

[46] "Le Comité zone sud du Front National et l'exécutif zone sud du Mouvement de la Libération Nationale à tous les responsables et comités du F. N. et du M. L. N.," 25 June 1944. Papers of Alban Vistel, Archives, CHG.

maintained certain reservations, and until the Allied invasion there was far more contact than effective cooperation. In its original statement of the *"Position des Mouvements de Résistance Unis à l'égard du communisme,"* the Directing Committee remarked:

> The courage of the communist militants in action against the enemy, the brutality of the repression of which the Communist Party is the object, finally the success—particularly in the northern zone—of the resistance organized by this Party, generally make [us] forget that from September, 1939 to June, 1941, the policy of the S. F. I. C. was defeatist.
>
> We must not have such a short memory and if needs be we will use this argument, for we ask the Communist Party to prove that its present patriotic attitude is indeed a profound transformation of its conceptions and not a momentary tactic.[47]

The *Directing Committee* demanded that their first arrangement with the PC be sanctioned unilaterally by the party in the form of "a Declaration of adherence to a French Government which will be established at once in North Africa under the Presidence of General de Gaulle"; and further "the French Communist Party commits itself in advance to support a Government which will be in the first place the expression of our resistance, and rejects, at the same time, any attempt to take power."[48]

Nevertheless, having demanded these guarantees the MUR hopefully extended its hand to the Communists, a policy that was followed closely in much the same spirit as proclaimed in its original announcement in April 1943:

> For our part, if we wish to act with loyalty, we must, in the most explicit manner, forbid in our ranks all anti-Communist propaganda. This will not prevent us from expressing the fundamental difference of our ideological position, nor from acting toward the Communist Party with the necessary prudence. But the Directing Committee has decided to apply the agreement concluded with total good faith and to obtain

---

[47] "Fouché à Toutes Régions," 16 April 1943, Papers of Alban Vistel, Archives, CHG, p. 3.
[48] Ibid.

from its members that if ever a break should occur it will never come from us.[49]

The same attitude is reflected in the MUR note *"Sur la necéssité de la fusion de l'A. S. et des F. T. P."* commenting on the projected accord of 29 December 1943.[50] In its final directives on the establishment of the FFI and the Departmental Liberation Committees, the Directing Committee declared:

> In both cases what is involved is putting into practice the policy, many times affirmed, of union with the Communists.
>
> Undoubtedly our *responsables* have had several disappointments in their relations with the P. C., the F. N., and the F. T. P. F. They complain of insufficient or intermittent contacts or meetings with underlings. It is also true that the almost general abstention of the F. T. P. F. with regard to the F. F. I. seems very systematic.
>
> It is not certain, however, that in these contacts, some of our *responsables* have repressed a narrowness of ideas which belongs to the past.
>
> Be that as it may, the interest of France, the interest of our movement, demands that we prevent by all possible means that there exist two resistances in France: two armies, one of communist influence, the other non-communist.[51]

Despite the MUR's desire to work closely with the Communists, it soon appeared that the affair was somewhat one-sided. For all their extravagant calls for unity, the PC and the FN retained a peculiar conception of this union. They were never anxious for a fusion in which the control of their forces might fall to non-Communists.[52] In northern France where the FN became the most important and by far the

---

[49] "Fouché à Toutes Régions," 16 April 1943, Papers of Alban Vistel, Archives, CHG, p. 3.

[50] Papers of Alban Vistel, Archives, CHG.

[51] "L'Exécutif Zone Sud de M. L. N. à Tous Directoires régionaux et départementaux," no date, but probably May 1944, from internal evidence, Papers of Alban Vistel, Archives, CHG, p. 2. Other examples of the MUR's determination to cooperate loyally with the PC are found in "S. G. du M. L. N. à Toutes Régions," 15 April 1944, and "Exécutif M. L. N. Zone Sud à Toutes Régions," 26 June 1944; both in Papers of Alban Vistel, Archives, CHG.

[52] See Alfred Rieber, *Stalin and the French Communist Party, 1941–1947* (New York: Columbia University Press, 1962), pp. 34, 92–93.

most active movement,[53] it was understandable that the Communists expected a dominant role in directing the Resistance. But in southern France the situation was quite different. The Communist party was slow to erect an underground apparatus in the South. When Georges Marrane arrived at Lyon late in 1941 to reconstitute the PC in southern France, he had so little success that he and Madeleine Braun, the other major Communist leader sent to the South, decided to put most of their efforts into the Front National and its FTP, which had a much better drawing capacity.[54] In fact, even the Front National had started so far behind the three movements that composed the MUR that it could never seriously challenge their preponderance in southern France. Naturally the MUR was piqued when in 1943 the Front National began to demand an equality of treatment, when it had very few really substantial contingents and was nonexistent in several regions of the southern zone.[55]

In the fall of 1943 the FN through the *délégué général* of the CFLN requested the creation of a southern zone coordinating committee in which the FN would sit as an equal with the other movements.[56] After they had expressed their dismay that the Front had not approached them directly and had pointed out that the *délégué* had no authority to create committees as he pleased, the MUR's Directing Committee rejected the idea that a new Committee of Coordination was needed. Instead, the FN should accredit its representative to the *Bureau* of the CNR and to the Comité Central de la Résistance to represent the Front in southern France. On the practical coordination of their efforts, the MUR suggested that it already existed in fact everywhere the FN existed, but that they would be happy to formalize these arrangements by the establishment of a permanent liaison between the two organizations.[57] It was evident that the MUR was ne-

---

[53] OSS Document 66534 C, report from OSS Algiers, 7 April 1944, notes that the Communist strength is centered around Paris and surrounding areas, the traditional stronghold of the party. Numerous *rapports* of Bingen, Serreules, Brossolette, and Morandat, Archives, CHG, attest to the strength of the PC in northern France.

[54] *Témoignage* of Bourdet, Archives, CHG. According to Bourdet, they were advised to do so by Farge and George Altman of Franc-Tireur.

[55] *Témoignages* of Frenay, Bourdet, Lévy and others, Archives, CHG. Morandat (*témoignage*) says the FN was, in the southern zone, a creation of Jean Moulin in an attempt to threaten the independent-minded leaders of the MUR and keep them in line.

[56] Bingen, "Rapport," Archives, CHG.

[57] C. D. M. U. R. au C. D. du F. N. Z. S.," 26 November 1943, Papers of Alban Vistel, Archives, CHG.

gotiating from a position of considerable strength. At that time, a fusion of the two movements would have meant simply the incorporation of several scattered FN groups into the MUR. Therefore, in its letter of 26 November 1943, to the FN, the Directing Committee did not hesitate to add:

> If you think that such a coordination would be insufficient, we will reply to you willingly that there can be a true unity of action only in union. We think that the very existence of the M. U. R. is a proof of our desire for union. We regret that you did not present yourselves to us at the epoch when the fusion between *Combat, Franc-Tireur* and *Libération* was achieved. We feel however that it is not too late; and we propose that you continue, according to procedures which remain to be arranged, to a complete fusion, arranged in good faith, between the *Front National Zone Sud* and the M. U. R.[58]

Later, in February 1944, when the MUR became the Mouvement de la Libération Nationale (MLN), including several northern zone movements, the Directing Committee renewed its offer of fusion to the FN. The proposed Union Nationale de la Résistance (UNR) would group in one organization all the resistance movements in France.[59] This time it was the Front National's turn to remind the MLN of the existence of the National Resistance Council and associated central organs, which in its opinion made the creation of another formation superfluous, amounting to no more than some new initials on the mastheads of their clandestine journals. More specifically the Front complained that this proposed UNR left out patriotic elements in the syndicates and political parties. Perhaps most significantly, the proposal envisioned a ninc-man executive committee on which the FN would have only one representative whose status would be equal to that of the other eight. According to the FN, such representation would mean the unfair subordination of their large activist movement to the decisions of smaller, less combative movements.[60] Actually, by

---

[58] Ibid.

[59] "4ème Partie—Le C. D. M. U. et les Mouvements," pp. 6–7 of Yvon Morandat's "*Rapport Général sur la Situation de la Résistance,*" received April 1944, by CFLN Commissariat à l'Interieur, Archives, CHG.

[60] See *Bulletin d'Information (du Front National de Lutte Pour la Libération de la France)*, no. 7, April 1944; and *Documents (édités par le Comité Directeur du Front National)*, no. 4 June 1944, which includes copies of a letter from the MLN and the four major non-Communist movements of the

the fall of 1943 the Communists had realized that they could most effectively exert their influence on the Resistance through the National Resistance Council. Pierre Villon, the Front National's delegate on the CNR's bureau, was generally considered the most dynamic member of the five-man committee.[61] Consequently, the Front's representative had systematically obstructed the operations of the *Comité Central*, on which the FN's influence was limited.[62] Thus, as explained earlier, the CC never played as significant a role as the directors of the MUR had hoped, and the CNR quickly absorbed most of its functions.

From November 1943 through spring 1944, relations between non-Communists and Communists in the Resistance were seriously strained by the manner in which the Communists used the CNR as a platform for their campaign against the *attentiste* and the *jour-jistes* (those with a more cautious philosophy of direct action who were inclined to "wait and see" when D-Day arrived).[63] The party's actions in this period in part reflected its disappointment at not being represented on the CFLN when de Gaulle reshuffled its membership in November 1943. Actually de Gaulle offered two posts to Communists of his own choice but thereby offended the party, which demanded that the General accept their nominations. Finally, in the spring of 1944 the Communists joined the CFLN on de Gaulle's terms.[64]

Within France the repercussions of this discontent in Algiers were

---

northern zone and their proposed *"Charte Constitutive de l'UNR,"* dated 28 March 1944, followed by Villon's response of 4 April 1944, stating the FN's reasons for opposing such a fusion.

[61] See the colorful description of Villon in Jacques Debu-Bridel, *Sous la cendre* (Paris: Gallimard, 1951), p. 239. Various reports of Bingen, Morandat, and Serreules, Archives, CHG, testify to the leading role of Villon on the *bureau* of the CNR.

[62] *Témoignage* of Bourdet, Archives, CHG, recalled that the FN objected strongly to its position of one against seven on the Comité Central, since it felt that its preponderant role in northern France justified a stronger Communist representation.

[63] Claude Bourdet, "La Politique Intérieure de la Résistance," Les Temps Modernes, no 112–13, 1955, pp. 1837–62, stated: ". . . it is certain that the principal political difficulties in the heart of the Resistance were caused by the relations between the Communist and non-Communist Resistance." The "Rapports" of Bingen, Serreules, and especially Morandat, for the period between fall 1943 and spring 1944, Archives, CHG, show that these relations were very strained during this period.

[64] Soustelle, *Envers et contre tout*, vol. 2, pp. 338–39, and Aron, *Histoire de la libération* (Paris: Fayard, 1959), pp. 308–10.

evident immediately. Although the Communists never dropped their nominal loyalty to de Gaulle, a member of the Gaullist Delegation reported: "The Communist Party bears a rather serious grudge against the C. F. L. N. since the incidents which led to its exclusion. They do not miss an occasion, directly or through the intermediary of the F. N., to accuse the Resistance of anti-Communism, to accuse the Délégation and the government of hostility, and everyone of playing a waiting game."[65] Some members of the CFLN's Délégation in France even warned of the possibility of a rupture between Communists and the Provisional Government or an outright confrontation between the Front National and the non-Communist movements centered around the MLN.[66]

Militants of the MUR were particularly irked by the indiscriminate nature of the PC's and FN's accusations. No one questioned the FTP's commitment to activism and immediate action. In depicting its impression of the role that direct action should play in the preparation of the National Insurrection, the FN used the metaphor of a steam engine: "In order for a locomotive to pull away, it is good to put it 'under pressure' for a time!"[67] This pressure was to be the function of the communist-inspired sabotage, assassinations, and strikes. It was when the Front National claimed, explicitly or by implication, that it was the *only* activist movement that the MUR took offense.

We have seen how the ideas of Henri Frenay clashed noticeably with those of Gaullists in London who wanted to convert his Armée Secrète into a force that was both "infinitely secret" and "infinitely

---

[65] Morandat, "Rapport" of April 1944 (received May 1944), "Suite du Rapport Général sur la Situation de la Résistance," Arnolphe à Merlin [Morandat to E. d'Astier]. Also see *Rapport* of Bingen, February 1944, p. 17; and "Note de Sauvier" [Scrreules], 11 March 1944; all in Archives, CHG.

[66] Serreules, "Note de Sauvier" on the attitude of the PC, 11 March 1944: "If I can give an opinion in light of my recent experiences, it is not excluded, that the Communist Party envisages a rupture with the rest of the Resistance and will not hesitate to put in cause its allegiance to the C. F. L. N." Also various *Rapports* of Closon; and Morandat, *Rapport* of 29 February 1944, to d'Astier, Archives, CHG.

[67] "Lettre du F. N. aux Mouvements de Résistance sur l'Insurrection Nationale," in *Bulletin d'information du F. N.*, no. 6, 15 February 1944, in which the F. N. contrasts its activism to the implied *attentisme* of the MUR. For a detailed elaboration of the Communist philosophy of direct action, see the six-page directive of the Front National, "Francs-Tireurs et Partisans Français: Comment faire la guerre?" (28 June 1944), in Papers of Alban Vistel, Archives, CHG.

inactive."[68] Actually, Frenay's position was somewhere between the *attentistes*—those in France and London who wanted to hold the AS in reserve for D-Day—and the FTP policy of constant and violent immediate action. Instead of random and spectacular sabotage of questionable harm to the enemy, Frenay advocated enough direct actions to train the men and keep them from "rusting."[69]

Unquestionably some of the cadres of the MUR's paramilitary forces, especially those few who had been recruited from Vichy's Armistice Army, were less enthusiastic about direct action than was the FTP. But such an attitude was never encouraged by the chiefs of the MUR. On the contrary virtually every directive from the Directing Committee stressed the importance of action. In announcing in April 1944 the integration of all the MLN's military elements into the Corps Francs de la Libération (CFL), the Directing Committee explained that it was responding to an urgent necessity: "TO GIVE THE RESISTANCE A TRUE ORGANISM FOR ACTION. It has clearly expressed its determination to finish once and for all with 'attentisme,' which, despite the sharp blows dealt it, persists much more than some believe in certain *milieux* of the Resistance."[70] Moreover, long before the creation of the CFL, the MUR's activist stance was clear. Even though occasional reports indicated that several officers were still not converted,[71] the official position of the leadership and the sentiment of the majority of MUR militants is well expressed in the following instruction, dated 13 December 1943, from the Secret Army's regional head for the region around Lyon to his departmental head:

---

[68] *Témoignage* of Bourdet, Archives, CHG.

[69] *Témoignages* of Bourdet and Frenay, Archives, CHG. For the MUR philosophy of effective rather than spectacular sabotage, see "S. G. des M. U. R. à Toutes Régions: Conseils au sujet du choix des sabotages à effecteur dans les usines travaillant pour l'Allemagne." Papers of Alban Vistel, Archives, CHG.

[70] Papers of Alban Vistel, Archives, CHG; also circulated in *B. I. M. U. R.*, no. 118, 20 April 1944.

[71] For example, "Rapport Général sur la situation de Service Maquis à fin Octobre"; and the 5 April 1944 "Note Sur la Création de Corps Francs de la Libération," which says of attentism: ". . . it is certain that it was during a long time, the very base of Resistance," but adds: "It is no less certain that if this conception is not completely destroyed, it is disappearing more and more. In every case, it appears sheepishly and is no longer avowed, even by those who were its warmest partisans." Both in Papers of Alban Vistel, Archives, CHG.

The value of the A. S.'s departmental head can only be appreciated according to their success in achieving the following goals (listed in the order of their importance):

I. Missions
1. —Execution of traitors and agents of the *Gestapo*.
2. —Cutting of rail lines, with the derailment of *enemy* trains.
3. —Cutting of enemy telegraphic or telephone installations.
4. —Cutting of the high tension networks in order to stop a specific factory or group of factories.
5. —Industrial sabotage of prioritary factories.
6. —Carrying off of material.

II. Organization of the Department
1. —Establishing liaison (perform frequent transmission exercises).
2. —Functioning of services.

III. Preparation for "D-Day"
1. —Preparation of communications disruptions and protection planned for D-Day.
2. —Preparation of the insurrection according to the instructions from the Departmental Directory.

A NEGATIVE MONTHLY RECORD FOR "MISSIONS" WILL AUTOMATICALLY ENTAIL THE REPLACEMENT OF THE CHEF DÉPARTEMENTAL.[72]

---

[72] "Logements, à Tous Départements," 13 December 1943, Papers of Alban Vistel, Archives, CHG. This directive was by no means exceptional. Compare: "S. G. des M. U. R. à Office du Logement," 8 December 1943, a copy of "Comité Central des Mouvements de Résistance à tous Chefs de Régions et Services," stating "1) All services without exception are mobilized for immediate actions against the enemy. 2) No stock of arms will be held in inaction for D-Day." "Circulaire" of 5 November 1943, "C. D. M. U. R. à toutes Régions"; "Le Chef Régional des F. F. I. à Bridoux, Esseiule, Magny, etc.: Note sur l'Organisation Régionale des

A train derailed by resistance saboteurs at Quierry-la-Motte (Pas-de-Calais), 25 March 1942. French railway workers were very active in the Resistance.

Whether or not they pointed it out, the original chiefs of the MUR must have seen the irony in their being labeled *attentistes* by the representatives of a party whose official line had kept it outside the Resistance before June 1941.[73]

As to the charges of anti-Communism the MUR's position as elaborated in the preceding pages would seem to belie the argument of the PC and FN. It was true that Henri Frenay had written a letter from London to the non-Communist members of the Comité Central

F. F. I.," 31 March 1944; "Référence à rappeler: 113/GR: Charte l'Action Ouvrière," 30 September 1943; "Rapport Général sur la situation de Service Maquis à fin Octobre," 31 October 1943; "Le C. D. des M. R. U. à tous Services Toutes Régions," 18 August 1943, which states (p. 4) that *chefs régionaux* must consecrate an important share of their budgets to immediate action, even if it means suppressing other services; and finally a declaration of the MLN, dated April 1944, states: "Action against the enemy and his agents is the fundamental task of the movement." All in Papers of Alban Vistel, Archives, CHG.

[73] In fact some Communists acknowledged that many of the MUR chiefs were not really *attentiste*. See Pierre Villon, "Juin-août 44 (1 La bataille contre l'attentisme and 2 Pourquoi Paris n'a pas brulé)," September and November 1964, pp. 57–58. See also *Témoignage* of Francis Cremieux, and *Témoignage* of Bourdet that Frenay's activism pleased Marrane.

de la Résistance in which he expressed his concern that the Communist party might try to use de Gaulle as a French Kerensky. He cautioned the non-Communist resisters to beware of the Front National's maneuvering.[74] Afterward the Communists referred repeatedly to this incident in their clandestine propaganda, in letters to the president of the CNR, and in a letter to members of the CFLN.[75] Nevertheless, Frenay later put his ministerial position on the line for the Communists, threatening to leave his post with de Gaulle if the Communist party was not represented on the CFLN.[76] To be sure, members of the MUR's Directing Committee—for example, Claude Bourdet and Guillain de Bénouville—were less partial to the Communists than others, but to tax with anti-Communism a movement that had offered loyal cooperation was manifestly unfair on the part of the Communist party. Henri Frenay declared after the liberation, when he was being viciously attacked by the party, "extra-Communism" was not the same thing as anti-Communism, and all non-Communists were not "fascists."[77]

In fact the Communists had cried "wolf"—anti-Communist—too often to be convincing, and probably more than concern about the personal attitudes of certain non-Communist resisters lay behind their charges. For it was after the fall of 1943 that the Front National first made a significant appearance in southern France, and particularly in 1944 that the competition between the FN and MUR became acute.[78] Curiously, at the same time the Front began to expand its operations in the South the Directing Committee of the MUR, having reached organizational maturity, decided to slacken its recruitment.[79] Rather

---

[74] Letter dated 29 October 1943, copy in Papers of Serreules, Archives, CHG.

[75] Copy in Papers of Serreules, Archives, CHG, of letter, dated 22 February 1944, Doucet (the PC representative on the CNR) to Bingen. Letter of seven pages from "Comité Central du Parti Communiste Français à Messieurs les members du Comité Français de la Libération Nationale," received March 1944, in Papers of Serreules, Archives, CHG.

[76] Granet and Michel, *Combat*, pp. 314–15.

[77] Henri Frenay, *Méthodes d'un parti "Alerte aux Démocrates"* (Paris: Les Éditions Universelles, 1945), pp. 9–10.

[78] *Témoignage* of Bourdet, Archives, CHG, recalled that the MUR's relations with the FN and PC were satisfactory until the *Comité Directeur* moved to Paris, when their first contacts with Villon put the MUR continually on the defensive.

[79] Bingen, "Rapport," end of November 1943, p. 4 (Archives, CHG), pointed out that this situation was leaving the way open to gains by the energetic FN.

than accept the MUR's proposals of cooperation in the formation of the southern zone's FFI and Departmental Liberation Committees, the Front National chose competition, which sometimes involved less than scrupulous attempts to lure militants away from MUR formations.[80]

In the military realm, despite agreements reached at the national level between MUR, PC, and FN representatives, no really effective coordination of the FTP and the CFL was reached before the Allied invasion. Except in areas where there was a very clear predominance of FN or MUR forces,[81] FTP and MUR Maquis bands roamed across the same territory without any permanent contact, a situation that occasionally led to open clashes. The FN continually complained that the FTP were being slighted in the distribution of arms and munitions,[82] and raids on the weapons caches of neighboring Maquis were not unheard of.[83] But the most serious implication of the lack of contact between the FTP and the CFL was that no common plan

---

[80] "R. S. G./A. (Alban) à S. K. F. (Corton)," 20 June 1944. Papers of Alban Vistel, Archives, CHG, concluded that the FN's policy of "unité à la base" was reminiscent of the PC tactic toward the Socialist party before the Popular Front era, and "unité" meant in essence seducing troops away from the MUR.

[81] In such areas there were fewer problems. For example, in the Auvergne (R6), Henry Ingrand, the MUR's regional head, very effectively controlled all aspects of the Resistance, and the FTP made up perhaps one-tenth at most of the total of resisters. (*Témoignage* and interview with H. Ingrand, 11 March 1970.) Also in the area around Limoges Guingouin, a Communist, had been the driving force behind the local Resistance even before the PC officially entered the anti-German fight. The MUR did not object to his appointment as head of the FFI for that region.

[82] "Arnold à Magny," 24 May 1944, Papers of Alban Vistel, Archives, CHG, and "Arnold à Magny," 19 May 1944, Papers of Alban Vistel, Archives, CHG. *Témoignage* of Bourdet, Archives, CHG, claimed that the MUR actually got no more arms than the FTP and that they were equally unhappy with the BCRA's policy, which left most of the arms from parachute drops under the control of the Regional Military Delegates or the BCRA operations officers (SAP or COPA), who considered the arms their personal property. Evidence shows, however, that in their distributions some of the BCRA operations officers did favor non-Communist formations over the FTP. For example, *Documents sur les Maquis Limousin* (Paris: Presses de l'Imprimerie E. Desfosses-Néogravure, 1946), quotes the testimony of Colonel Charles, who said he received arms in his own name for Guingouin because the Gaullist agents would not give arms to the FTP.

[83] "Arnold à Magny," 19 May 1944, Papers of Alban Vistel, Archives, CHG. Francis Cremieux, *Témoignage*, Archives, CHG, relates his experience of stealing arms when he deserted an MUR maquis group to join the FTP.

of action was established. The persistent refusal of the FTP chiefs to parley with MUR delegates inevitably aroused suspicions about their intentions and posed a threat of anarchy or even armed conflict between resisters during the liberation period.

Complaining of the absence of contact with the FTP, an MUR military leader reported to his regional head: "The F. T. P. question is still at the same point. Is it so difficult to obtain honest cooperation in our common work? Action without coordination corresponds to *a true sabotage . . .* to the profit of whom?"[84] On the eve of D-Day the FFI's *délégué général* for the southern zone and chief of the MUR's CFL, Marcel Degliame, wrote:

> As to relations with the F. T. P. F. I must observe that in almost all the regions contacts are nonexistent. In spite of the efforts of our *responsables,* it has been impossible until now to constitute regional F. F. I. staffs with the effective participation of the F. T. P. F.; this situation is profoundly regrettable at the moment when decisive operations are developing. It is unthinkable that the Resistance be divided at the hour of combat. I have sent a note on this subject to our comrades of the F. N. and F. T. P. F. at the national echelon, asking them (urgently) to intercede with their regional and departmental leaders in order to hasten the formation of the F. F. I. Even if these leaders were able to say at a certain epoch that they refused to establish contact with directors of an *"attentiste"* Resistance not oriented towards action, this argument no longer holds; our men are fighting everywhere that they have the means, just as well as their comrades of the F. T. P. F.: all old quarrels must dissolve before the higher interests of the Nation at war.[85]

Finally, after the invasion the MUR had to content itself with local agreements with FTP units whenever possible.[86] During the opera-

---

[84] "Arnold à Magny," 19 May 1944, Papers of Alban Vistel, Archives, CHG. See also "Didier à Brioux: Note sur le Rapport d'Efficacité de l'E. M. des F. F. I.," 23 February 1944, Papers of Alban Vistel, Archives, CHG, for similar complaints about the unsatisfactory cooperation.

[85] "Fouché, Délégué Général F. F. I. Zone Sud à toutes régions Zone Sud —tous Responsables F. F. I," 1 June 1944, Papers of Alban Vistel, Archives, CHG.

[86] "R. S. G./J Arnold à EMNFFI à titre de compte rendu: Alban, Chef régional des MUR: Rivière, responsable F. T. P., etc.: Ordre du 5 Juin 1944," Papers of Alban Vistel, Archives, CHG, announced that the *Chef*

tions of the liberation, relations showed some improvement,[87] although they were never completely satisfactory.

These military problems were paralleled in the political sphere by dissension over the makeup of the southern zone's Departmental Liberation Committees (CDL). Recall that these committees included members of political parties and syndicates as well as the resistance movements, though the movements normally dominated the executive committees or *noyaux actifs* of the CDLs. In theory these committees were to reflect as nearly as possible the political tendencies present in a given area, with representation allowed for all patriotic organizations. The Front National, however, developed an ingenious tactic in attempting to gain a large share in the control of the CDL. In addition to representatives for the PC and FN, the Communists demanded mandates for the unitary tendency of the CGT, the Femmes de France, the FTP, the FUJP (Forces Unies de Jeunesse Patriotique), and for all of the other PC tributaries.[88]

Actually the MUR had at first tended to monopolize all of the CDL in the South,[89] which was not surprising because of their preeminent position. But when the Communists threatened to form their own separate committees, members of the Gaullist *Délégation* had persuaded the Directing Committee to give the FN the benefit of the doubt and allow them entrance to the CDL where they had a real existence in southern France.[90] They were even to give special con-

---

Régional (RI) had decided to conclude a provisory accord with the FTP chief for the Rhône, and hoped that such arrangements could be extended to other departments as well as at the regional level.

[87] A 1 July 1944 "Rapport Sur la situation de R. I.," noted: "Our relations are sensibly ameliorated with the F. T. P. since last month." Papers of Alban Vistel, Archives, CHG.

[88] *Témoignage* of Closon, and *Rapports* of Closon, no. 2, 10 November 1943, and no. 4, 1 April 1944, Archives, CHG. Guyot, Claude, *Historique du Comité Départemental de Libération de la Cote d'Or* (Copyright M. Guyot, Néo-Typo-Besancon, 1962), pp. 116–17; and "R. S. G./A (Alban) à S. K. F. (Corton)," 20 June 1944, Papers of Alban Vistel, Archives, CHG, in which Vistel describes this process in the CDL at Grenoble. Also Pascal Copeau, interview, 23 January 1970.

[89] Papers of Serreules, a note from the MUR received in London 17 October 1943, concerning the CDLs and *commissaires de la république*, states that obviously the president and the dominant voices in the CDLs would come from the ranks of the MUR. See also "Secrétariat Général de M. U. R. à la Région" (24 October 1943), Papers of Alban Vistel, Archives, CHG, which states: ". . . the president of the CDLs will be by right the regional and departmental leaders of the M. U. R."

[90] Bingen, *Rapport*, end of November 1943, Archives, CHG; also Closon, "Rapports," no. 2 and no. 4 of 10 November 1943 and 1 April 1944, Ar-

sideration to the FN when a choice between the FN and an extra MUR representative was possible.[91] Nevertheless, the FN's claims were blatantly exaggerated, often including the requested representation of an organization without any troops in the given territory. A note from the MUR's *Exécutif* in southern France in the spring of 1944 was very explicit in its desire for cooperation with the Communists but nonetheless firm in rejection of such designs:

> The principles for the composition of the active nuclei of the *Comités de Libération* have been indicated to you. To permit the functioning of this nucleus, we have been very accommodating on its composition: it may be well to note that it is preferable that two representatives of the M. U. R. be members of the nucleus that, in certain cases, it is not possible for nuclei to be formed with three Communists (P. C., F. N., C. G. T. U.) and one M. U. R. (this is not in the interest, of course, of anyone, not even the Communist Party); that our leaders should support the presence of a socialist delegate in the nucleus wherever his presence can be justified objectively.[92]

In addition to these difficulties in organizing the FFI and the CDL, some non-Communist resisters were troubled because several Communists held important positions in the MUR hierarchy. During the early months of the occupation, numerous Communist militants as individual patriots had joined the movements that later became the MUR. Even after the German attack on the Soviet Union, Communists in southern France unable to make contact where the Communist clandestine organization was either newly begun or non-existent,[93] adhered to the resistance movements. Some revealed their Communist origin, others did not. Naturally the presence of these PC militants was most noticeable in Libération, reputedly the most

---

chives, CHG; and *témoignage* of Max Juvenal, Archives, CHG, for the concessions to the PC and FN in the Bouches-du-Rhône.

[91] Bingen, "Rapport," end of November 1943, Archives, CHG.

[92] "L'Exécutif Zone Sud du M. L. N. à Tous Directoires régionaux et départementaux," no date, but probably April or May 1944, from internal evidence, Papers of Alban Vistel, Archives, CHG. See also letter of 15 April 1944, "Comité Directeur du Mouvement de la Libération Nationale au Comité Exécutif du Parti Socialiste," Papers of Alban Vistel, Archives, CHG.

[93] *Témoignage* of Bourdet, Archives, CHG, notes that Degliame came to Combat because he could not find the PC in the southern zone.

leftist of the three major movements.[94] Marcel Degliame was the only Communist who held an important post in Combat's organization, though other Communists were among the rank and file. In view of their presence in all of the movements, it was not particularly surprising that some Communists rose to positions of leadership. After the MUR fused, the ascension of three Communists, Degliame, Pierre Hervé, and Maurice Kriegel-Valrimont, to major responsibilities did not pass unnoticed, especially among Socialists and non-Communist syndicalists who were inclined to be suspicious of the Communists.[95]

In addition, the attitude of Pascal Copeau, who felt that cooperation with the Communist party was essential to the success of the Resistance,[96] seemed to support occasional charges that he was a fellow-traveler (*communisant*).[97] After Claude Bourdet's arrest on 25 March 1944, the Communist influence in the Directing Committee appeared to be confirmed by the selection of a Communist, Kriegel-Valrimont, to be the MUR's representative on the CNR's national military directorate, the COMAC. Did this choice not suggest that through an adroit policy of infiltration the Communist party had gained control of the Mouvements Unis de la Résistance?[98]

First, the very nature of the MUR's clandestine organization argues against this contention. The six regional heads, none of whom were Communists, enjoyed considerable latitude in the interpretation of orders from the Directing Committee and normally retained the essential executive power over their own territories.[99] In many cases at

---

[94] Étienne Bauer, interview (January 1970), said that Libération-Nord, controlled by Socialists, always refused unity with the southern zone's Libération on the grounds that too many Communists were in its ranks.

[95] Vistel, *La Nuit*, pp. 96, 273–76, points out that the Socialists and syndicalists were the most wary in their contacts with the Communists.

[96] Copeau, interview, 23 January 1970.

[97] See Passy, *10 Duke Street Londres*, p. 269, and Soustelle, *Envers et contre tout*, vol. 2, pp. 301–4.

[98] See Bourdet, "La Politique Intérieure," pp. 1853–54, Rieber, *Stalin and the French Communist Party*, pp. 88–98. In fact Kriegel-Valrimont was at first Degliame's second, replacing him when later, on 29 April 1944, the CD was dispersed. Then Degliame and Copeau assured the *exécutif* in the South and Avinin and Lacoste remained at Paris.

[99] Recall chap. 3. See *Combat*, chart on pp. 233–40. *Témoignage* of Bourdet, Archives, CHG, notes that in one case, Gilbert de Chambrun in R-3, Montpellier, the *chef régional* was influenced strongly by the activist doctrines of the PC.

the local level involving the nuclei of the Departmental Liberation Committees, the apparent numerical predominance of Communist elements (including the FN, PC, and CGT) was deceptive. In the South the complete CDL's, which assumed their functions at the liberation, were almost always controlled by the MUR. Alban Vistel, regional head of R. I—Lyon, offered this explanation.

> A first reason for this: the solidity of the M. U. R.'s structures, their seniority in the Resistance, their clearly superior power on every plane. I always figured that a well chosen representative of the M. U. R. was sufficient to dominate the nucleus, in which there could be a numerical superiority of the communist elements, moreover that was a matter of isolated cases. But the policy I had adopted for the plenary *Comité* obliged the representatives of the other organizations to furnish members able to direct the specialized *Commissions*. Now, they did not have such people, and since the M. U. R. possessed a qualitative superiority, the result was the numerical predominance of representatives of the M. U. R. in all the *Comités de Libération.*[100]

Finally, a closer look at the Directing Committee itself suggests that caution must be used in applying head-counting formulas to the examination of clandestine organizations. Antoine Avinin's exclusive right to propose the MUR's nominees for the provisory administration of southern France after the liberation precluded any Communist influence over the choice of these critically important officials.[101]

In fact, the role of calculation compared to that of chance in the rise of individual Communists in the MUR hierarchy is impossible to measure accurately. The exact nature of the relationship between Communist members of the MUR and the PC is unclear. What is certain is that the atmosphere and vocabulary of the Cold War have significantly colored many postwar accounts. The general tendency has been to overrate the cohesion and efficacy of the Communist

---

[100] "Observations sur C. D. L.," a note from Vistel to the author, along with several documents that support his statement: "R. S. G./A (Alban) à Martial," giving composition of the ten CDLs in his region; "R. S. G./A à tous départements," 2 July 1944, instructions for the enlargement of the CDLs' and "R. S. G./A. à tous départements," 29 June 1944. These documents are from Vistel's personal papers.

[101] See chap. 3.

party during the clandestine period.[102] Certainly in southern France the image of a monolithic organization encompassing the FN, PC, FTP, and the party's agents within the MUR is false. Even the party's control over its own formations (FN and FTP) in the South was not clear-cut.[103] Among Communists who held important places in the MUR, only Kriegel-Valrimont was an outspoken advocate of the party.[104] Pierre Hervé had joined the MUR in 1942 after a dramatic escape from jail in the northern zone, and he did not immediately reveal his party membership to all his MUR comrades.[105]

Marcel Degliame before the war had been active in the *unitaire*, Communist, wing of the CGT. His actions in Combat and the MUR, if naturally reflecting the influence of his background, by no means

---

[102] One of the most common assertions is that the PC controlled the CNR. René Hostache in his excellent work, *Le Conseil*, has convincingly demonstrated the fallacy of this view, expressed by Alfred Rieber, Robert Aron, and many others, that the *bureau* of the CNR was controlled by the party. In fact only Villon, the FN's representative, was a spokesman for the party. Copeau and Saillant, the other two members often said to have given the PC a three–two majority on the *bureau*, were not members of the party. Saillant, who joined the party after the war, was at this time being attacked violently by the Communists as not fit to represent the CGT on the CNR. (See in addition to Hostache, "Rapport" of Bingen, Archives, CHG; and interview, Pascal Copeau, 23 January 1970.) Actually, the COMAC was the only central organization of the Resistance that the Communists dominated, and its direct control was very narrowly limited to a small area around Paris where Communist strength was prevalent. Copeau's situation is discussed below.

[103] Bingen, "Rapport," end of November, *Vert*, p. 5, Archives, CHG, notes "Gaston" (Georges Marrane) was at times a bit at odds with the national directors of the PC. The Party according to their own admission did not rigorously control the FN and the FTP in the South. Tillon, the national head of the FTP, was occasionally in disagreement with the heads of the party organization. Recalling his earlier experience with them, one can imagine how close Guingouin, the leader of the most important FTP groups in the South, was to the Parisian leadership. This is not to imply that the most important leaders of the FN and FTP were not Communists. It is simply necessary to understand the relative autonomy that existed, even for the Communists, in a clandestine situation that required considerable individual initiative.

[104] Raymond Aubrac, who recruited him for Libération, called Kriegel an *emmerdeur doctrinaire No. I, Témoignage*, Archives, CHG.

[105] Étienne Bauer, interview, 5 January 1970, remarked that Hervé was always "rather independent" of the party's central organization. Hervé was not the least among many Communists, who had been very important resisters but were later excluded from the party because of their independence of mind.

indicated a role as the puppet of any Communist apparatus. It was Degliame who had expressed the MUR's reservations toward the party's early defeatist attitude, and the same Degliame who in June 1944 complained sorely about the impossibility of achieving a working contact with the FTP.[106] A party functionary does not openly criticize his superiors. Furthermore, Degliame was at the liberation by far the most powerful Communist in the MUR's hierarchy with nominal command over its military forces. That individual importance he owed to the MUR and not the party, in which he commanded no particular influence. The interesting observation of his friend Étienne Bauer, Libération's secretary general, provides this helpful insight: "Degliame-Fouché was a man of action . . . he was surely very much leftist; but if he was anyone, it would have been a Tito rather than a Thorez."[107]

Perhaps most crucial for an understanding of the relationship between the Communists and the MUR was the case of Pascal Copeau. No one played a more important part than Copeau in the direction of the MUR during the last year of the Occupation, and his sentiments seem to reflect very well those of many of his comrades. Copeau freely admits that he had many Communist friends who may have influenced him indirectly, but he was not a member of the Communist party, nor was he ever, in his own words, "a submarine" for the party.[108] He was, on the other hand, thorougly committed to the unity of the Resistance, which in his opinion absolutely required an understanding with the Communists. If Copeau often supported a point of view that the Communist party shared, it was for the simple reason that he agreed with them.[109] Like most of the resisters, he desired a profound renovation of France after the war, involving a truly revolutionary transformation of society.[110] This change, Copeau

---

[106] See above, this chapter. Quotes from various reports of Degliame (*Fouché*).

[107] Étienne Bauer, interview, 5 January 1970.

[108] Copeau, interview, 23 January 1970.

[109] Ibid.

[110] Ravanel, addressing himself to the question of the Communist influence over the Resistance, stated: "It is certain that in many cases, the responsible directors were men of advanced ideas. But there is nothing astonishing in that: the Resistance was largely progressive. One has only to reread the program of the C. N. R. to be convinced of that. . . ." *Progressiste*, rather than *communisant* (fellow traveler), which is often used much too carelessly, is certainly a much better term to use in describing men such as Copeau.

believed, could not be brought about without the cooperation of the French Communists.

The Exécutif MLN Zone Sud on 26 June 1944 declared:

> It is clear that we cannot, without injustice and without endangering the true democracy that we desire to build, expel the Communists from the French community.
>
> In the degree that the task of the M. U. R. is equally a political task, it is necessary, on the contrary, to maintain our communist comrades in the broad community of the Resistance even if, by chance, they are tempted to withdraw from it; even if, against every expectation, the P. C. now represented on the C. F. L. N. appears one day to wish to loosen the bonds which tie it to the various patriotic formations.[111]

The MUR was from the first determined to retain the Communists within the national community, even if it sometimes appeared, as in the Exécutif's declaration, they might have to do so against the party's will! And yet it was almost certainly not against the party's will. With regard to the influence of its resistance experience on the Communist party, Henri Michel has written: ". . . the Party had struggled too much, suffered too much in the patriotic fight for patriotism to have been for its members only an ephemeral and superficial sentiment. It had had its baptism of fire, and the fire had marked it."[112]

It was precisely the Communist party's identification with intransigent patriotism and its tremendous sacrifices in the service of France that, aside from any ideological considerations, made the party extremely attractive to thousands of young Frenchmen, and in part explain its phenomenal growth during and after the liberation.[113] Thus the use of terms such as *communisant* in the context of this period in French history can be seriously misleading, for such words conjure up inappropriate visions of underhanded maneuvering that serve only to obstruct the path of those who seek understanding.[114] One should

---

[111] "Exécutif M. L. N. Zone Sud à Toutes Régions," Papers of Alban Vistel, Archives, CHG.

[112] Michel, *Les Courants de pensée*, p. 721.

[113] See David Caute, *Communism and the French Intellectuals, 1914–1960* (New York, 1964), and H. Stuart Hughes, *The Obstructed Path* (New York: Harper & Row, 1966, 1967, 1968). See also Rieber, *Stalin and the French Communist Party.*

[114] Étienne Bauer's comment (interview, 5 January 1960) that the PC of the resistance era had nothing in common with the PC today or in the

remember that the MUR policy toward the Communist party was established before individual Communists held major posts in the hierarchy. The attitude of the MUR leadership was formulated from a position of relative strength. In effect, the party's late entrance into the Resistance meant that it could never challenge the MUR's position in southern France.[115] The facile implications of occult Communist manipulations overlook the nonsectarian spirit in which the resisters opened their clandestine fraternity to all active patriots.

In extending its hand in an offer of loyal cooperation with the Communists, the MUR observed: "In the course of events, the P. C. is becoming a great party. Enclosed in its proletarianism and cut off from social strata which represent French tradition and French humanism, this party can only owe foreign loyalties; it is up to us to make of it a national party, a Gallican party, and that we can do by gaining its confidence through an enlightened collaboration."[116]

If in retrospect this generous attitude could be considered politically naïve, at the time it seemed natural to join with all who shared the common goal of liberating France. In their decision to act in a straightforward, sincere manner, and in their ardent desire to see transformed what Léon Blum had termed a "foreign nationalist party," the resisters displayed the same hopefulness and idealism revealed in their programs for the future and in their relations with other political parties.

---

prewar era is undoubtedly accurate. Annie Kriegel, *Les communistes,* who points out that in the present-day party only 3.1 percent of the members joined during the Occupation, makes the interesting point that almost all those Communists who were really prominent during the Resistance have in common their failure in the postwar party. Certainly, those members of the MUR were too independently minded to follow docilely a policy line that failed to accord with their ideas. Thus most of them were either purged from the party or left of their own volition.

[115] See Bourdet, "La Politique Intérieure," p. 1849, for the interesting observation that if the Party had not delayed its entrance into the Resistance, France might have followed the path of Yugoslavia. Also comments that the leadership roles of various Communists at the national level made almost no differences for the operations of the MUR on the local level.

[116] "Sur la Necéssité de la Fusion de l'A. S. et des F. T. P.," note joined to an "Accord d'Action Commun Entre les F. T. P. et l'A. S.," 29 December 1943. Papers of Alban Vistel, Archives, CHG.

CHAPTER 5

The Movements and Political Parties

THREE WEEKS before the liberation of Paris, the readers of *La France Libre,* a clandestine journal of limited circulation in northern France, were told: "Liberated France will expect new, mature, and pure men. She has nothing but disgust for the old cliques, for whom financial dealings and money were the only thoughts. We must listen to those good men who tell us: 'Above all, do not bring back the rotten, the spoiled, the *operators,* the prewar politicians."[1]

Countless examples of this nature could be cited as evidence of the resisters' hostility to the political personnel of the Third Republic. One of the most recurrent themes in their underground tracts and papers, their conversations, and their reports to the outside world is their desire to be rid, once and for all, of any remaining vestiges of the weak politicians and sectarian parties of the past.[2] The debacle

---

[1] *La France Libre,* no. 162, 5 August 1944.

[2] This was perhaps the most frequently mentioned idea in reports from political agents to the BCRA (Archives, CHG). In their clandestine journals Libération, Franc-Tireur, and especially Combat, whose ranks contained the smallest percentage of representatives from the former parties, were unanimous in their condemnation of the Third Republic's political failures. Typical of most resisters' attitudes was an early report to the BCRA from Colonel Rémy, one of the most successful organizers of

of 1940 left all of the traditional political parties in shambles, and few resisters had any desire to see them restored. At first the condemnation was unequivocal: "At the crucial hour of its history," said *Combat,* no. 34 (September 1942), "the Third Republic did not defend itself: indeed, it committed suicide. It belongs to the past."[3]

In question was not so much the republican form of government as the particular degeneration of the French Republic in the interwar period.[4] When the Vichy regime in a trial at Riom attempted to place the blame for France's collapse on certain prewar leaders, *Le Franc-Tireur* denied that the government had any right to use these men as scapegoats: "The political parties of all kinds, bear part of the responsibility for our disaster," but "The main fault of the parliamentary democratic regime was its weakness, which engendered its impotence and its incoherence . . . this fault cannot be imputed to only one party. If there was a mess in 1936, the egotism and the incomprehension of the rich classes are just as much responsible as the pretentious demagoguery of the working class leaders."[5] Similarly, it was not so much that all politicians were pernicious but, rather, that they were of insufficient stature to cope with the problems at hand. While not completely absolving Blum, Daladier, Reynaud, Gamelin, and the other leaders of the interwar period of their share in the Republic's failure before the Nazi menace, *Le Franc-Tireur* argued: ". . . the essential weakness of these men is to have been only Daladiers, Reynauds, and Gamelins, at a moment when, faced with the enemy and defeatism, the country had need of Poincarés, Clemenceaus, and Fochs."[6] Indeed, those most guilty were the ones who had profited by the defeat. Specifically, *Le Franc-Tireur* of January 1942

Gaullist intelligence networks, who commented: "Nobody in France wishes to hear any more of the old political parties, presently dying and discredited. General de Gaulle would disappoint all patriots if he took on a political label of any kind" (Passy, *10 Duke Street Londres,* p. 52).

[3] *Combat,* no. 34, September 1942.

[4] Most resisters were staunch republicans and rejected Vichy's simplistic explanation of what they realized was a complicated problem. In *Les Cahiers politiques,* no. 2, July 1943, several resisters explained "Pourquoi je suis Républicain." Marc Bloch's *L'étrange defaite, (témoignage écrit en 1940 suivé d'écrits clandestins, 1942–1944)* (Paris: André Colin, 1957), and Alban Vistel's *Héritage spirituel de la résistance* represent two of the best examples of individual resisters' thoughtful attempts to come to grips with France's disaster.

[5] *Le Franc-Tireur,* December 1941.

[6] *Le Franc-Tireur,* January 1942.

concluded: "We designate the one chiefly responsible . . . Pétain."[7]

Possibly the gallant behavior of the defendants before the Riom Court helped to reduce somewhat the stigma attached to the politicians and the Republic.[8] But undoubtedly more helpful for their rehabilitation was the continuing occupation and the unpopularity of Vichy, which lead many Frenchmen to think back on the Third Republic as the "good old days."[9] Nevertheless, if the general trend soon turned toward indulgence, certainly in this respect the resisters lagged considerably behind public opinion. Most of the resistance movements' principal leaders never were reconciled fully to the re-emergence of the old political parties.[10] Instead of the "anarchic parties" of the past, the resisters hoped French political life in the future would revolve around broad "ideological movements."[11] More explicitly *Combat* suggested:

> In the France of tomorrow there will certainly exist the Communist Party, which has proved its vitality in the Resistance, and without doubt, a conservative or "moderate" grouping. And there will be also a great republican and revolutionary party which will renovate the political life of France and will build the IVe Republic. This will not be the

---

[7] Ibid.

[8] See Colton, *Léon Blum*, pp. 405–27, for a succinct account of the Riom Trial. Daniel Mayer, *Les Socialistes*, pp. 55–61, and Robert Verdier, *La Vie clandestine du parti socialiste* (Paris: Éditions de la Liberté, 1944), pp. 10–14, suggest that the gallant behavior of the defendants before the Riom Court reduced the stigma attached to the politicians and the Republic.

[9] Recall chap. 1.

[10] Baudot, *L'Opinion publique*, p. 157. Taking the instance of the Riom Trial as one example: most resisters appreciated the outcome—an abrupt suspension of the proceedings after it became clear to Hitler that the prosecution would not demonstrate French responsibility for the war, and after the defendants had successfully shown that responsibility for a military defeat could not be attributed to civilians alone—only in so far as it proved embarrassing to Pétain's government. Only the Socialist CAS seemed concerned about the particular fate of the accused, notably Léon Blum. The Comité Directeur of the MLN sharply criticized the CAS for using its journal, the clandestine *Le Populaire*, more as a political leaflet than an organ of combat, citing its February 1943 issue, which consecrated the greatest part of its front page to the anniversary of Riom rather than to the young Frenchmen who were then engaged in a deadly struggle with the Milice. "Le Comité Directeur du Mouvement de la Libération Nationale au Comité Exécutif du Parti Socialiste," 15 April 1944, Papers of Alban Vistel, Archives, CHG.

[11] *Combat*, no. 34, September 1942.

party "of the Resistance" but . . . a party heir to the spirit and the mission of the Resistance."[12]

We have seen that the creation of the National Resistance Council (CNR) in May 1943, which implied the resistance movements' formal recognition of the political parties, was achieved after assurances that the political members would represent "sectors of opinion" rather than the parties as they had previously existed. Later the CNR became an effective organization only when the chiefs of the movements realized that they and not the parties' representatives would control its activity. In its instructions for the formation of regional committees charged with planning the insurrectional takeover of political power, the MUR's Directing Committee on 17 May 1943 stressed the importance of including only true militants of the Resistance.

> It is absolutely not a matter of a distribution of seats among the more or less nebulous political parties. . . . We insist that the delegate charged with this question [of purges of government officials] have a truly new spirit and understand fully that we have no intention to restore without modification the IIIe Republic, or, according to de Gaulle: "to whitewash the sepulchers."[13]

In creating local and departmental liberation committees from the fall of 1943 until the Allied invasion, the movements required evidence that a nominee could offer a genuine contribution to the Resistance. Only such aid could justify a party or individual politician's representation on the committees.[14] The resisters naturally were infuriated by local politicians such as the Socialist chief at Limoges, who demanded two places on the regional liberation committee on the grounds that all of the prewar deputies from that area were Socialists.[15]

---

[12] Ibid., no. 54, February 1944. Several *rapports* of Bingen, Archives, CHG, reflect this same idea, which had gained much support within the ranks of the MUR.

[13] "Turgot à Toutes les Régions," 17 May 1943, Papers of Alban Vistel, Archives, CHG.

[14] "Circulaire" of 5 November 1943, "Le Comité Central des Mouvements de Résistance à tous Chefs de Régions et Services," Papers of Alban Vistel, Archives, CHG. Also Papers of Serreules, *Rapport "Corot,"* received March 1944, Archives, CHG.

[15] The movements obviously rejected this idea, and even the CAS on the national level agreed that such a position was untenable. Closon, "Rapport" no. 3, 11 November 1943, p. 8. Archives, CHG.

As the liberation approached, political parties and politicians who had previously shown few signs of life began to resurface, ardently proclaiming their allegiance to Gaullism. Talents desirable for clandestine resistance had no necessary correlation to skills useful in the political arena; and the movements' delegates to the CFLN and the Consultative Assembly at Algiers often found themselves outshone by the more experienced politicos whose expertise lay in public debate and parliamentary maneuvering.[16] The resisters made no attempt to hide their bitterness toward leaders of the former Republic "whose sole act of courage has been to take the plane to North Africa."[17] Their criticisms were frequently heavy-handed and sometimes manifestly unfair. Obviously a well-known politician, especially one from a leftist background (and thus by definition suspect at Vichy), could not participate actively in an underground organization so easily as relatively unknown resisters. In fact the participation of such men, probably under police surveillance, could only undermine the movements' already precarious security. After the war some resisters acknowledged this problem,[18] but during the Occupation conditions were not conducive to such impartial reflections.[19]

The resisters understood de Gaulle's interest in using some former parliamentarians whose reputations carried some weight with the Allies.[20] They also conceded that the eighty deputies and senators who had voted no when Pétain was given full powers might offer a "symbol of continuity,"[21] but they warned against going too far in this direction. The resisters wanted guarantees that none of the wrecks of the former regime would hold real power.[22] Their future Republic was to be *autre chose*[23]—something different in which no influence would belong to the men of the past responsible for the defeat of

---

[16] Bingen, "Rapports," November 1943, p. 4, and January 1944, p. 5. Archives, CHG.

[17] Bourdet, *Témoignage*, Archives, CHG. Hostache, *Le Conseil*, cites many reports of this widespread hostility to the old politicians, pp. 119–20.

[18] Bourdet, "Histoire de la Résistance française."

[19] See *rapports* of Morandat, 29 February 1944, March 1944, received 4 May 1944, and April 1944. All in Archives, CHC. The April report includes the comment: "Moreover their names [those of former deputies, etc.] one should well understand, are detested by most of our people. The attacks of *Combat* against the Auriols, Cots, and Rucarts, if they are maladroit and often unjust, nonetheless represent very deep feelings. . . ."

[20] *Combat*, no. 51, 15 November 1943.

[21] Ibid., no. 52, December 1943.

[22] Ibid., no. 51 and 52, 15 November and December 1943.

[23] Ibid., no. 54, February 1944.

1940 and now trying to jump on the bandwagon with cries of "For you, the prisons and cemeteries; for us, the offices."[24]

These same prejudices were extended to politicians who remained in France, and all rumors of any activity on their part aroused immediate suspicion. In the fall of 1943 Marshal Pétain proposed that if he disappeared before the promulgation of a new constitution his powers would revert to the National Assembly from which he had received them.[25] The CNR, however, warned all the former parliamentarians that any convocation of the former Assembly under the German Occupation would be illegitimate, and any deputy or senator who attended would be held responsible before the nation at the liberation.[26] The plot proved abortive when the Germans refused to allow Pétain to broadcast his message over the radio. But all the same, to thwart future attempts the MUR's Directing Committee ordered its regional organizations in southern France to inform all parliamentarians, resisters or not, that "they must oppose this maneuver, or run the risk of subsequent punishment, and must abstain from any National Assembly which might be convoked under German pressure."[27] The movements would not in any circumstances permit the resurrection of an Assembly that three years earlier had committed political suicide.

Despite their extreme dislike for the parties and politicians of the past, the resisters were not so blind in their views about France's political future as their exaggerated attacks on the former regime occasionally suggested. On 16 April 1943, the MUR realistically defined its relationship to the political parties.

> There exists in our ranks a rather legitimate mistrust towards anything which touches closely or distantly the politics of

---

[24] Ibid.

[25] See Aron, *Histoire de Vichy*, IVᵉ Periode, chap. 3: "Ultimes Sursauts du Maréchal," for details of this episode. Also Papers of Alban Vistel, Archives, CHG. "C. D. M. U. R. à Office du Logemont (R. I.)," 20 November 1943, which includes all the pertinent documents, including text of Pétain's planned radio message and new constitutional acts, plus the CD's evaluation of the political situation at Vichy, especially the conflict between Pétain and Laval.

[26] *Le Franc-Tireur*, 1 December 1943, quotes the text of the CNR's warning and says any politician acting contrary to these orders will be guilty of high treason.

[27] "C. D. M. U. R. à Office du Logement (R. I.)," 20 November 1943, Papers of Alban Vistel, Archives, CHG.

the Third Republic. We must, however, take realities into account and we cannot claim—if we consider with some humility the weakness of our cadres—to represent by ourselves the political future of France.[28]

In the following months the movements clarified their position. They were not opposed to parties per se; their existence was deemed necessary to a democratic, republican society.[29] Still, *Combat* insisted that they be renovated parties; ". . . new parties, with new methods and new men . . . none of these foul-smelling mummies."[30]

The movements realized that within their ranks were many members of the different parties, but they felt that these men had joined the Resistance not as party men but simply as patriots. Henri Frenay said:

> It would be ridiculous to pretend that, in the great test of France, men died for the "Radical Party" or the "*Alliance Démocratique*," but there were certainly men, formerly belonging to the Radical Party or the *Alliance Démocratique*, who died in the Resistance for France.[31]

As long as the immediate fight against the occupant was their major concern, the movement chiefs had no doubts about the loyalty of former party militants. But as the liberation became more imminent, would these men not look to their customary political milieus when they envisioned the reconstruction of postwar political life in France?

The resisters knew all too well that they had touched only a very small segment of the population. In the fall of 1943 the CFLN's acting *délégué général* Claude Serreules observed that even though all of France had become Gaullist and certainly hoped for a profound renovation of political mores, the French were incontestably still attached to their traditional political families. The *délégué* maintained that a syndicalist, for example, joined a resistance movement just as in

---

[28] "Comité Directeur des Mouvements de Résistance Unis: Fouché à Toutes Régions," 16 April 1943, Papers of Alban Vistel, Archives, CHG.

[29] See *Libération*, no. 29, 1 June 1943, and no. 32, 1 August 1943; "Le Comité Directeur des Mouvements de Résistance Unis à tous les Directoires Régionaux," 14 May 1943, Papers of Alban Vistel, Archives, CHG.

[30] *Combat*, no. 52, December 1943.

[31] Michel and Guetzévitch, *Les Idées*, p. 114, quoting *Combat* (of Algiers), 13 February 1944.

peacetime he might have joined a football club, but he remained first and foremost a syndicalist.[32] This attachment to prior associations was clearly illustrated, continued Serreules, by the "chronic inquietude" of the chiefs of the movements toward the parties and syndicates in contrast to the "perfect calm with which the parties and labor unions watch their men participate in the movements."[33]

That the resisters in southern France were concerned about the possible dislocation of their movement because of the rebirth of the parties was evident as early as the spring of 1943. In April the Directing Committee of the MUR commented on the reconstitution of various groups.

> The active members of the Socialists and the Syndicalists have been in the ranks of the Resistance since the first day. They were in *Combat*, they were in *Franc-Tireur*, they were in *Libération*. It would be childish to oblige these courageous people, whose republican sentiments can be in no way subject to doubt, to choose between the Resistance and their reconstructed parties or labor unions.[34]

The resistance movements, affirmed the Directing Committee, did not oppose the restoration of these organizations, "who are contemplating a more distant future than we have wished to think about up until now. But what we do wish, and what we can do, is to prevent this reconstruction from being made in the ruts of the past or against the unity fostered by the Resistance."[35]

The depletion of their ranks in the present rather than defections

---

[32] Papers of Serreules, *Courrier*, no. 6 of 10 September 1943, Archives, CHG, pp. 1–2. Shortly after the liberation, André Siegfried, "The Rebirth of the French Spirit" (*Foreign Affairs*, July 1945), pp. 561–62, wrote: ". . . in the provinces the masses of the people regretted the old regime, with its elections, its horsetrading, its easygoing ways. . . . If one believed the talk in drawing-rooms and the press, public opinion had come to despise the Deputy, but the fact was the Deputy retained his influence in the electoral district. For this reason the antiparliamentarianism of the Resistance does not mirror the mood of the country at large."

[33] Papers of Serreules, *Courrier*, no. 6 of 10 September 1943, Archives, CHG, pp. 1–2.

[34] "Comité Directeur des Mouvements de Résistance Unis: Fouché à Toutes Régions," 16 April 1943, Papers of Alban Vistel, Archives, CHG, p. 4.

[35] "Comité Directeur des Mouvements de Résistance Unis: Fouché à Toutes Régions," 16 April 1943, Papers of Alban Vistel, Archives, CHG, p. 4.

at a later date most worried the resisters. Their determination to avoid any disperson of their troops was stated very frankly in instructions of 14 May 1943 to the lower echelons.

> Concerning the political parties: the M. R. U. are not disposed to pay the expenses of their subsequent reconstruction. . . . The Resistance has counted in its ranks since the first hours numerous militants of the former parties and labor unions. But it remains absolutely understood that the *ACTION* of Resistance is carried out *within* the movements, and that the legitimate reconstruction of the Socialist Party (like all parties in general) and of the M. O. F. (like all union organizations in general) will not lead to the disruption of the M. R. U.[36]

Members of the MUR's regional directories were explicitly forbidden to retain regional responsibilities in a political party.[37]

The Directing Committee's selection of the Socialist party as an example was almost certainly not a fortuitous choice. In fact, among the former parties only the Communists and Socialists were really active during the German Occupation and participated in the Resistance enough to justify attention.[38] We have examined the MUR's relations with the Communist party; but the Socialists actually were most heavily represented in the southern zone's movements, and not surprisingly the Directing Committee often clashed with the Comité d'Action Socialiste (CAS—the party's clandestine leadership).

The unity of the French Socialist party (SFIO) had been terribly strained by the collapse of the Popular Front and was further divided by the defeat and coming of the Vichy Regime. Thirty-six of the eighty deputies and senators who had refused to vote Pétain full powers were Socialists, but almost five times that many Socialist representatives had voted yes.[39] A minority—the segment that resur-

---

[36] "Le Comité Directeur des Mouvements de Résistance Unis à tous les Directoires Régionaux," 14 May 1943, Papers of Alban Vistel, Archives, CHG, p. 8.

[37] "Le Comité Directeur," p. 9. It was argued that recruitment would suffer from identification with a specific shade of republican opinion, and also security required that the members of the regional directing committee have no connection with organizations outside of the movement.

[38] Michel, *Les Idées*, pp. 6–7.

[39] Mayer, *Les Socialistes*, pp. 9–10, and Verdier, *La Vie clandestine*, pp. 5–6.

rected the party under the Occupation—regrouped around their chief, Léon Blum. Although imprisoned by the Vichy government, he remained their doctrinal and inspirational guide and was personally responsible for several major tactical decisions.[40] Before Blum was turned over to the Germans on 31 March 1943, Daniel Mayer, head of the CAS, visited him sixteen times without being molested—an interesting commentary on the vigilance of Vichy's police.[41] Recreating a visit to the prison at Bourassol, Jean Pierre-Bloch recalled his surprise that Blum was so aware of the Socialists' activities: "I had nothing to teach him. On the contrary: he knew everything."[42]

Early in the Occupation the Socialists made two crucial decisions, rigorously adhered to until the liberation, that conditioned in large measure the party's fortunes throughout the clandestine era. From the beginning Blum declared his unequivocal confidence in Charles de Gaulle as the essential symbol of French unity in the Resistance. Even before some movement leaders, Blum recognized in de Gaulle more than simply a symbol. In October 1942 the Socialist chief, urging the establishment of a Provisional French Government to replace Vichy at the liberation, wrote:

> This interim government can only be built around one man, around one name, General de Gaulle. He was the first to arouse in France the will for resistance and he continues to personify this spirit. He will be therefore the indispensable man, or rather, the only possible man, at the hour when the idea of the Resistance and the fact of the liberation will form the bond between Frenchmen.[43]

---

[40] Daniel Mayer's introduction to Blum's "La Prison et le Procès," part 2 of *L'Oeuvre*, vol. 5, refers to the paradox of Blum's cell at Bourassol becoming a "command post in the battle against the government of the time" (p. 138), and says that Blum was indeed the director of the clandestine party.

[41] Mayer, *Les Socialistes*, pp. 23–25.

[42] Jean Pierre-Bloch, *Mes Jours heureux*, p. 149. See pp. 143–59 for details of this visit.

[43] De Gaulle, *Mémoires*, vol. 2, p. 377, "Extrait d'une note adressée par Léon Blum au Comité de la Libération Nationale à Alger," [*sic*]—should read *Comité National Français à Londres*. Also see Blum, *L'Oeuvre*, vol. 5, pp. 382–84, "Note Adressée au Général de Gaulle pour le President Roosevelt et M. W. Churchill," which expresses similar ideas, with Blum vouching for de Gaulle's "republican spirit."

Blum added that he did not share the suspicions of those who were apprehensive about de Gaulle's political stance.[44]

The Socialists persisted unwaveringly in their support for de Gaulle's CNF at London and the CFLN at Algiers. In the spring of 1944 a Gaullist political agent reported: "Its position *vis à vis* Algiers is of perfect loyalty; for the Socialist Party the *Comité* is the true, the only Government. Its leaders are taboo: to criticize them is treason, to question their decisions a grave assault on National Unity."[45]

This unstinting commitment to de Gaulle evidently led to the Socialists' second major decision—to encourage their militants to join the Gaullist resistance movements.[46] In essence, with this decision the Socialists had opted to leave the action of the Resistance to the movements, rejecting the possibility of forming a separate Socialist paramilitary force. Therefore, the first step in reviving the party as such was the formation of the Comité d'Action Socialiste (CAS)—a reorganization of the party's cadres rather than the birth of a mass movement.[47] After an initial inventory of their potential support, a renewal of contact with reliable comrades, and a preliminary meeting in March, the Socialists held a small "congress" of forty people at Toulouse on 21 June 1941. At that time an executive committee was established to direct the CAS in southern France.[48]

Daniel Mayer, appointed secretary general of the organization at its Toulouse meeting, was soon in contact with the leaders of several southern zone resistance movements, in particular Emmanuel d'Astier whose movement Libération included the largest percentage of So-

---

[44] De Gaulle, *Mémoires*, vol. 2, p. 378. These included a group of Socialists, *Le Cercle Jean Jaurès,* at London. See Blum's letter to Felix Gouin, 21 October 1942, *L'Oeuvre*, vol. 5, pp. 370–71.

[45] Morandat, "Suite du Rapport général sur la Situation de la Résistance," to Commissariat à l'Intérieur du CFLN, April 1944, received May 1944, Archives, CHG.

[46] See *Le Populaire*, 15 June 1942.

[47] See Daniel Ligou, *Histoire du socialisme en France, 1871–1961* (Paris: Presses Universitaires de France, 1962), p. 500, and Mayer, *Les Socialistes*, pp. 66–67.

[48] Mayer, *Les Socialistes*, pp. 14–38, passim; Pierre-Bloch, *Mes Jours heureux*, pp. 101–3; and Verdier, *La Vie clandestine*. In the northern zone a separate and fairly autonomous CAS was established. Not until Daniel Mayer's trip to London in the spring of 1943 was the fusion of the two committees accomplished and headquarters established in Paris. Mayer was selected *secrétaire général* of the combined executive.

cialists. From their first contacts d'Astier, not wanting his movement to assume any particular political coloring, had refused Mayer's request that Libération distribute only socialist tracts.[49] Nevertheless, the two agreed that a CAS representative would join the movement's executive committee, and later Libération also assured the clandestine printing of *Le Populaire*.[50] In return the CAS agreed not to threaten the precarious unity of the Resistance by grouping its members into a band apart. Therefore, while many Socialists were active in the resistance movements the CAS had under its direct control no troops fully engaged in the immediate action of the Resistance.

The wisdom of this policy was brought into question after the belated but total commitment of the Communist party to the Resistance in June 1941. We have seen that the Communists' dynamic contribution to the direct action of the Resistance quickly brought the party enormous prestige and admiration in resistance circles. Étienne Bauer, a student at the outbreak of the war and later the secretary general of Libération, remembered the sharp contrast the Socialist and Communist parties presented to the youth of his generation who were active in the Resistance. Compared to the SFIO, which seemed destined to disappear, Bauer recalled the extraordinary attraction of the PC. "The Communist Party was absolutely the party of France, of liberty, of effectiveness in the fight against Nazism. . . ."[51] No less an authority than Daniel Mayer acknowledged this superior attraction of the Communist party. "From the moment the Communists entered the Resistance . . . it was very evident that we would be at a disadvantage in comparison to them."[52]

Faced with the increasing influence of the Communist party, several Socialist leaders demanded that in order to demonstrate clearly

---

[49] Eschalier, *Étude*, and d'Astier, *Témoignage*, Archives, CHG. Similarly, d'Astier refused to exclude Communist militants from Libération, as the CGT chief, Léon Jouhaux, had desired, though he did tell Jouhaux that no Communists would serve on the directing committee.

[50] Vistel, *La Nuit*, pp. 76–92, gives a good picture of the importance of the Socialist members in Libération. For the agreements between the Socialists and Libération, see d'Astier, "Rapport Général sur la situation des Partis et des Mouvements de Résistance, sur le role actuel de la Résistance et l'incidence des elections." Bibliothèque Nationale, Paris [4ºL59b 6]; Eschallier, Étude, pp. 4–9, 11–12; *Témoignage* of Morandat, Archives, CHG; Passy, *10 Duke Street Londres*, pp. 258–60, and *Missions secrètes en France*, pp. 31–33.

[51] Étienne Bauer, interview, 5 January 1970.

[52] Mayer, *Les Socialistes*, pp. 69–70.

the Socialist contribution to the Resistance their party form its own action groups in imitation of the Communist FTP.[53] When the CAS broached this possibility to Léon Blum, his advice was unequivocal. "We cannot take it upon ourselves to weaken in any manner whatsoever the resistance organizations, either in pulling out our friends, or in breaking discipline."[54]

Eventually Blum's decision would prevail as the official CAS policy, but some individual federations were at first reluctant to follow this line. Most notably a Marsaillais lawyer, André Boyer, with the support of Gaston Defferre and Eugène Thomas, ventured beyond the operations of his Gaullist intelligence network Brutus to aid in the organization of Socialist paramilitary units, the so-called Groupes Veni under Colonel Lefevre (Veni or Vincent).[55] The growth of these units did not go unnoticed by the chiefs of the MUR, and the spring of 1943 witnessed several explosive arguments between Daniel Mayer and Emmanuel d'Astier. Mayer used the Groupes Veni and threats of Socialist withdrawal from the movements as levers in the CAS's bid for a seat on the MUR's Directing Committee, and d'Astier accused the CAS of breaking its agreements with Libération.[56]

Actually one may legitimately question the seriousness of Mayer's threats. Boyer claimed in December 1942 that the Socialists within the movements were ready to form separate milices "immediately and on a single call from the C. A. S,"[57] and Léon Blum repeatedly reminded Charles de Gaulle of the Socialists' "unselfish" gesture of ordering their men into the resistance movements.[58] However, Henri Frenay maintained that the CAS did not order the Socialists to leave the movements for the simple reason that the men probably would not have followed such an order.[59] In fact the majority of Socialists,

---

[53] Ligou, *Histoire*, pp. 502–3.

[54] Blum, "Consultation au pied levé," for the party, 7 March 1943, in *L'Oeuvre*, vol. 5, p. 394. Also Mayer, *Les Socialistes*, pp. 72–73.

[55] Boyer was known as Brémond or Brutus. The original organization was an intelligence network called Froment, then Brutus. The paramilitary groups were most often tagged *groupes Veni*, but later changed to *France au Combat*. See Passy, *10 Duke Street Londres*, Mayer, *Les Socialistes*, and Ligou, *Histoire*.

[56] Passy, *Missions secrètes en France*, pp. 4, 222.

[57] Report to London (to the BCRA) on the political situation in France. Quoted in Jean Pierre-Bloch, *Le Vent souffle sur l'histoire* (Paris: Éditions S. I. P. E. P., 1956), p. 255.

[58] Blum, *L'Oeuvre*, vol. 5, letter of 15 March 1943, pp. 399, 403.

[59] *Témoignage* of Henri Frenay, Archives, CHG.

like resisters in general, had not entered the movements on anyone's orders. Instead they had volunteered from their own personal motivations, many before the CAS existed or began to encourage Socialists to join the movements. Furthermore many Socialists in the ranks of the MUR were opposed to the rebirth of the SFIO,[60] which the CAS represented, despite its unquestionable dedication to the "purification" of the party.[61] Finally, we have seen that because the Communist party had a late start in southern France, it could not match the MUR's strength in that area. Surely we can assume the Socialist party over a year later and with less spectacular resistance credentials would have had even less success.

In any event this drastic step, which Blum correctly opined would have served mainly to further divide the resisters,[62] was never taken. Jean Moulin, de Gaulle's *délégué général* and Moulin's successor in southern France, Jacques Bingen, both agreed with the movements that the Groupes Veni should be incorporated into the MUR's Secret Army.[63] Moulin supported the MUR's stand against including representatives of any political party on their Directing Committee, and he advised Mayer to seek an increased influence through Socialists who held important offices in Libération.[64]

Still, Mayer's demands for representation were not completely unjustified. With the creation of the MUR in January 1943, Combat, Libération, and Franc-Tireur had suppressed their individual executive committees so that the *patrons* alone made even more decisions. Thus the CAS representative at Libération lost even his former

---

[60] *Témoignages* of Frenay and Bourdet, Archives, CHG. Also, like a few Communist militants within the MUR (see chap. 4), many of these Socialists had helped create the MUR and, holding numerous important offices within its structure, had no interest in leaving or disrupting the movement.

[61] See various issues of the clandestine *Le Populaire*, and letters of Blum to de Gaulle (*L'Oeuvre*, vol. 5), also Christian Pineau, *La Simple vérité*, pp. 294–95, for description of Mayer's strong concern for a thorough purge of the ranks.

[62] Letter to de Gaulle, 15 March 1943, *L'Oeuvre*, vol. 5, p. 399.

[63] After a personal inspection Bingen reported ("Rapport" of November 1943, pp. 7–11, Archives, CHG) that the Socialist forces represented at best only two thousand men, and he was very unfavorably impressed with their leaders on the regional and departmental level. Mayer had claimed twenty thousand men for the *Groupes Veni*. (Passy, *Missions secrètes en France*, pp. 31–33.)

[64] Passy, *Missions secrètes en France*, pp. 31–33, 222–23, quoting reports from Moulin.

advisory and consultative role.[65] Perhaps with this in mind, Bingen and the MUR at one time envisioned adding André Boyer, whose exceptional abilities were universally recognized, to the Directing Committee.[66] But at the end of September 1943, the CAS disassociated itself from the Groupes Veni,[67] and Daniel Mayer turned to the National Resistance Council in his quest for more equitable Socialist representation within the Resistance. Shortly thereafter the Groupes Veni were simply absorbed by the AS under the label France au Combat,[68] and the Socialists never enjoyed the benefits of direct representation on the MUR executive.[69] To the Socialists' dismay, the CNR was no more receptive to their pleas than was the MUR. A plenary session in December 1943, including representatives of the parties and trade unions, rejected Mayer's request for a socialist representative on the CNR's *bureau*.[70]

In retrospect it is evident that the leadership's original decision not to organize its own paramilitary groups had placed the CAS in

---

[65] This event undoubtedly increased the CAS's tendency to think exclusively in party terms. Similarly, at Combat the suppression of the executive committee left Georges Bidault and other Christian Democrats without an active role in the movement. They subsequently turned to thoughts of the future and began to lay the foundations for the postwar MRP.

[66] Bingen, "Rapport" of November 1943, Archives, CHG; Passy, vol. 2.

[67] Bingen, "Rapport" of November 1943, Archives, CHG. Mayer, *Les Socialistes*, claimed (p. 121): "The liaison between the *Groupes Veni* and the Socialist Party were sporadic and fragmentary." But the connection was evidently more important than he suggests, at least until this disavowal in the fall of 1943. Henri Noguères, *Histoire*, vol 2, p. 633, states emphatically that the creators of the *Groupes Veni* had obtained "the full accord of Daniel Mayer, national chief of their party."

[68] BIMUR, 14 December 1943.

[69] Passy, *Missions secrètes en France*, pp. 31–33, claims that after Gaston Deferre's trip to London in September 1943, France au Combat was allowed a representative on the Directing Committee, but I have found no evidence of this. Bingen's reports do not indicate any further developments in this direction. Claude Bourdet, who was at that time Combat's most important chief, remembered (*témoignage*, Archives, CHG) their "great mistake" of having opposed CAS entry to the MUR. At the time of the formation of the MLN (see Marie Granet, *Defense de la France*, p. 152), Boyer was not a member of the Directing Committee. Boyer was arrested through the treason of a double agent and did not return from deportation. The only Socialist who was a member of the CD of the MUR was Robert Lacoste, a syndicalist who opposed the reconstruction of the SFIO. (See Passy, *Missions secrètes en France*, pp. 25–26, and Hostache, *Le Conseil*, pp. 54, 58.)

[70] Hostache, *Le Conseil*, pp. 162–63.

an extremely awkward position with respect to the MUR and the resistance movements in general. Late in November 1943 the Gaullist *délégué général* observed: "The reconstituted Socialist Party finds itself, in all of the directing bodies of the French underground, in a position of conflict with all the other organizations."[71]

The main reason for this situation was readily apparent. Since the Communist party's activities in the Resistance were fully recognized and rewarded by a large, almost excessive, share in the command of the Resistance, the Socialists felt that by comparison they were being slighted. Yet the logic of their own policy clearly argued against the Socialists. The chiefs of the movements insisted that they spoke for the Socialists within their ranks along with all the other resisters. Why should the Socialist party, not involved as an independent force in the immediate action of the Resistance, have a voice in the direction of those operations? The Communist party's presence was amply demonstrated by the FTP, but where were the socialist FTP? From the movements' point of view, the principal interest was immediate action, and the CAS had no legitimate claim to the equality of treatment it was demanding.

During the Occupation the "old traditional distrust of hostile brothers"[72] continued unabated under a thin veneer of patriotic comradeship. The Communists ceremoniously sidestepped a few half-hearted Socialist attempts to extend a fraternal hand to their fellow proletarian party.[73] And despite the Socialists' official statements to the contrary, in conversations with Gaullist agents Mayer expressed sharply anti-Communist opinions.[74] Léon Blum urged General de Gaulle: "Above all do not attribute to me any thought of jealousy of communism";[75] but his evident apprehension clearly showed through in this and later correspondence with de Gaulle and the Socialist

---

[71] Bingen, "Rapport," end of November, received February 1944, Archives, CHG.

[72] As Bingen termed the all too evident competition between Socialists and Communists in the Resistance. "Rapport," end of November, received February 1944, Archives, CHG.

[73] Mayer, *Les Socialistes*, pp. 118–19. Four letters exchanged by the two parties during the Occupation are found in Papers of Alban Vistel, Archives, CHG; one of these letters is reproduced in Mayer, Appendix 16, pp. 226–28. See also *Le Populaire*, February 1943, 15 June 1942, and 1 July 1943.

[74] Passy, *Missions secrètes en France*, pp. 33–36.

[75] Letter of November 1942, *L'Oeuvre*, vol. 5, p. 381.

party.[76] The obvious advantage the Communists enjoyed resulted in unmistakable traces of paranoia among the Socialist leaders, which led them to exaggerate the significance of various agreements between the Communist party and the resistance movements.

For example, within twenty-four hours after the demonstrations of 16 October 1942, protesting Vichy's forced labor draft, the CAS complained that the resistance movements were discriminating against them by signing tracts with the Communist party that claimed to speak for all resisters.[77] Actually this combined action had been taken on the initiative of the movements' local elements with the simple intention of preventing the deportation of French workers to Germany. The standing policy of the southern zone resistance movements' leadership at the time was not to sign tracts with the Communist party unless the Socialist party signed as well.[78] The Socialists' attribution of some sinister political design to the joint action was as misguided as Colonel Passy's assertion that by this action the movements "signed their political death warrant for the future"[79] by bringing politics into the Resistance. The reconstruction of the political parties and the problems thus posed for the movements would have been no less real without mutual signatures on a few clandestine pamphlets.[80]

We have seen that most of the accords signed at superior echelons between the MUR and the Communist party remained essentially dead letters, resulting at most in occasional discussions of common goals or targets for direct action. Furthermore, the MUR's Directing Committee refused to endorse the Communist's minimization of the Socialists' role in the Resistance and insisted, for example, that a CAS representative be present when plans were made for the organization

---

[76] For example, "Consultation au pied levé," 7 March 1943, *L'Oeuvre*, vol. 5, pp. 394–95, and letter to de Gaulle, 15 March 1943, *L'Oeuvre*, vol. 5, pp. 399–404.

[77] Passy, *10 Duke Street Londres*, p. 269, and *Missions secrètes en France*, pp. 4–5. See above, chap. 4. Compare to Noguères, *Histoire*, vol. 2, pp. 620–23.

[78] See *Témoignage* of Pascal Copeau, quoted in Noguères, *Histoire*, p. 623.

[79] Passy, *10 Duke Street Londres*, p. 269.

[80] Noguères, *Histoire*, vol. 2, p. 620, notes: ". . . what some call the 'politicization' of the Resistance . . . is in fact only the avowal of the existence beside the movements and of Fighting France, of political parties rebuilt clandestinely."

of the liberation committees in southern France.[81] Nevertheless, the CAS persisted in its suspicions that the movements wanted to deny the Socialists their proper place in the Resistance.

In a note to the CAS about an accord allegedly signed 5 February 1943, between the Communist party and the resistance movements, Léon Blum wrote: "It is clear that they wish to get rid of us. They consider us a negligible element."[82] And a week later he warned General de Gaulle that this "contract" was "an error of orientation fraught with dangers."[83] The Socialists, continued Blum:

> . . . judge inadmissible . . . that the fact of having entered *en masse* into the ranks of the organizations of Resistance . . . while the Communists jealously created their distinct action groups, today places them under the orders of a command in which the Communist Party shares equally and from which their party is excluded. . . .[84]

It is unclear exactly what accord is involved here.[85] Blum was certainly mistaken in speaking of "the contract concluded between all the resistance organizations and the Communist Party,"[86] since no joint agreements whatsoever were made between the northern and southern zone resistance movements before formation of the CNR on 27 May 1943. A slight possibility exists that the accord in question was the coordination of direct action for southern France between the MUR and the Communist party.[87] If so, the Socialists clearly

---

[81] "Le Comité Directeur du Mouvement de la Libération Nationale au Comité Exécutif du Parti Socialiste," 15 April 1944. Papers of Alban Vistel, Archives, CHG.

[82] "Consultation au pied levé," 7 March 1943, *L'Oeuvre*, vol. 5, p. 394.

[83] Letter to de Gaulle, 15 March 1943, *L'Oeuvre*, vol. 5, p. 403.

[84] Ibid.

[85] Blum is the only source I have found for the 5 February date. George Ligou, *Histoire* (pp. 502–3) picks up the date from Blum and erroneously cites Colonel Passy, allegedly commenting on this agreement, when in fact Passy is talking about the demonstrations of 16–17 October 1942. Also Ligou curiously notes that Passy "had to intervene" (*dut intervenir*), perhaps suggesting that Passy could have canceled such an agreement had it indeed been made by the movements. But Passy had no such authority over the resistance movements.

[86] Letter to de Gaulle, 15 March 1943, *L'Oeuvre*, vol. 5, p. 403.

[87] See chap. 4. Unfortunately I have been unable to pinpoint the date of this accord. The fusion of the MUR occurred 26 January 1943, and it is improbable that this agreement could have been made so soon thereafter. The first mention of the accord with the PC in directives to the MUR

misinterpreted the movements' intention and Blum considerably overrated the importance of this understanding with the PC. The chiefs of the MUR merely hoped to coordinate the efforts of their paramilitary forces with the only other clandestine organization, which at that time controlled troops that offered a real potential for immediate action. Even this limited aspiration came to naught when the Communists declined to return the MUR's loyal cooperation.

Undeniably involved in the Resistance yet always remaining on the fringe where direct action was concerned, the CAS was unable to extract itself from the embarrassing situation its own policies had created. This difficulty explained in part the Socialists' continual "feeble and grumbling attitude"[88] toward the directing organizations of the Resistance. The bitter competition with the Communists in which the Socialists could claim few victories also must be reemphasized. In the spring of 1944, a Gaullist political agent, Yvon Morandat, noted:

> The P. S. remains the place of refuge of everyone who fears communism. And, if it adopted a dynamic and realistic policy, it would be understandable. Instead, it is involved in systematic opposition, offering complicated, moderate, and tardy counter-proposals, splitting hairs, reflecting mistrust and *attentisme*. Their great fear is that the Resistance [movements] might unite, their even greater fear is that once unified, it might come to an understanding with the P. C. They are maneuvering in every fashion to prevent this occurrence.[89]

---

regional organizations was on 16 April 1943 (*Fouché à toutes régions*, Papers of Alban Vistel). The text of the accord, perhaps with the date, was attached to the original document, but unfortunately was missing from the copy that I have consulted. It is possible that Blum was mistaken about the date, or even that the CAS was disturbed by a less important local arrangement, if their reaction to the 16 October 1942 demonstration can be judged typical.

[88] Morandat, Letter to d'Astier, 29 February 1944, Archives, CHG.

[89] Morandat, "Suite du Rapport Général sur la Résistance," April 1944, received May 1944, p. 3. Archives, CHG. Morandat mentions as an example of this maneuvering Libération-Nord's failure to join the MLN because of pressure from the CAS. Étienne Bauer, interview 5 January 1970, recalled that Libération-Nord had never fused with Libération-Sud, because the Socialist directors of Libération-Nord told him: "You have too many Communists in your movement." See Marie Granet, *Un Journal socialiste clandestin pendant l'occupation, Libération-Nord* (two brochures, supple-

But underlying all of the conflicts between the CAS and the resistance movements, and beyond historical quarrels of long standing with the Communist party as well, lay a fundamental and apparently unbridgable difference in conceptions of the Resistance.

Because their roots were deep in French political history, the Socialists could view the defeat and Occupation as just another hurdle to be overcome in their progress toward socialism. In this broad context they naturally looked beyond the present hard times to a better future for France, and especially for the Socialist party. On the other hand, the resistance movements were creatures of the defeat, conceived of and developed in the framework of a struggle against Vichy and the Germans. Thus the leaders of the resistance movements were concerned above all with their immediate problem—the organization and action of the Resistance. Only as the liberation appeared imminent did the movements turn more attention to questions of the future, and even then specific proposals for the future were unquestionably of secondary interest to the immediate task of an insurrectionary seizure of power.[90]

Léon Blum's suggestions to the CAS about the action of the proposed executive committee of the Resistance (the CNR) on 1 March 1943 are remarkable for their revelation of the Socialists' mentality.

> It is, I think, before the future Executive Committee that we must finally bring our offer to prepare a common program, or more precisely our initiative aimed at a preliminary agreement of principle on *the immediate problems: orientation of the peace negotiations; reconstruction of the national economy.*[91]

Nothing could have been further from the resistance movements' view of what were the "immediate problems" at that time. Indeed, a

---

ments to *La Revue Socialiste*, nos. 192 and 193 [Arras: Imprimerie S. E. P., 1966], pp. 12–14.

[90] A comparison of the subjects treated in the clandestine Socialist journals *Socialisme et Liberté* and *Le Populaire* with those the movements produced reveals a striking contrast in orientation. Beginning in 1943 the resistance movements produced a few special journals—*Cahiers de la Libération, L'Avenir, La Revue Libre*—devoted to postliberation France, and some leaders began to plan, as we shall see, for a resistance-based political party. But these activities filled only a small fraction of their time, and organizations devoted exclusively to the future were closely associated in the resisters' minds with *attentisme* and came under sharp criticism.

[91] Blum, *L'Oeuvre*, vol. 5, p. 393.

year later when Mayer did eventually offer the CNR the Socialists' project for a common program, it was rejected in favor of the version drafted by Pierre Villon, the *Front National*'s representative. Villon's version emphasized the need for immediate action.[92]

It was their preoccupation with the future for which MUR leaders most reproached the Socialist chiefs. In April 1944 the MUR's Directing Committee very clearly defined its position with regard to the Socialists in a letter to the CAS.

> . . . In what concerns the actual direction of the Resistance's action the C. D. of the M. L. N. does not share the point of view of the P. C. and F. N., who contest any effective participation of the Socialist Party in the present struggle against the enemy. In making such a severe judgment the C. D. of the M. L. N. fears committing a cruel injustice to numerous militants of the Socialist Party who are active in the ranks of the M. L. N. with a devotion which, for many of them, has meant the sacrifice of their freedom and of their lives.
>
> Nevertheless, the C. D. of the M. L. N. feels that the Executive Committee of the Socialist Party has not always appeared to place immediate concerns of action against the enemy before political concerns for the future, and that it has most insufficiently utilized its local, departmental, and regional channels in the transmission of directives of action or in calling all the strata of the population reached by its channels to come *en masse* to fill out the ranks of the Resistance.
>
> The C. D. of the M. L. N. also believes that the national

---

[92] Letter of Morandat to d'Astier, 29 February 1944, Archives, CHG, reported: "It [the CAS] has offered a *Charte de la Résistance* which was not accepted. One must say that it had little chance of acceptance. Treating only the future, it was extraordinarily moderate. Something like the program of the *Cartel des Gauches* of 11 May 1924." Specifically, the Socialists had said nothing about the immediate distribution of all parachuted weapons and those held in clandestine caches, which was a major demand of the resisters in 1944 and something the Communists had long advocated. The Communist proposal presented by Villon, which became the so-called charter of the Conseil National de la Résistance, did however, as Daniel Mayer pointed out, resemble much of the Socialist program, especially in all that concerned the future. Mayer, *Les Socialistes*, p. 119.

edition of *Le Populaire* is certainly more of a political leaflet than an organ of combat, and it is astonished that, at the moment when whole departments of France are put to fire and blood by the *Milice* of Darnand and when young Frenchmen are falling with arms in hand fighting for the honor of their country, the February issue of *Le Populaire* devoted the greatest part of its first page to the anniversary of the Riom Trial. . . .[93]

Unquestionably many resisters were skeptical of Socialist claims that the CAS was not the partisan "party of yesterday."[94] Although the Socialists had temporarily loaned their militants to the movements, they left no doubt about the duration of this arrangement.[95] The future, they assumed, belonged to socialism and to the Socialist party. The CAS's first clandestine newspaper, *Socialisme et liberté*, proposed a program for the triumph of "Social Democracy or *better still Socialist Democracy*."[96] From this first issue of *Socialisme et liberté*, one perceives something of the tone that was to characterize all of the Socialist party's clandestine literature, especially its peculiar definition of the action called for before the liberation. Since public action was temporarily impossible, reasoned the Socialists, "what we must above all demand of our comrades, is to stand ready for open, public action, from the moment that this will have become pos-

---

[93] "Le Comité Directeur du Mouvement de la Libération Nationale au Comité Exécutif du Parti Socialiste," 15 April 1944, Papers of Alban Vistel, Archives, CHG. The CD added that it was pleased to observe an apparent change in the Socialist attitude in recent weeks, and vowed to exert all its influence toward a greater representation of the CAS in the direction of the Resistance on the condition that this was indeed the case. But the actions of Socialists within the MLN could be credited to the PS as well "only in the measure that the Socialist Party pushes its militants towards action just as the MLN was doing."

[94] *Le Populaire*, 15 June 1942.

[95] Emmanuel d'Astier, "Rapport Général," remembered the frequent reminders from the CAS that the Socialist militants in *Libération* were "our" men or "our property." Léon Blum and the Socialist paper, *Le Populaire*, and others following Blum's lead were very consistent in their opinions that the role of the resistance movements was specific and limited. After the liberation, their task finished, the cadres of the movements should enter the political parties, which should benefit from the fresh blood and new ideas of these men. See *Le Populaire*, no. 31, February 1944: "Une Concentration des Partis, sera-t-elle possible?"

[96] No. 1, December 1941, my italics.

sible."[97] To those who might interpret these words as *attentisme*, the Socialists replied, "Ah, No!" There was much to be done now, and specifically the first task was "to prepare ideologically and materially for the reconstruction of socialism and of the Party."[98]

Some resisters construed such statements as these to mean that the Socialists were above all concerned with the reconstruction of their party.[99] Certainly, to the directors of the MUR the Socialist party was the political party par excellence and as such was by definition suspect.[100] In a report on the opposition of the MUR and the Socialists over the Groupes Veni, Jacques Bingen related his impression that it was very easy to find people—"They are legions, I dare say"— who had no love for the Socialists.[101] Since Bingen was the Gaullist agent most familiar with and deeply involved in the operations of the MUR, we can imagine these legions were found within their ranks.

The broadness of mind and generosity that characterized the MUR's attitude toward the Communist party was never extended to the Socialist party.[102] The announcement that André Le Troquer would be de Gaulle's minister of war meant that a Socialist leader would hold ultimate authority over the military forces of the Fighting French and in theory would be capable of giving orders to such celebrated FFL officers as Leclerc and Koenig. *Combat* complained bitterly about this "appalling disproportion: the defender of Léon Blum cannot give orders to the defender of Bir-Hakeim."[103] In August 1942 Léon Blum, advising his fellow Socialists to work toward the elaboration of a common program around which the Resistance

---

[97] *Socialisme et Liberté*, no. 1, December 1941.

[98] Ibid.

[99] For example, *témoignage* of Zerapha, Archives, CHG.

[100] *Témoignage* of Bourdet, Archives, CHG.

[101] Bingen, "Rapport," November 1943, Archives, CHG. The same impression is reflected in interview, Étienne Bauer, 5 January 1970; "Rapports" of Closon, 10 September and 10 October 1943, Archives, CHG.

[102] Bingen, "Rapport," November 1943, Archives, CHG; interview Étienne Bauer, 5 January 1970; "Rapports" of Closon, 10 September and 10 October 1943, Archives, CHG; and Granet and Michel, *Combat*, p. 315.

[103] *Combat*, no. 53, December 1943. The CAS protested sharply about Combat's declarations. After Morandat's intervention with Copeau, the MUR eventually apologized for the personal nature of their criticisms, which nevertheless clearly reflected their deep-seated resentment toward the politicians of the former republic. *Le Populaire*, April 1944, decried *Combat*'s attacks on Le Troquer and Auriol, pointing out that the CNR had repudiated all such personal attacks. See various *rapports* of Morandat, Archives, CHG, for his involvement in the affair.

could unite, remarked: "I am thinking naturally—it is impossible for me not to recall it—of the program of the Popular Front, and it is a democracy of the same type that I envisage."[104] But when the resistance chiefs thought of the Popular Front, so closely identified with the Socialist party, they remembered not the temporary enthusiasm and accomplishments but the failures, along with all of the other frustrated hopes and disappointments that colored their image of the Third Republic—a long history of "Reformers without reform, Revolutionaries without revolution."[105] As if in response to Blum, *Combat* wrote: "We no longer want the Republic of Comrades, an impotent parliamentary system, programs which remain only programs; [we do not wish] to recommence the experience of the Popular Front, ministries falling every fifteen days only to be reconstituted by the same men. . . ."[106] In general the Socialists were unable or often unwilling to disavow their close association with the former and, in the eyes of the resisters, discredited regime. Perhaps this fact alone precluded a satisfactory understanding with the resistance movements.

Ironically these same movements, which throughout the Occupation disparaged the Socialist party, anticipated the future establishment of socialism in France as a matter of course. In April 1944 an American observer remarked:

> Both in France and in Algiers, Socialism is apparently losing in importance as a specific party, while gaining in influence as a generalized political philosophy. Delegates to the Consultative Assembly, who consider themselves Socialists in principle, complain of the Party's poor discipline and unimaginative leadership.[107]

Daniel Mayer observed that even though the particular draft the Socialists had offered to the CNR as a charter for the Resistance was turned down, the final version incorporated many of the Socialists' proposals, especially those for the postwar period.[108]

---

[104] Blum, "Schéma d'une sorte d'instruction pour mes amis," Paris-London, 28 August 1942, *L'Oeuvre*, vol. 5, p. 368.

[105] *Combat*, June 1942.

[106] No. 53, December 1943.

[107] OSS Document 66534 C, Report from Algiers, 7 April 1944.

[108] Mayer, *Les Socialistes*, p. 119. Compare Hostache, *Le Conseil*, Annexe 1 "Programme d'action de la Résistance" (adopted 15 March 1944) and Mayer, Annexe 17 "Projet de Contenu d'un Programme Commun" (11 December 1943). See also Verdier, *La Vie clandestine*, p. 27.

Although critical of the Socialists for giving so much attention to the future, the more activist resisters did not reject the conceptions elaborated by these men they accused of *attentisme*. Their guerrilla activities were less spectacular than those of the Communists and the movements, but the Socialists' political, social, and economic theories became the common property of all of the movements.[109] Mosts resisters assumed nationalization of the trusts, social security, stricter control over banks and financial exchanges, and other Socialist propositions to be reasonable and indeed necessary.[110] Ten years earlier such thoughts might have horrified many who had associated these doctrines with the destruction of the French social fabric.

Despite their reticence toward the Socialist party, not surprisingly, given the large number of Socialists within their ranks, the resisters were strongly influenced by Socialist ideas. But the Socialists' influence was by no means limited to this indirect assimilation of ideas. At least twice the Socialists figured significantly and directly in the evolution of the Resistance. First, a Socialist, Christian Pineau, was most instrumental in General de Gaulle's decision to enunciate a thoroughly republican and progressive political platform in 1942[111]— a major step in gaining the movements' adherence to Gaullism. Later, several Socialists, including Pierre Brossolette, Louis Vallon, Jean Pierre-Bloch, Georges Boris, and André Philip, held important posts in the BCRA, the CNF, and the CFLN. Their presence in London and Algiers, along with the active correspondence Blum maintained

---

[109] *Combat*, no. 34, September 1942: "Our revolution will be socialist. . . ." *Combat*, no. 54, February 1944, description of projected "new society" includes evident assimilation of Socialist watchwords. *Le Franc-Tireur*, no. 15, 20 February 1943, article under the rubric "Our Socialism: ". . . Socialism and democracy go together. . . ." Finally, Hauriou, *Le Socialisme humaniste*, p. 89: "The constructive thought of the Resistance has progressively organized itself around two themes: liberty and socialism."

[110] See chap. 6 for a more detailed discussion of the resisters' ideas. It might of course be argued that these ideas were to some degree the common property of all of the French Left, notably the Communists and Syndicalists, but no other group during the Occupation so clearly formulated their ideas or so actively propagandized in their favor as did the Socialists. The Communists, indeed, said nothing of their plans for the future, refusing to speak of anything but patriotism and the immediate struggle.

[111] Passy, vol. 2, pp. 63–64, 71–74.

with de Gaulle, undoubtedly furthered the steady leftward drift of the Gaullist movement.[112]

In addition, perhaps because the movement chiefs had denied them full access to the superior organs of the underground, the Socialists more than any other group were the originators and strongest advocates of the idea of a "national political council," to include representatives of the political parties and syndicates as well as the resistance movements.[113] In conversations with Gaullist agents and at the time of his visit to London in April 1943, Daniel Mayer argued that such an organization would demonstrate to the Allies that de Gaulle enjoyed the total support of the French people.[114] Mayer insisted that a union of all parties:

> . . . from Marin to Thorcz [hcads of the conservative *Fédération Républicaine* and the Communist party] ought to be allowed to participate in the direction of the clandestine action in France, on the political plane; on the condition that these political parties and syndical movements turn over their troops to the Secret Army and the Forces of Fighting France. Thus, the day of the Liberation; General de Gaulle would have automatically the guarantee of French unanimity acclaimed by its representatives at his sides.[115]

Another idea that Socialists in both London and France consistently championed was the importance of a variety of organized political parties to the proper functioning of a democratic republic. Apprehensive that some resisters might be tempted in their disgust with the parties of the Third Republic to demand the Resistance's transformation into the single official political party, Léon Blum, writing to General de Gaulle, admitted that partisanship in the French political parties in the past often had been detrimental to the national community. Nevertheless, he reasoned:

> . . . a democratic State—whatever its constitution, whatever the part played by parliamentary representation— cannot exist or even be reasonably conceived of without

---

[112] See Michel, *Les Courants de Pensée*, passim.

[113] Hostache, *Le Conseil*, pp. 111–16, and Michel, *Jean Moulin*, pp. 163–72.

[114] Passy, *Missions secrètes en France*, pp. 28–30; Mayer, *Les Socialistes*, Annexe which reproduces a report of "Manuel," and passim.

[115] Passy, *Missions secrètes en France*, pp. 28–29.

the existence of political parties. The pure and simple denial of political parties means the denial of Democracy. . . .

It is in dictatorial regimes that parties disappear and a single party fuses with the totalitarian State. Men who have wished to found a totalitarian State have invariably begun by destroying or outlawing political parties.

. . . the organizations of Resistance which have arisen from the French soil at your call cannot substitute to any degree for them. When France has regained her sovereignty and restored her stability, the useful role of these organizations will be exhausted. This role will have been very important, not only for the decisive participation in the work of Liberation, but for the spontaneous formation of a fresh, young elite. Nevertheless, the men who compose this elite will be necessarily led to redistribute themselves into different parties which they will rejuvenate and refresh.[116]

Curiously even the success of these causes, certified by the recognition of political parties within the National Resistance Council, may have rebounded against the Socialists in their relations with the resistance movements. By their bold insistence on the importance of political parties had they not confirmed the resisters' conviction that the CAS indeed represented the political party par excellence?

The history of the French Resistance holds no more striking phenomenon than the contrast between the success of the Communist party and the failure of the Socialist party in their relations with the resistance movements. In view of the earlier defeatist, or at least neutralist, attitude of the Communists and the severe repression that decimated their party, it is all the more astonishing that at every turn the Socialists seem to have emerged second best. An OSS study of the political orientation of the European Resistance, completed shortly after the liberation of France, suggests that the crucial difference was the Communists' complete identification with the policy of activism in the immediate struggle. "Experience shows," the report concluded, that a more quietist policy "fails badly to meet the emotional needs of people suffering under Nazi military occupation." In this respect the European Socialist and Social Democratic parties "have . . . failed to make a successful adaptation, in spite of the degree to which their

---

[116] Blum, letter to de Gaulle, 15 March 1943, *L'Oeuvre*, vol. 5, pp. 397–98.

prewar programs would seem to correspond to the present mood of the Resistance."[117]

Claude Bourdet added three other explanations for the particular failure of the Socialists and the MUR to cooperate harmoniously.

> 1. The rancor towards politicians prevalent in all of the Resistance from the base to the summit. 2. The failure of the socialist leaders to adapt to the problems of the Resistance. 3. Finally, the blindness of the Resistance which . . . believed Social Democracy prematurely buried.[118]

Bourdet later acknowledged: "We did not understand that the Resistance would have a brief existence, and, that after the war, political formations better adapted than we to life in peacetime would regain their importance."[119]

In a report on the political situation in France in November 1943, Jacques Bingen dwelt at length on the paradoxical position of the French Socialists.

> . . . The directors of the reformed Socialist Party feel a mixed complex of inferiority and of superiority. . . . They recall with good reason that their party was the largest in the last Chamber; they underline, with an insistence, occasionally displeasing, that the present Commissioner of the Interior is a Socialist; finally, they proclaim correctly and with a somewhat aggressive pride that they are the only ones able to maintain their traditional program and that in reality the national unanimity is realized—with the single exception of communism, perhaps—around Socialism.
>
> To resume this too long exposé of the problem of the

---

[117] OSS R&A (Research and Analysis Branch) Document 97368 S. The Communists were extremely clever in concealing any plans they might have had beyond the immediate fight. Villon, the FN representative on the CNR *bureau,* simply refused to discuss any projects for the future (Morandat, letter to E. d'Astier, Commissariat à l'intérieur, 29 February 1944, Archives, CHG.)

[118] *Témoignage* of Bourdet, Archives, CHG.

[119] Bourdet, *Histoire de la Résistance française.* Bourdet and a few others later regretted that the resisters had overlooked a chance to radically change the structures of the Socialist party through a postwar fusion of the movements and the SFIO. Étienne Bauer, interview, 5 January 1970, remembered the exaggerated pretensions of many resisters who were sincerely convinced that they alone represented "France, all of France."

Socialist Party, I would say that the Socialist Party, if it were born in France as a Party, without ever having existed before the war and without having been exposed to the redoubtable test of power, . . . could legitimately claim to be at the head of all the French Resistance and to effect future national unity based on its traditional program, its active party members and sympathizers.

Unfortunately, the Socialist Party has faced a test of power; its directors were worn down by it; they cling too desperately to the formulas of its traditional structure (a little like so many reformers confuse the prewar parlementarianism and republican democracy); finally there is the rising tide of communism with the prestige of the moral and economic power of the U. S. S. R.; the aureole of the well-orchestrated publicity of its numerous martyrs; so much so that today one wonders if the Socialist Party is not going to die in France at the very moment when "Socialism" will be established there.[120]

On 1 March 1943, Léon Blum had written: "In my opinion there is no reason to modify the title of the Party. There is a Socialist Party, because there is socialism. The Socialist Party must continue to exist with its name, just as the French Republic must continue to exist with its name"[121]—the conflicting prophecies of equally honorable men.

The resisters were generally in agreement in wanting to avoid a return to the political system of the past and in sharing common aspirations for the reinvigoration of French political life. They were, however, far from unanimous when confronted with certain problems inevitably posed by the liberation. Was the role of the Resistance to end once the Germans had been driven out of France? If the resisters had refused to allow the political parties a full share in the direction of the Resistance, could they now entrust the future transformation of French society to those same parties? Most of the movements' directors were understandably disinclined at the liberation to witness the immediate effacement of their organizations before the reemergent parties. Under the Occupation the clandestine newspapers often had

---

[120] Bingen, "Rapport," end of November 1943, pp. 1–2, received February 1944, Archives, CHG.

[121] Blum, "Note au Parti," *L'Oeuvre*, vol. 5, p. 392.

referred to the resisters as *les inconnus* (the unknown) who, after the enemy's defeat, would become *les connus*, those who would build the new Republic.[122]

As the liberation approached, *Combat* proclaimed:

> We who for three years have led the combat of the Resistance do not want to be considered paid for our efforts by several eulogies, several ribbons, and several monuments. Speaking in the name of our comrades who are still fighting and in the name of those who have fallen in this struggle, we announce that we wish no other recompense than the realization of our ideal. Our war aim is the construction of the new, strong, and pure France that Charles de Gaulle promises. The Resistance will not dissolve itself until this ideal has been totally attained, *envers et contre tout.*[123]

In a similar vein, among the final clandestine directives that the MUR circulated in southern France was the Exécutif's declaration:

> The men who every day have placed their lives in the balance in an unequal fight have in fact reflected the spirit of the living Nation. They intend indeed to assume tomorrow public responsibilities without doubt less dangerous but equally representative of the victorious Nation. The Resistance will not pursue the sterile myth of war veterans but will fully enter into French public life.[124]

Still aside from such statements of intent, the resisters before the liberation devoted little serious thought and even less actual preparation to converting the movements into a peacetime political force. First, most resisters were much more concerned with the liberation itself than worried about what would follow.[125] Besides, would Gen-

---

[122] *Combat,* no. Special, January 1943, and no. 51, 15 November 1943. *Le Franc-Tireur,* no. 17, 30 April–May 1943: "des hommes nouveaux" will run the new Republic. *Le Franc-Tireur,* no. 35, 14 July 1944, argues that the *"gens très bien"* are the resisters. The resisters prefer men formed in the Maquis to graduates of the *Sciences Politechniques.*

[123] *Combat,* no. 55, March 1944.

[124] "L'Exécutif Z. S. du Mouvement de la Libération Nationale à toutes régions, tous départements, toutes P. D.," 5 August 1944. Papers of Alban Vistel, Archives, CHG.

[125] Étienne Bauer, interview, 5 January 1970. The resisters at the base "did not give a damn about politics."

eral de Gaulle not take care of all that? At the end of November 1943 Jacques Bingen, in an analysis of the resistance movements reported: "The political ideas of the great majority of the militants are sane and banal: these are above all democrats who desire a better Republic; they have put their confidence in de Gaulle and expect miracles from him."[126]

Even the leaders of the movements could simply not agree on what should be done after the victory. Some, including Henri Frenay, Antoine Avinin, Alban Vistel, and Claude Bourdet, favored the creation of a progressive, socialistic, resistance-based party that would advocate sweeping reforms along the lines of the CNR Charter.[127] The Socialists suspected that certain resisters harbored plans for a *parti unique,* but the movements in southern France had explicitly opposed such a concept.[128] Their party was envisaged as one progressive alternative to the Communist party. Predictably the resisters, still distrustful of the label *party,* preferred to retain their clandestine title, the Mouvement de la Libération Nationale (MLN).

Other leaders of the MUR—notably the Communists, such as Pierre Hervé and Maurice Kriegel-Valrimont, and the Christian Democrats, including Georges Bidault and François de Menthon—felt that the Resistance could not become a political party.[129] Instead,

---

[126] Bingen, "Rapport," end of November, *Beige,* Archives, CHG, p. 3. The same sentiment is seen in Bingen, "Rapport," January 1944, p. 8; and Morandat's "Rapports" of March 1944, received May 1944: "L'Opinion Publique," and of April 1944, received May 1944, "Suite du Rapport Général sur la Situation de la Résistance," and letter of 29 February 1944, to d'Astier: "The General still enjoys incomparable prestige. . . . For the moment he is the only one who is known to the masses."

[127] Letter of Alban Vistel to the author, 7 May 1971; *témoignages* of Bourdet and Avinin, Archives, CHG; and Frenay, quoted in BIMUR, 7 March 1944.

[128] *Le Franc-Tireur,* 23–25 August 1944, *Libération,* no. 29, 1 June 1943, pointedly rejected a *parti unique. Combat,* no. 54, February 1944, imagined there would be at least a Communist party, and a conservative or moderate grouping in addition to their party. Papers of Serreules, Archives, CHG, a letter to de Gaulle, Christmas 1943, urging him to head a *parti unique* was evidence that such sentiment existed in resistance circles though not in the MUR.

[129] Hervé, *secrétaire général* of the MUR, was the author of the "Rapport Chardon," written at the end of 1943 when the MUR was encouraging the fusion of all the resistance movements in France. Reproduced in Michel and Guetzévitch, *Les Idées,* pp. 107–9. Hervé, chief spokesman for the Communist elements in the MUR, was categorically opposed to any attempt to transform the Resistance into a party. Like the FN and

the resisters should continue their activity through the traditional parties or in the case of the Christian Democrats, within the framework of a new party that rested on a base broader than the Resistance. Bidault, de Menthon, and Pierre Henri Teitgen as members of Combat's executive committee had, during the first years of the occupation, represented a strong contingent of Christian Democrats within the ranks of that movement. But when the three southern movements formed the MUR in January 1943, the separate executive committees were suppressed, and the Christian Democratic leaders, left without any real influence on the direction of the MUR, assumed positions with the Gaullist Délégation.[130]

As they gradually lost their earlier intimate association with Combat and the other movements, these men turned more freely to thoughts of the future and in particular began to nurture the idea of a new confessional party that would champion social justice as well as spiritual liberty.[131] Before the liberation little was accomplished beyond rudimentary soundings, the establishment of a skeletal network of contacts in various regions, and the drafting of a manifesto, but the foundations were laid for the Mouvement Républicain Populaire (MRP), one of the Fourth Republic's most important political parties.[132]

A third group—Pascal Copeau, Emmanuel d'Astier, and others mostly associated with Libération—rejected the notion that the Resistance could be transformed into a political party but did not want the resisters simply parceled out among the traditional parties after the liberation. They argued that the resisters should stay united within the MLN, which would act as a powerful force of moral suasion as it remained above what *Le Franc-Tireur* termed the "party jungle."[133] They never made clear, though, exactly how an organization that voluntarily assumed a position outside the normal political

---

PC, Hervé insisted that the Resistance should remain a patriotic union dedicated only to the immediate problem of liberating France.

[130] *Témoignages* of Bourdet and Frenay, Archives, CHG. Tietgen and de Menthon worked on the CGE. Later de Menthon went to Algiers as a member of the CFLN. Bidault, as we have seen, became president of the CNR, after working on the BIP.

[131] Bidault allegedly believed that granting the vote to women, an idea that all the resisters supported, would greatly increase support for a Catholic party. (See Jacques Duquesne, *Les Catholiques français sous l'occupation* [Paris: Bernard Grasset, 1966], pp. 377–78.)

[132] See "Origines et Mission du M. R. P.," Numéro Spécial of *Forces Nouvelles*, Paris, 1952.

[133] *Le Franc-Tireur*, 23–25 August 1944.

channels might operate with any real effect. But then what had the Resistance been, if not continual improvisation? There would be time enough to decide after the Germans had been driven out of France. A few days before the liberation of Paris, *Combat* proclaimed its distaste for "ready made schemes and theoretical plans," in affirming that the course of events would define the meaning of the "Revolution" they desired.[134]

Indeed, in its last clandestine instructions to the regional directories the MUR deliberately delayed any concrete decision about the movement's future activity until after their primary objective of liberation was secured.[135] To be sure, since Pascal Copeau's share in drafting them was predominant these directives heavily reflected the idea that the Resistance should remain united as an independent political force. In May 1944 the Exécutif Sud envisioned the restoration of a regular government.

> This government will be the expression of the Resistance ... but it is crucial that the Resistance subsist as a Movement and not disperse itself in a bureaucratization which, under the guise of a "revolutionary takeover of power" would be a pure and simple disappearance.[136]

Since one primary interest of the Resistance would be to actively demonstrate to the Allies that widespread popular support existed in France for the Provisional Government, the major task of its chiefs immediately after the liberation was to be "a task of political action and distribution of information."[137] But this action should rest within the framework of the movements' existing organization. Therefore, the Exécutif concluded: "No competition for official posts ... the Resistance must remain independent, young, dynamic, must support the Government and also its agents, but it must also push them."[138]

---

[134] *Combat*, no. 59, 21 August 1944.

[135] "L'Exécutif Zone Sud du M. L. N. à Tous Directoires régionaux," May 1944; and 2 Circulaires of 5 August 1944, from "L'Exécutif Zone Sud du Mouvement de la Libération Nationale," one concerning "Mesures pratiques à prendre dès la libération," and another concerning "Les Congrès de la Résistance," all in papers of Alban Vistel, Archives, CHG, clearly affirm the MUR's intention to play a major postwar role, but show that no real preparation had been made during the Occupation.

[136] "L'Exécutif Zone Sud de M. L. N. à Tous Directoires régionaux," May 1944.

[137] Ibid.

[138] Ibid.

In August the Exécutif again emphasized this independence of the Resistance when it forbade MLN members to accept public or administrative functions without authorization of their superiors in the movement. "If all our militants became bureaucrats," insisted the Exécutif, "there would be no independent movement. Do not forget that the principle of every democratic state is the separation of powers."[139] Yet in the final analysis the movement's directors had not determined how they might push the government and its agents and thus presumably assure adoption of the Resistance's programs. This problem was left to the Congress of the Resistance, which was to be called immediately after the Germans were driven out of France. Communal congresses would elect delegates to a departmental congress, which in turn would elect representatives for the National Congress of the MLN. The Éxecutif concluded:

> Meeting in liberated Paris, the delegates of the National Congress of the *Mouvement de la Libération Nationale* ... will choose freely their directors; they will treat any unresolved questions concerning the Union of the Resistance; they will define the place of the Movement and of all the Resistance in French public life and its position towards the former parties. . . .[140]

It is beyond the scope of this study to examine in detail the postwar fortunes of the MLN, but it is important to distinguish between the postwar and clandestine organizations. In reality the two were quite distinct—so much so that less than three years after the liberation Combat, the single largest component of the wartime MUR and MLN, disavowed any association with the MLN. In May 1947 Jacques Dhont, president of the bureau of the Comité National de la Fédération des Amicales "Combat," advised members of Combat against joining a projected MLN Amicale.

> At the present time, that is to say more than two years after the Liberation, the M. L. N. appears in the eyes of the public, as to the Resistance itself, like a formation, much more marked by its political action since 1944, than by its

---

[139] "L'Exécutif Zone Sud . . . : Mesures pratiques," 5 August 1944. Papers of Alban Vistel, Archives, CHG.

[140] "L'Exécutif Zone Sud . . . : Les Congrès," 5 August 1944. Papers of Alban Vistel, Archives, CHG.

clandestine action. This political action, upon which we do not wish to offer here any value judgment, has had as a result that the majority of the *clandestine* members of the M. L. N. have left it. To attempt now to build an *Amicale* under this same politically tainted label is an error. It is perhaps also an impossibility; for it would be difficult to reunite men that political divergences have placed in violent opposition.[141]

Actually, in light of the resister's conflicting projections about the movement's role in postwar France, it is not surprising that the MLN failed to retain its cohesion after the liberation removed the principal goal that had united all resisters. Once the Nazis were defeated and French independence in face of the Allies was assured, ideological differences were bound to appear. For, as Pierre Hervé suggested and even those resisters most hostile to the Third Republic's parties recognized, all the political struggles of the past were not "stupid and without foundation."[142]

In particular a confrontation between those who favored and those who opposed active cooperation with the Communist party was unavoidable. At the first National Congress, in Paris 23–28 January 1945, the majority by a 250 to 119 vote rejected Pierre Hervé's motion requesting organic fusion with the Communist Front National.[143] A contemporary observer noted:

> Thus, the M. L. N. presents from the beginning its essential features: many tendencies, brilliant individuals, but a real lack of homogeneity. It is torn between a *tendance communisante*—in minority—and a *tendance anticommuniste*, which dares not admit it too much, but which refuses energetically to establish close ties to the "*Front National.*"[144]

Although the original Congress elected an executive committee with members of both tendencies, it was only a matter of a few months before the MLN broke apart. In June 1945 the majority formed the Union Démocratique et Socialiste de la Résistance (UDSR), and the

---

[141] *Bulletin Intérieur des Amicales "Combat,"* May 1947.

[142] Hervé, in "Rapport Chardon," p. 107, Michel and Guetzévitch, *Les Idées.*

[143] *L'Année politique, 1944–1945,* pp. 93–94.

[144] *L'Année politique,* p. 11.

minority cleverly adopted the label of the Mouvement Unifié de la Renaissance Française (MURF), thus attempting to appropriate for itself the clandestine prestige of the MUR.[145]

Even without the division between sympathizers and opponents of the Communist party, which eventually destroyed the MLN, the movement's prospects for success in the peacetime political arena were problematic at best. In the fall of 1943 Jacques Bingen had predicted that if it were to succeed, a progressive party formed around the MLN would need "the official or tacit patronage of General de Gaulle."[146] Later many of the resisters felt that the General's refusal to head a coalition of the Resistance and other progressive groups had prevented the profound reform of French society that they all desired.[147] Additional handicaps, though, might have checked the resisters' ambitions even with de Gaulle's sponsorship.

Aside from Charles de Gaulle none of the major resistance personalities were known to the public.[148] Furthermore, the resistance chiefs often lacked the temperament conducive to a political career. For example, Henri Frenay, recalling his brief and stormy foray into politics, confided to Alban Vistel: "Yes, I have renounced all active political life. My experience taught me that the rules of the political game excluded any possibility of friendship between men. Rather than lose my friends, I prefer to abstain. For me, friendship is the essence of existence."[149] Étienne Bauer commented that compared to the representatives of the political parties, most of the resisters were children when it came to politics. (*"On a été des enfants, des enfants!"*)[150] Others were without personal political ambitions, wishing simply to return to their prewar occupations.[151] Some (perhaps those with the most political savvy) who did aspire to political careers in the new

---

[145] *L'Année politique,* pp. 227–30.

[146] Bingen, "Rapport," end of November, p. 5; same idea expressed in Bingen, "Rapport," January 1944, pp. 7–8, both in Archives, CHG.

[147] Bourdet, "Huit Ans Après," pp. 7–8, Frenay, "De Gaulle et la Résistance."

[148] See Crane Brinton, "Letters from Liberated France," *French Historical Studies* 2, no. 1 (Spring 1961): 18. Bingen, "Rapport," end of November 1943, *Beige,* Archives, CHG, commented on the definite advantage of former professional politicians in being "known" even if they were unfavorably viewed.

[149] Vistel, *La Nuit,* p. 54.

[150] Étienne Bauer, interview, 5 January 1970.

[151] Jean Bruller (Vercors), *The Battle of Silence,* pp. 282–85, 272–73, notes his desire for anonymity after the war.

France realized that the Socialists[152] and others who said that the Resistance could not become a party were correct. For despite their temporary fraternity the resisters did not have, as *Le Populaire* pointed out in February 1944, the "common thought, a framework, common memories, tradition, and above all, a doctrine" essential to a political party.[153]

Finally, the active resisters in France always were a very small percentage of the population. An effective political party requires a more widespread base than the resistance movements could offer. Only by establishing some form of dictatorship could the resisters have imposed their will on the French people. But, they, like General de Gaulle, would stand by their original promise to allow the French to choose freely their representatives and political institutions. After the gallantry, sacrifice, and trauma of the liberation, they would relinquish voluntarily their power and the fate of their revolution to the ballot box.

[152] Bingen, "Rapport Beige," November 1943, p. 3. "The weakness of the program, if not to say the absence of constructive policies, disrupts the movements and seems to condemn them to death with reprieve—the reprieve will end the day after the liberation." OSS Document 97368 S, R&A Report 2009, 4 October 1944. The possibility exists that after the emotional pressure of the occupation is gone these groups "may lose their political cohesiveness entirely and cease to exert any political influence."

[153] *Le Populaire*, no. 31, February 1944. BIMUR, 7 March 1944. The Socialist Bordier noted that several major tendencies were present in the Resistance, united by their present common aspiration, and added: "Mais la résistance, un parti? . . . allons donc, la Résistance, c'est la France, c'est toute la France."

CHAPTER 6

The Liberation

"Après ce que j'ai vu la vie ne pourra être gaie, comme avant, mais je crois qu'elle peut être encore belle."

(Extract from a letter, 10 May 1945, of Pierre Kaan, assistant to Jean Moulin, former philosophy professor, died 18 May 1945, as a result of treatment sustained after his arrest and deportation to Buchenwald. Quoted in "La Résistance Francaise," Textes & Documents, *N°20, 4°Trimestre, 1964.)*

THE SPRING of 1944 was for France a season mixed with hope and despair. The "signs of a profound anarchy"[1] that an intelligence informant for the Americans had noticed as early as October 1943 had taken on some aspects of civil war. In January 1944 Vichy enlarged the powers of Joseph Darnand, head of the notorious Milice, and encouraged him to undertake an all-out campaign to exterminate the Resistance. The organized resisters replied in kind.

A circular of 10 January 1944 from the Directing Committee of the Mouvements Unis de la Résistance declared: "To terror there is no other reply than a more powerful and more implacable terror. Assassination of any French patriot which is not immediately followed by the execution of those responsible for the crime or of another of their people is a dishonor for the Resistance."[2] *Le Franc Tireur* passed on the message to its readers in no uncertain terms. "Joseph Darnand and all members of the Milice, decreed public enemies and traitors to the Nation, are put outside the law. From today every

---

[1] OSS Document No. OB-8838.

[2] "S. G. des M. U. R. à: Toutes régions Tous Services: Représailles contre le Terrorisme Vichyssois," Papers of Alban Vistel, Archives, CHG.

milicien must be thought of as a mad dog and treated as such. . . . Fire on the Milice!"[3] In every region of France bombings, sabotage, and political assassination became commonplace and increased with each passing week.[4] A letter to the family of a prefectoral administrator in the Massif Central expressed in a few words the situation of most Frenchmen: "I tell you straight away that we are living in a state of panic."[5]

This pervasive atmosphere of terror had developed in a vacuum of political leadership. The Vichy government and particularly its chief, the venerable Marshal Pétain, had enjoyed the support of most Frenchmen during the first months after the armistice, but four years of German occupation had taken their toll. The Marshal's policy of collaboration was discredited as soon as its implications were made manifest by the German annexation of Alsace-Lorraine, the occupation of southern France, and most damaging, the deportation of hundreds of thousands of French workers to Germany. By 1944 the theoretically loyal administration of Vichy was so thoroughly undermined with resistance sympathizers that Laval resorted to massive shifts in the prefectoral ranks in order to weaken the links between these officials and the Resistance. An American intelligence observer remarked that even this desperate measure was not very effective. Referring to the increased powers of the Milice and the transfers of the prefects, he concluded: "While all of these measures result in severe losses, the French Resistance cannot be crushed in this way, or by any other means which the Germans have at their disposal."[6] To secure at this late date a local administration completely loyal to its policy of collaboration, Vichy would have had to fill every post with

---

[3] *Le Franc-Tireur*, 5 February 1944.

[4] A comparison of the number of index cards for the OSS Records, recording acts of sabotage during 1942, 1943, and 1944 is indicative of this increase in activity. Even more detailed is a *fichier* at the CHG, which attempts to record on cards every act of resistance during the occupation. The file contains as many cards for the last few months of the Vichy regime as for the whole preceding year. Georges Beau and Leopold Gaubusseau, *R. 5 Les S. S. en Limousin, Périgord, Quercy* (Paris: Presses de la Cité, 1969), pp. 173–95, and Pierre Trouillé, *Journal d'un préfet pendant l'occupation* (Paris: Éditions Gallimard, 1964), passim, capture well the atmosphere of France during the spring and summer of 1944.

[5] Beau and Gaubusseau, *R. 5 Les SS en Limousin, Périgord, Quercy*, p. 177.

[6] OSS Document No. 62365 R, dated 15 March 1944.

German soldiers or miliciens. The postal and railroad administrations had been among the most willing accomplices of the resisters from the first,[7] but now even the police often actively abetted the movements.[8] The mechanics of French society were disintegrating. Clearly the average citizen, caught up in the throes of a civil war, had reason to despair.

But the French had had ample cause for dismay long before the spring of 1944. Executions of hostages, economic plunder, and Gestapo raids had not begun in 1944; they were merely intensified and compounded by the open fratricidal struggle between miliciens and resisters. The novel factor in the spring of 1944 was the expectation that all this misery would soon be over. With German armies in poorly veiled retreat in the East and Allied troops finally victorious in Italy, everyone felt the long-awaited invasion of France was imminent. For the Resistance an early invasion was a necessity. The chief of de Gaulle's intelligence services, recalling the hard winter of 1943–1944 ("the snow was stained with blood during those months"), concluded: "the spring of 1944 was the springtime of the last hope; for it seemed impossible that the nation could survive if deliverance did not come before a new winter."[9]

These hopes and fears were not restricted to resistance circles. True, the internecine strife that had terrorized the countryside since the past winter was the work of a small minority of active resisters and an even smaller minority of fanatic collaborators. The great majority of Frenchmen during the Occupation were concerned principally with survival and food for the next day. They had assumed that this affliction must someday pass, and although they had grown to hate their occupants they had cloaked their resentments in an embittered silence. Prudence, concern for family, or a conviction of the ineffective-

---

[7] See M. Paul, *Histoire des PTT pendant la deuxième guerre mondiale (1939–1945)*, (four vols., completed 1956, published posthumously in ronéotype by the ministère des PTT, Paris, 1967) and Paul Durand, *La S. N. C. F. pendant la guerre* (Paris: Presses Universitaires de France, 1968).

[8] "Rapport: L'Opinion publique" to CFLN Commissioner of the Interior, from Yvon Morandat, received May 1944, Archives, CHG. Also Warner, *Pierre Laval*, pp. 372–73, quoting a report from Knochen, a high ranking SS chief in France; and OSS Document No. 62365 R, 15 March 1944.

[9] Soustelle, *Envers et contre tout*, vol. 2, pp. 368–69.

ness of clandestine activities had kept most Frenchmen from open commitment to the Resistance. But a dramatic revolution in public opinion was evident on the eve of the liberation. The bankruptcy of political leadership within France, along with the propaganda of the underground newspapers and the BBC, had created a new symbol of *honneur et patrie.* By 1944 to most Frenchmen Charles de Gaulle represented resistance to the Germans, and Gaullism was, in the midst of several contradictory tendencies within French society, the meeting point around which a new political unity would be shaped.

Thus when de Gaulle insisted that a France in arms must contribute significantly to its own liberation and urged the French people to give all possible assistance to the Allied armies, large numbers of Frenchmen realized the time had come to transform simmering hatred of the Boche into positive action. On the night of 5 June 1944, the BBC broadcast a series of "personal messages," which were received in France as the call for a national uprising.[10] Thousands of men responded to the calls of local resistance chiefs and streamed into the countryside to join Maquis or Secret Army units and share in the fight. Sabotage operations entailing the interruption of rail traffic were evident all over the country.[11]

The enthusiastic response of the French far exceeded Allied expectations. An American intelligence officer in Algiers reported:

> Since D-day the French Resistance has given the final answer to those who over the past months had talked of de Gaulle's "so-called mandate to lead the so-called Resistance groups." All over France, with action concentrated in mountainous terrain, Frenchmen have risen against the enemy on a scale that only the most sanguine had anticipated. The demand for arms and aid has exceeded the possibilities of supply, and the principal problem is now one of restraining, not inciting, the movement. . . .[12]

---

[10] Foot, *SOE in France,* pp. 387–90; also Aron, *Histoire de Vichy,* pp. 143–54.

[11] Soustelle, *Envers et contre tout,* vol. 2, p. 396, rated rail destruction under *plan vert* as 95 percent effective. See Capitaine Mathis, "Comment furent actionnées, par l'état-major français de Londres, les Forces Françaises de l'Intérieur," *Revue Historique de l'Armée,* no. 2, May 1959, pp. 39–60, for an excellent description of the various plans for sabotage and an evaluation of their success.

[12] OSS Document No. 78747 S.

According to plans of long standing, the insurrection in France was to have been phased carefully with the approach of friendly armies. Neither the Gaullists outside France nor the interior resistance organizations had planned to call out forces which, isolated from the support of Allied armies, stood little or no chance against the superior armament of the Germans.[13] The Allied High Command, however, decided to call out the Resistance simultaneously all over France. In order to heighten the possibility of a successful invasion, it was felt essential that the first landing attempts succeed.[14] In so far as the insurgent actions helped to distract the Germans and delay reinforcements to the landing areas, the eager response of the French to the "personal messages" was highly gratifying to the Allied leaders. But the situation thus created was potentially explosive, particularly in southern France where the arrival of regular troops was not expected for months. Premature actions unsupported by Allied troops could prove disastrous—as indeed they did in several instances where early liberation of an area was followed by brutal reconquest when German troops passed through.

The tragedy of the Vercors Maquis was probably the most dramatic example of the consequences of a premature rising. Shortly after D-Day about four thousand resisters were trapped by twenty thousand German troops with overwhelming firepower on the Vercors Plateau, a towering natural fortress between the valleys of the Rhône and the Isère. Because of the excellent natural protection their location offered, the Maquis held their ground for over a month; but without exterior intervention their position was untenable if the Germans chose to launch a determined, vigorous assault. On 21 July forty gliders full of what seemed to be desperately needed Allied reinforcements appeared above the plateau. The resisters cheered their safe and unobstructed landing on the airfield prepared for Allied planes, but the

---

[13] "Le Comité Central des Mouvements de Résistance Française à Tous Chefs de Région et Tous Chefs de Service," 5 November 1943, is but one of many directives on the insurrection, found in Papers of Alban Vistel, Archives, CHG, which stress the importance of correct timing of the rising.

[14] The French had no significant role in planning the invasion of France. The Gaullists were asked for their approval after the decisions had been made, but a refusal would not have changed things. See Aron, *Histoire de la Libération de France* (Paris: Fayard, 1959), pp. 147–50. See also, *The Papers of Dwight David Eisenhower, The War Years*, vol. 3 (Baltimore: Johns Hopkins University Press, 1970), pp. 1903–8, for references to the last-minute briefings for the French.

"reinforcements" returned the greetings with a hail of machine gun fire. Behind the weapons were five hundred crack SS troopers. The defenders of the Vercors, lacking significant quantities of heavy arms, were quickly driven off their redoubt and forced to disperse. Those who failed to escape were massacred along with the local civilians.[15]

At the Vercors and in later operations during the liberation, the differing mentalities and opposing conceptions of warfare that had earlier marred relations between the interior and exterior resistance commands occasionally revealed themselves again, flaring up in regrettable and unpleasant incidents. The original plan for the use of the Vercors Maquis (code-named *Plan Montagnards*) had been conceived in France and later received the approval of the military chiefs in London.[16] On 5 June 1944, Eugène Chavant, civilian chief at Vercors, returned to the plateau with orders from Algiers to apply *Plan Montagnards* as previously agreed. The plan in January 1943 had received enthusiastic endorsement of General Delestraint, who hoped to command the operations there during the liberation.[17] As outlined by one of the Vercors' commanders, the plan was intended:

> . . . to create at the enemy's rear, either by spontaneous generation—the *maquis*—or better, by exterior support—massive parachuting of perhaps a division—an important center of disruption, *destined to act offensively, toward the exterior, in coordination with allied operations.*
>
> It was on these grounds that the whole organization was established. The clandestine phase was to allow the Vercors to serve as a depot for arms and material for the Isère and the Drôme; to prepare the eventual establishment of the peripheral defense of the plateau, *during a very short time—on the order of several days—*necessary for the parachuting, regroupment and entry into action of the men parachuted.[18]

---

[15] Descriptions are found in Foot, *SOE in France,* pp. 391–93; Charles Tillon, *Les F. T. P.* (Paris: René Julliard, 1962), chap. 15, pp. 303–30; Roland Bechmann (dit Lescot), "Le Vercors," *L'Armée Française,* No. Spécial (June–July 1948), pp. 3–15; Colonel Costa de Beauregard, "Vercors 1944," *L'Armée,* no. 6 (September 1960), pp. 7–20; and Pierre Tanant, *Vercors, haut-lieu de France* (Paris: B. Arthaud, 1966).

[16] Bechmann, "Le Vercors," p. 4; Costa de Beauregard, "Vercors 1944," pp. 9–10; and Tanant, *Vercors, haut-lieu de France,* pp. 24–25.

[17] Bechmann, "Le Vercors," p. 5.

[18] Costa de Beauregard, "Vercors 1944," pp. 9–10.

Evidently, the interior commanders of the Vercors never intended to hold the plateau as an armed bastion.[19] The Maquis remained in their defensive positions rather than breaking up into small guerrilla bands because for weeks they continued to hope that the promised arms and French or Allied troops would arrive from the exterior. Despite direct radio contact with Algiers,[20] the illusion that aid would arrive persisted until shortly before the resisters were overwhelmed and ordered to disperse on 23 July.

The Allies did offer one spectacular and highly publicized demonstration of their support on 14 July, Bastille Day, when forty-eight flying fortresses in broad daylight covered the reception zone with a massive drop of tricolored parachutes bearing light arms and munitions. But no significant quantities of heavy arms, mortars, or artillery were dropped; and at least one participant questioned the utility of the exaggerated publicity, which served mainly to remind the Germans that the resisters were still there.[21] His skepticism was not relieved when the men who dashed out to recuperate the treasures under the colorful parachutes were strafed and bombed by German planes from the nearby airfield at Chabeuil. In the final moments of a heroic but futile combat, the military command at the Vercors in desperation demanded that the Allies bombard the German positions at Vassieux. When this request was not granted, all of the resisters' frustrations boiled to the surface, and this bitter message was radioed to Algiers.

> If you do not take any immediate measures, we will be in agreement with the population in saying that those who are in London and Algiers have understood nothing of the situation in which we find ourselves, and we will consider you as criminals and cowards. We say indeed: criminals and cowards.[22]

---

[19] Foot, *SOE in France*, pp. 391–95, and other accounts that imply that the French intended to hold defensive positions are misleading. At the Vercors and in similar situations, such as the Maquis at Glières, the resisters held their ground only because they were led to believe that Allied reinforcements were coming.

[20] Tanant, *Vercors*, pp. 48, 112–13, 118.

[21] Bechmann, "Le Vercors," pp. 12–13. Marcel Vigneras, *Rearming the French* (Washington, D.C.: Office of the Chief of Military History, Department of the Army, 1957), pp. 301–4, points out that the Americans gave a great deal of publicity to these drops in order to revise the then prevalent opinion that only the British were aiding the resisters.

[22] Bechmann, "Le Vercors," pp. 13–14.

This distemperate and unfair charge in a moment of extreme exasperation was to a degree predictable in light of the resisters' repeated disappointments over the limited and always insufficient aid they had received from the exterior.[23] The Gaullists in London argued that they had always done their utmost to supply the Resistance, but in the final analysis they could do no more to satisfy the ever-increasing needs of the resisters than was allowed by the British and Americans, whose planes carried the material.[24] There was undeniably much justice to this argument; clearly a direct correlation existed between the fortunes of the BCRA and the state of de Gaulle's relations with Churchill. But another fundamental reason was that the exterior French as well as the Allied High Command certainly attached a much lower priority to arming the resisters and expected much less from them than the interior fighters anticipated.

On 17 March 1944, one of Churchill's aides, Major D. J. F. Morton, told Claude Serreules that the High Command estimated it was possible to arm perhaps forty thousand resisters in small groups of ten to twenty men who would be assigned very specific tasks, such as the destruction of bridges. The groups would act always on the direct orders of the Allies. Morton remarked that patriotic bands had been very useful to the Russians when they acted on the orders of the regular army, but the groups "complicated its task and caused trouble each time they acted on their own initiative."[25] Thus Morton concluded:

> The High Command expects from the French Resistance very effective aid of the sort that we have just defined, during a very short time, the most often no longer than several hours. Once this aid has been given at the determined time, the High Command does not want the French Resistance, by spontaneous and impetuous actions, to disrupt its plans; in a word, it hopes that it [the Resistance] will disappear.[26]

---

[23] De Gaulle, *Mémoires de guerre*, vol. 2, p. 155, recalled: "It goes without saying that the resisters, terribly short of supplies and constantly menaced, often had the impression that London and Algiers were not doing all that they could for them."

[24] Passy, *10 Duke Street Londres*, pp. 141, 149–51, 170–71.

[25] "Note de 'Sauvier'" (i.e., Serreules), 20 March 1944, a description of his conversation, three days before, with Major Morton. Archives CHG, Papers of Claude Serreules.

[26] Ibid.

The Allies planned to use their decisive air superiority as the principal means of preventing German reinforcements; and although they hoped the resistance movements might help out, they regarded their support "as a bonus, which could be enjoyed, but was not to be relied on."[27]

The resisters' opinions occasionally prevailed, as when in certain areas the Allies stopped bombing and strafing because sabotage attacks by the Resistance involved less loss of civilian lives and proved adequate and even more effective. More often, though, the underground forces were discounted as unreliable or were even viewed as potential troublemakers. Certainly in February 1944, after Churchill pledged to arm the French Resistance, British aid sharply increased.[28] And beginning in May the Americans augmented their assistance, which though long in coming eventually surpassed the British contribution.[29] Nevertheless, although Churchill was finally convinced of the desirability of a special effort to arm the Resistance he told Emmanuel d'Astier that he wanted guarantees that the weapons would

---

[27] Foot, *SOE in France*, p. 387. For the Allies' low expectations contrasted to high returns from the FFI. See also: Marcel Baudot, "La Résistance en France et les Alliés," in *European Resistance Movements 1939–45* (London: Pergamon Press, 1964), pp. 369–71; Forrest C. Pogue, *The Supreme Command* (Washington, D.C.: Office of the Chief of Military History, Department of the Army, 1954), pp. 237–39; and *La France et son empire dans la guerre*, vol. 2 (Paris: Éditions Litteraires de France, 1947), p. 118.

[28] Jacques Bingen, the acting *délégué général* in France, reported that the special effort of the British had saved the Resistance from catastrophe. "Rapport," February 1944, Archives, CHG. Unfortunately, after Churchill's attention was diverted and the question of arming the resisters left in the hands of the British military chiefs who did not share his commitment, the increase in aid was not so great as had been promised earlier. See telegram of Boris to D'Astier, 5 March 1944, and other documents appended to *témoignage* of d'Astier, Archives, CHG.

[29] Vigneras, *Rearming the French*, pp. 301–4, and table 4, p. 307, which details the material the Americans airdropped into France January–October 1944. Unhappily, when arms and material did begin to arrive in significant quantities, the distribution was very uneven. The officers in charge of receptions of the parachutes continually complained that it was impossible to transport arms to other regions at that late date, when German patrols were constantly on the alert. (See "Courrier de Pacha au B. C. R. A. de Londres," May 1944, pp. 3–4, 11, in Papers of Henri Guillerman, Archives, CHG; and a message from Colonel Grandval to London, 3 July 1944, in *Journal*, 3ᵉᵐᵉ partie, Papers of Gilbert Grandval, Archives, CHG.)

not be used in a civil war and that the French would obey General Eisenhower's orders without reservations "inspired by political reasons."[30]

For reasons of his own, Charles de Gaulle also was concerned about what the resisters might do with their weapons. We have seen that the interior's conception of the "national insurrection" was quite different from that of the exterior command. The Gaullists in Algiers and London had created a network of military delegates and operations officers apart from the resistance movements to oversee the reception and distribution of arms and hopefully to control their use.[31] De Gaulle fully endorsed the idea of an insurrection and encouraged a widespread uprising in support of the invasion, because he felt only the French people's enthusiastic participation could secure France its proper place in the war's final settlement.[32] But he expected the uprising to be coordinated under his direction. De Gaulle and his associates saw a serious potential danger in the existence of numerous, relatively autonomous bands of armed men whose first loyalty belonged to a local resistance leader. So despite his compliments about the exceptional valor of the resistance forces, one of the General's first steps immediately after the liberation of Paris was to order disbanded the irregular forces of the Resistance and to incorporate the FFI within the ranks of the regular French army that had been reorganized in North Africa.[33]

In view of the Allied High Command's skepticism and the suspicions of their own countrymen who comprised the exterior leadership, the resisters' military contribution to the liberation of France was all the more remarkable. To be sure, as the MUR chiefs had expected, in each locality the effectiveness of the Resistance and the FFI's behavior varied greatly and was closely related to the leadership in the local resistance organizations. One writer has noted: "The story of the liberation . . . must be that of 36,000 *communes* and of 90

---

[30] *Compte Rendu* of meeting, Thursday, 27 January 1944, with Churchill at 10 Downing Street, London; Annexe 3 to *témoignage* of d'Astier, Archives, CHG.

[31] De Gaulle, *Mémoires de guerre*, pp. 254–56, and Soustelle, *Envers et contre tout*, vol. 2, pp. 308–10.

[32] De Gaulle, *Mémoires de guerre*, pp. 249–57.

[33] Vigneras, *Rearming the French*, pp. 319–25; De Gaulle, *Mémoires de guerre*, vol. 2, pp. 317–18, 711–12; and *Mémoires de guerre*, vol. 3, pp. 312–14.

départements."[34] Nevertheless certain elements were common to the liberation in most areas.

Almost everywhere the invasion was greeted with enthusiasm.[35] Sometimes the response to the calls of the resistance organizations and de Gaulle's radio appeals was truly spectacular. In the Auvergne the resisters' order of 20 May 1944 for the constitution of the "Army of the Liberation" sparked a massive flood of humanity to the Maquis camps in the mountains.[36] Henry Ingrand, the MUR's regional head, had to turn back three thousand men who could not be equipped and incorporated into the burgeoning volunteer units.[37] An astonished German officer visiting near Clermont-Ferrand described the phenomenon as a "true general mobilization."[38] Similarly, an officer at the Vercors recalled having absolutely no manpower problem there; " 'recruitment' was merely a task of selection."[39]

As the events at the Vercors have illustrated, it was the cruel fate of many patriots that their generous enthusiasm led to tragedy. But after the Allied Command's original decision to call out all of the Resistance on D-Day, such incidents probably were unavoidable. It was difficult for local resistance chiefs to organize and hold in check the stream of volunteers who were anxious to fight the Germans and collaborators. Having called them out, the Resistance could not without risk send them back to their homes until the liberation was complete, since they would become obvious and defenseless targets of reprisals by reinforced German troops or the Milice. The dangers of this situation were soon recognized both in London and in France. On 29 June a regional FFI commander appealed to his chiefs in

---

[34] Aron, *Histoire de la libération,* p. 5.

[35] Aron, *Histoire de la libération,* p. 5. Chap. 3 points out that the only exceptions were areas, especially in Normandy, that suffered greatly from the Allied bombings, which meant that liberation was bought at a very high price for the local citizens.

[36] G. M. Levy, "Un épisode crucial de la Résistance française en mai–juin 1944: La Concentration des maquis d'Auvergne," *Revue Historique de l'Armée* (no. 3, 1968), pp. 43–62; *Témoignage* of Henry Ingrand, Archives, CHG; Capitaine Gilles, "Il y vingt, ans. Un épisode glorieux de la Résistance" (La véritable histoire de la concentration des Maquis d'Auvergne), *Revue de la Haute-Auvergne* (Tome 39, 66ᵉ année, July–September, 1964), pp. 141–74.

[37] *Témoignage* of Ingrand, Archives, CHG.

[38] Levy, "*Un épisode crucial . . . ,*" p. 51.

[39] Costa de Beauregard, "Vercors 1944," p. 12.

London: "I insist that the BBC stop inciting men to join the *maquis*. . . . An influx of men into the *maquis* when there is nothing with which to arm them can only lead to catastrophe."[40]

In London General Pierre Koenig, who had recently been appointed head of the FFI by de Gaulle, confronted this potentially explosive situation. At first he advised the resistance movements to slow down. On 10 June 1944, he ordered: "Maximum restraint of guerrilla activity—Impossible at present time to supply you with arms and ammunition in sufficient quantities—Everywhere break contact as far as possible to permit reorganizational phase. Avoid large assemblages. Form small isolated groups."[41] But it was immediately evident that in France Koenig's orders were received with consternation.[42] From the Southeast an MUR regional head replied:

> F. F. I. population *départements* Ain, Saône-et-Loire, Ardèche, Drôme have exceeded objectives called for by plan—We are trying to contain action—In these *départements* impossible to back-pedal—no retreat, if so peril to sedentary population—Armed help urgent—massive rising —Enthusiasm—Germans nervous, demoralized—If back up, disaster.[43]

Consequently, six days after his initial order Koenig revised his instructions in a "General Order of Operations, No. 1," prefaced by the comment: "The mission of all of the army of the interior is to fight."[44] He warned that virtually all of the aviation at the disposition of the

---

[40] Grandval, *Journal*, 3eme partie, p. 25. Papers of Gilbert Grandval, Archives, CHG.

[41] Grandval, *Journal*, 3eme partie, telegram of 10 June from Koenig.

[42] See Grandval's message of 12 June to Koenig: "Have noted your orders relative to moderation ardour troops—Their transmission which I am beginning is delicate; for troops, among which some, notably those of the Vosges, are already fully engaged, risk to not understand why, after their actions have been set off by the High Command, I am coming to preach moderation and ordering them to break contact." (*Journal*, 3eme partie); also see Maurice Kriegel-Valrimont, *La Libération, les archives du COMAC (mai–août 1944)*, (Paris: Les Éditions de Minuit, 1964).

[43] Message from *chef régional* MUR: Alban to Allied Commands in Algiers and London, 10 June 1944, in response to General Koenig's orders of 10 June to restrain guerrilla activities. Papers of Alban Vistel, Archives, CHG.

[44] Grandval, *Journal*, 3eme partie, p. 11, Archives, CHG, and Kriegel-Valrimont, *La Libération*, pp. 49–52.

These men from the "Henri Bourgogne" maquis unit did not live to see the liberation for which they had fought. This photo was taken just before their execution by the Germans, 25 May 1944, during the final days of the Occupation.

Allied Command would be directed toward support of the bridgeheads established during the invasion, so that the supply of the FFI would have to be effected progressively as the battle developed. Men who had joined the Maquis and could not safely return home were to be organized into small, dispersed groups, which could be regrouped when arms and the proper moment arrived. However, groups that were armed already were ordered to carry on a relentless campaign of guerrilla activity against the enemy's communications and transport.[45]

Koenig's orders were applied with varying degrees of success.[46] Fortunately the tragedy at the Vercors had few parallels. In the Auvergne the large Maquis concentrations, after several engagements with large

---

[45] Grandval, *Journal*, 3eme partie, p. 11, Archives, CHG; and Kriegel-Valrimont, *La Libération*, pp. 49–52.

[46] Some units interpreted Koenig's orders in a restrictive sense and planned to refrain from any further action until the arrival of Allied troops. But the MUR chiefs were quick to condemn this attitude as a reemergence of *attentisme*. See for example, "Bayard à Alban," 16 July 1944, and "RSF/A Alban à tous chefs départementaux F. F. I," 18 June 1944, Papers of Alban Vistel, Archives, CHG.

German units, were able to disperse into guerrilla units without being trapped in the mountain strongholds.[47] In other areas, such as the Limousin, the FFI were most adept at guerrilla tactics. The harried enemy unable to seize his elusive antagonists, all too often revenged himself on the hapless civilian population. The senseless atrocities committed by the SS division *Das Reich* and its French accomplices, the Milice, at Oradour-sur-Glane, Tulle, and Magnac-Laval,[48] bore solemn testimony to the limits of the resisters' capabilities. Without significant quantities of heavy arms, the resisters could irritate or cripple their opponents but could not stand fast before heavily armed units or prevent them from exacting a horrible price in retaliation for the trouble the resisters had caused them.

It is difficult to find any very precise measure for the military value of the Resistance. In his final report on operations in Europe, General Dwight D. Eisenhower, Supreme Allied Commander during the liberation, estimated the FFI's effectiveness as equal to fifteen regular divisions.[49] Eisenhower later wrote:

> Throughout France the Free French [the interior Resistance] had been of inestimable value in the campaign . . . Without their great assistance the liberation of France and the defeat of the enemy in western Europe would have consumed a much longer time and meant greater losses to ourselves.[50]

The supreme commander considered that the Resistance's action "played a very considerable part in our complete and final victory."[51] However, a leading authority on the Resistance in France Henri Michel has pointed out that Eisenhower's generous postwar estimates may

---

[47] Levy, *"Un épisode crucial"*; Gilles, *"Il y a vingt ans . . ."*; and *témoignage* of Henri Ingrand, Archives, CHG.

[48] For details of these tragic incidents, see Trouillé, *Journal d'un préfet;* also Jacques Delarue, *Trafics et crimes sous l'Occupation* (Paris: Fayard, 1968); J. Delperrie de Bayac, *Histoire de la Milice;* and *International Military Tribunal, Trial of the Major War Criminals* (Nuremberg, 1947), 6: 388–416.

[49] Dwight D. Eisenhower, *Eisenhower's Own Story of the War* (New York: Arco Publishing Co., 1946), p. 8.

[50] Dwight D. Eisenhower, *Crusade in Europe* (Garden City, New York: Doubleday and Co., 1948), p. 296.

[51] Letter of Eisenhower to Gubbins, Chief of the SOE, 31 May 1945, cited in Foot, *SOE in France,* p. 441.

have been influenced by considerations of diplomacy.[52] Michel painted a more sober picture of the contribution of the Resistance:

> What characterized its activity first of all was a long period of shadow and silence; then when it appeared in the open, a dispersion in small operations. Its daily victory was to survive. It is probable that it received more blows than it dealt, that it had more deaths to grieve than it inflicted upon the adversary.[53] It is also probable that many actions carried out spontaneously, as the occasion permitted, were barely effective, if not useless.[54]

The military value of the Resistance certainly should not be overestimated. The major operations of the liberation involved regular army units, and Allied forces might possibly have liberated France without the help of a single underground unit. Although the French claimed to have liberated on their own twenty-eight *départements* in central and southwestern France,[55] these areas were often only casually defended by the Germans, and liberation was sometimes simply a matter of German withdrawal.[56]

Nevertheless, very few German troops withdrew in peace. The resisters did not seriously threaten with annihilation complete German units, but patriotic bands constantly harassed them at every step of their retreat from French soil. Also, the resisters clearly achieved one of their major goals as they enveloped the enemy in an unrelenting climate of insecurity.[57] By 1944 the occupation troops' days of carefree sightseeing were over. The threat of sniper fire or exploding *plastic* was ever present for the German soldier and generally produced the desired psychological effects. The Germans often were led to over-

---

[52] Henri Michel, "L'aide apportée aux Alliés par la Résistance clandestine française," *Revue des Travaux de l'Académie des Sciences Morales & Politiques* (115e année, 4e série, 1962), p. 63.

[53] About 25,000 FFI were killed in action or executed by the enemy during the liberation in operations through October 1944.

[54] Michel, "L'aide," p. 66.

[55] Henri Michel, *Histoire de la Résistance*, p. 115.

[56] Foot, *SOE in France*, pp. 144–45.

[57] See Xavier de Virieu, *Radio journal libre*, pp. 352–53, for an interesting description of the goals of clandestine warfare. Also, Michel, "*L'aide* . . . ," pp. 67–70, and pp. 70–72, comments of General Pierre Koenig, following Michel's presentation.

estimate the strength of the Resistance's forces and in many cases were seriously demoralized by their persistent and elusive foe.[58]

In some instances German units even surrendered early to the regular Allied armies in order to avoid capture by the FFI, at whose hands they feared less gentle treatment.[59] Very probably such fears were justified. After all, the Germans had refused to treat the FFI according to the conventions of warfare. Hitler rejected the Allied High Command's appeal that men organized in FFI units and wearing special armbands be treated as regular soldiers;[60] so resisters were not made prisoners; they were executed on the spot. Thus it would not have been surprising had FFI units treated their prisoners less well than the Americans. As a general rule, though, the French command encouraged the FFI to act according to the conventions of regular warfare despite the German attitude. On 21 August 1944, headquarters in London ordered one of the FFI's regional commanders to discontinue the posting of warnings that threatened the Germans with ten prisoners killed in reprisal for each Frenchman executed, and ten German villages burned for every French village destroyed.[61]

In view of their organization and armament, sabotage was the tactic that offered the resisters the greatest possibilities for action, and as saboteurs the resisters were highly successful. On D-Day the various plans for the sabotage of rails and communications, worked out months in advance in cooperation with the Allies in London, were carried out very effectively. The arrival of German reinforcements was delayed for several crucial days or even weeks in some instances.[62] Even operations that ended tragically, such as the Vercors, helped to draw the Germans' attention away from the main Allied thrust and thus played some positive role in assisting the liberation. The inadequately armed resisters could not destroy large German units, but the

---

[58] At Nuremberg, Field Marshal Gert von Rundstedt called the Resistance in southern France a "tremendous threat to the troops fighting in the Mediterranean area." (IMT, *Trial of the Major War Criminals*, vol. 21, p. 27.) An interesting example of the demoralization of the German troops is found in General Adeline, "La Libération de Bordeaux," *Revue Historique de l'Armée* (17e année, no. 4, December 1961), p. 144.

[59] Michel, "L'aide," pp. 67–70, and pp. 70–72, Koenig's comments, following Michel's presentation.

[60] See Von Rundstedt's testimony, IMT, *Trial of the Major War Criminals*, vol. 21, p. 28.

[61] Grandval, *Journal*, 4eme partie, 21 August 1944.

[62] Michel, "L'aide," passim, and Koenig's comments, pp. 72–74; and especially Mathis, "Comment furent actionnées . . . les F. F. I."

bottlenecks provoked by the blown bridges and rails they had sabotaged often gave Allied pilots easier targets for their bombs.[63]

Also of incalculable value was the precise information derived from the resisters' widespread intelligence networks, which permitted the Allies to follow closely each step taken by every German unit in France.[64] If their part was small in comparison to that of the Allied armies, the resisters had nonetheless made a significant contribution toward the liberation of their country. And we can be certain that had they been given heavy arms and been more fully supported by the High Command, they would have played a much greater role.[65]

In describing the liberation of southern France it is often impossible to distinguish between actions carried out by the MUR and those that might be credited to other groups. We have seen that following the formation of the CNR the resisters moved toward effective coordination of their military activities in creating the FFI, and that they formed Departmental Liberation Committees (CDLs) to execute the political takeover at the local level. The insurrection and liberation were carried out within the framework of these combined organizations. The MUR cooperated with representatives of the political parties, the trade unions, and the Communist resistance organizations, and it is in that framework that we shall follow the resisters' actions. But it should be borne in mind that unquestionably the Mouvements Unis de la Résistance formed the backbone of the Resistance in southern France. It was they who had chosen the commissioners and prefects, provided the mass of the troops and leadership, and dominated the CDLs.

Although it is somewhat artificial to separate these two closely entwined aspects of the liberation of France, it seems clear in retrospect that the movements' seizure of political power was even more significant than their military achievements. In the political realm the resisters' two major goals were the elimination of the Vichy administration with a minimum of trouble and the establishment of a de

---

[63] Michel, "L'aide," passim, and Koenig's comments, pp. 72–74.

[64] Michel, "L'aide," and Passy, *10 Duke Street Londres*, p. 306.

[65] Comments of Major Sir Colin Gubbins in preface to Henri Bernard, *Histoire de la Résistance européenne* (Verviers: Marabout Université, 1968); and Michel, "L'aide," pp. 67–71, and Koenig's comments, p. 74; and F. Feral and A. Ressigéac, "Notice Explicative de la Carte de la Résistance F. F. I. en Tarn-et-Garonne," December 1963, Bibliothèque CHG, argue that the effectives "would easily have been doubled if the parachute drops had been more numerous."

facto authority in every region, which would force the Allies to recognize the legitimacy of the Gaullists' claims that they alone could provide the necessary leadership within France and command widespread loyalty from the population. In both respects the resisters' plans were carried out to perfection. Nowhere was there any serious challenge to the Gaullist takeover. Depending on the extent of their involvement in collaboration with the occupant, the former Vichy officials either fled or quietly stepped aside; some aided the resisters in assuring an orderly transition to the new administration.

Commenting on the transfer of power to the Gaullist commissioners and prefects, an American OSS officer who had entered France with the liberation armies remarked: "Vichy has faded away, like Lewis Carroll's Cheshire cat, but not even the leer has remained."[66] And after an inspection tour that covered most of liberated France in October 1944, the same observer added: "I need hardly tell you that the question as to whether the de Gaulle government is accepted simply doesn't exist."[67] The collapse of what had remained of the Vichy regime was complete and immediate.

The months of coordinated planning between the Gaullists at Algiers and the resistance movements before the insurrection were richly rewarded by this amazingly simple overthrow of the Vichy regime. But the resisters probably were not too surprised at their success. Their persistent efforts had thoroughly undermined an administration that had long been without any significant popular support. What Frenchmen was going to fight to preserve the Vichy regime? The Gaullist commissioners, prefects, and the Departmental Liberation Committees faced no real threat of civil war between Frenchmen. On the other hand, the new officials were definitely concerned with the possibility of an Allied attempt to limit French sovereignty. They anticipated no serious challenge to their authority from their fellow Frenchmen, but might not the Allies rob the resisters of their just due?

In the past the resisters had been greatly alarmed by Allied (especially American) dealings with Darlan and Giraud in North Africa and by their refusal to accept de Gaulle's claim to represent French

---

[66] Crane Brinton, "Letters from Liberated France," *French Historical Studies* 2, no. 1 (Spring 1961): 12. These "Letters" are a reproduction of Brinton's reports from France in 1944.

[67] Brinton, "Letters from Liberated France," 2, no. 2, p. 147.

interests.[68] The precedent of an Allied Military Government (AMGOT) in Italy aroused the suspicions of the Resistance. Was something similar in store for France?[69]

Before D-Day nothing was done to calm the resisters' fears. As early as 19 January 1944, General Eisenhower had urged recognition of the CFLN, so that satisfactory arrangements for the civil administration could be made prior to the invasion. In a letter to the Combined Chiefs of Staff and Combined Civil Affairs Committee, he wrote: "It is essential that immediate crystallization of plans relating to civil affairs in Metropolitan France be accomplished. This requires conferences with properly accredited French authorities. I assume, of course, that such authorities will be representatives of the Committee of National Liberation."[70] But despite Eisenhower's appeal, when the invasion began no satisfactory arrangement had been reached between de Gaulle and the Allies on the official status of the CFLN which had declared itself the Provisional Government of France.

Although President Roosevelt denied any interest in "policing" France,[71] General Eisenhower, the Supreme Allied Commander, was empowered to take whatever measures he felt necessary in order to secure his military goals. In the civil administration in France, Eisenhower was given a free hand to deal with any groups willing to fight the Germans, and he was ordered not to deal exclusively with de Gaulle's CFLN.[72] President Roosevelt believed that such a course

---

[68] See chap. 3.

[69] In numerous issues in the months preceding the invasion, the *Bulletin Intérieur des Mouvements Unis de la Résistance* (BIMUR) and the individual journals of the movements reflected the resisters' strong suspicions that the Allies wanted to rule France under an AMGOT.

[70] *The Papers of Dwight David Eisenhower: The War Years*, vol. 3, p. 1667; but as fully revealed in later correspondence in "The Papers" (pp. 1782–87, 1834–35, 1852–53, 1857–58, 1866–67, 1881, 1904–8) and in *Foreign Relations of the United States, Diplomatic Papers: 1944*, vol. 3: *The British Commonwealth and Europe* (Washington: United States Government Printing Office, 1965), pp. 634–703, no agreement between the Allies and the French had been reached before the invasion, a situation that considerably hindered Eisenhower's preparations. Pogue, *Supreme Comamnd*, Funk, *De Gaulle*, and Harry L. Coles and Albert K. Weinberg, *Civil Affairs: Soldiers Become Governors* (Washington, D.C.: Office of the Chief of Military History, Department of the Army, 1964) all offer useful discussions of this matter.

[71] Eisenhower, *Papers*, vol. 3, pp. 1726–27.

[72] Eisenhower, *Papers*, vol. 3, pp. 1784–86, and Coles and Weinberg, *Civil Affairs*, pp. 667–68.

would be tantamount to a formal recognition of the CFLN, a step he stubbornly refused to consider despite the almost unanimous encouragement of his advisers.[73] Indeed, Roosevelt pigheadedly maintained his refusal to recognize de Gaulle's government until two months after the liberation of Paris, by which time all of liberated France was in fact under the control of a Gaullist administration.

The resisters had clearly foreseen that the Allies might be reluctant to accept their authority to speak for all French people, and they had laid their plans accordingly. As early as 5 October 1943, their directives for the establishment of liberation committees and the installation of commissioners and prefects emphasized the importance of putting these officials in place before Allied troops arrived "so that they will find themselves before a new administration, incontestable and ready to operate."[74] Pascal Pia, who helped supervise the organization of the liberation committees in southern France, stated very succinctly the MUR's intention in forming these committees:

> The Resistance wished at all costs to prevent the Allies from proceeding after landing as they had in North Africa anywhere on French soil. It was absolutely necessary to have at hand authorities loyal to the Resistance and ready to replace the Vichy officials. Otherwise, we would risk another imbroglio like that which occurred at Algiers.[75]

The long-delayed formal recognition of de Gaulle's government, which finally occurred on 23 October 1944, attested to the resisters' success in carrying out their design. In virtually every liberated French village, the Allies were greeted by officials whom the Resistance had selected and de Gaulle's Provisional Government had certified. It was perhaps the greatest single achievement of the resisters that, because of their farsighted actions, France had been spared an AMGOT, and the French were free to work out their political future unobstructed by Allied interference.[76] (It should be noted that most of the Allied officials—General Eisenhower in particular—were probably

---

[73] Funk, *De Gaulle*, p. 301 and passim; and Norman Kogan, "American Policies towards European Resistance Movements," *Deuxième Conference Internationale d'Histoire de la Résistance* (Milano, 1961), p. 10.

[74] "Note concernant Les Comités de la Libération," 5 October 1943: "Projet confidential à titre d'informations aux Régions Sud," Papers of Claude Serreules, Archives, CHG. See chap. 3, especially footnotes on this issue, for numerous similar examples.

[75] *Témoignage* of Pascal Pia, Archives, CHG.

[76] See Robert Aron, *Histoire de la libération*, p. 139.

A makeshift barricade constructed during the Parisian insurrection of August 1944 on the rue du Renard, just around the corner from the Hôtel de Ville.

happy to leave the administration in French hands. Eisenhower had long been convinced of the justice of many Gaullist arguments, and as early as January 1944 had urged President Roosevelt to recognize the CFLN, whose assistance he felt essential to the success of operations in France.[77] Generally, the misunderstanding that always embittered relations between de Gaulle and Roosevelt did not prevent Frenchmen and Americans at lower echelons from working together harmoniously toward their mutual goal of driving out the Germans.)[78]

Also, thanks to the resistance movements, the civil war or chaos that some had predicted for France at the liberation failed to materialize. In northern France, where liberation usually coincided with the arrival of Allied troops, little disorder had been anticipated and almost none occurred. But in southern France a highly explosive situation existed in many areas liberated by the Resistance before regular troops arrived. Reports to de Gaulle and his intelligence services warned that FFI bands were completely out of control and

---

[77] Eisenhower, *Papers*, vol. 3, p. 1667.

[78] See Funk, *De Gaulle*, passim, and Coles and Weinberg, *Civil Affairs*, passim; and especially Passy, *10 Duke Street Londres*, pp. 142–43.

constituted a serious threat of anarchy.[79] Some feared the Communists might take advantage of the situation, using their confederates in the resistance movements to establish "red soviets" wherever possible.[80]

Sometimes these fears appeared to be justified when rival groups or individuals claimed the right to control the local administration. Occasionally, justice was by personal vendetta. Bands of men, some true resisters but others remnants of Milice formations or simply outlaws, roamed the countryside. De Gaulle's *commissaire de la république* for Lyon was stopped six times in one day by various gangs of men who demanded his credentials.[81] Occasionally local resistance chiefs would reject the imposition of a Gaullist official sent from Algiers with orders from the CFLN.[82] Some isolated Maquis groups had never submitted to control by the organized Resistance, and the creations of the FFI had seldom resolved all the differences that hindered cooperation between FTP, ORA, and CFL units.[83]

Still, challenges to Gaullist commissioners and prefects were the exception, not the rule, and the disorder in the southern zone should not be exaggerated. If isolated objections to the installation of certain officials occurred, they can usually be attributed to personal rivalries at the local level that did not involve questions about the legitimacy of the CFLN's powers. The resistance movements were not competing with de Gaulle and the CFLN. They were making every effort to secure recognition of Gaullist legitimacy in the face of the Allied powers. No challenge to de Gaulle was ever presented or sanctioned by the directors of the resistance movements or the CNR.[84]

---

[79] De Gaulle, *Mémoires de guerre*, vol. 3, pp. 297–99, 316–18; and Soustelle, *Envers et contre tout*, vol. 2, p. 442.

[80] De Gaulle, *Mémoires de guerre*, vol. 3, pp. 316–18; and Soustelle, *Envers et contre tout*, vol. 2, pp. 419, 425–35.

[81] Farge, *Rebelles*, p. 223.

[82] *États Généraux des C. D. L. de la Zone Sud à Avignon les 7–8 Octobre 1944, Procès-Verbaux des Déliberations* (Avignon: Imprimerie Rulliere Frères, 1944), p. 16 and passim.

[83] Generous documentation for these difficulties in the area around Lyon is found in the Papers of Alban Vistel, Archives, CHG. For example, "*Alban à Colonel Bayard*," 28 August 1944; concerning the impending insurrection at Lyon, Vistel wrote: "I am refusing to set off any premature folly, but I regret to tell you that discipline is not the quality of our appointed leaders."

[84] Hostache, *Le Conseil National de la Résistance*, p. 315, passim, notes that in general commissioners, prefects, and local CDLs worked well together.

Investigation of the reputed seedbeds of red power, such as Toulouse, Montpellier, Limoges, and Marseilles, where Communists or their sympathizers were the leading political or military figures at the liberation, reveals no evidence to support myths alleging the creation of autonomous soviets in the Southeast.[85] To be sure, in these areas tense moments of confrontation occurred between different groups whose cooperation had seldom been perfect.[86] But in every case the need to present a united front before the Allies overrode all other considerations. Recalling the liberation of Toulouse, Serge Asher-Ravanel, the FFI commander who helped direct the insurrection, wrote:

> Were there never any problems? Of course, there were. All the more because we were living among problems that had to be resolved. But the important thing was the manner in which they were handled. I must insist that a sincere spirit of cooperation developed among us. The desire of any single group of resisters to seize power . . . was never manifested.[87]

When prominent Gaullist officials from Algiers were flown into areas of reported unrest in southern France, they were welcomed by well-disciplined units exercising control in de Gaulle's name.[88] The commissioners and prefects, aided by the Departmental Liberation Committees, set to work as best they could in a troubled situation.[89]

---

[85] In his *Histoire de la Libération*, Robert Aron is very misleading in most of his comments concerning the Communists, particularly with regard to their intentions at the liberation. Crane Brinton's "Letters From Liberated France," and Coles and Weinberg, *Civil Affairs*, quoting extensively from firsthand reports covering most areas of southern France, clearly demonstrate that the widespread rumors of disorder were rarely justified. Almost everywhere the Gaullists were in firm control of the local administration and there were no "Communist Soviets."

[86] For example, see Pierre Bertaux's description of the early moments of the liberation at Toulouse, in Theodore H. White, *Fire in the Ashes* (New York: William Sloane Associates Publishers, 1953), pp. 113–20. Bertaux was the *commissaire de la république* at Toulouse.

[87] Serge Asher-Ravanel, "Le récit du colonel Ravanel," *L'Express*, 26 March 1959, pp. 7–9.

[88] Jean Pierre-Bloch, *Le Vent souffle sur l'histoire*, pp. 237–42; Soustelle, *Envers et contre tout*, vol. 2, pp. 442–43, points out that they had left expecting to find a troubled atmosphere.

[89] In response to questions about the CDLs, a number of documents transmitted to the author by M. Alban Vistel, from his personal papers, demonstrate the multiple activities of these organizations, faced with the

They tried to preserve "republican order" and wherever possible to suppress all groups that attempted to take the law into their own hands. The resistance leaders were faced with enormous problems (disruption of communications, transport, food supply) and had extremely limited means to impose their authority. Georges Bidault remarked: "You cannot administer a nation in full rebellion the way you would run the Mortgage Registration Office."[90] By the time of de Gaulle's tour of the liberated areas in southern France in the fall of 1944, Gaullist administrators were installed everywhere, and in every city enthusiastic and loyal supporters greeted the president of the Provisional Government.[91]

The specter of a Communist conspiracy to seize power for the party, which had haunted some non-Communist resisters, was laid to rest at the liberation. The Communist party did not try to take power, despite the possible disappointment of individuals who were convinced that the party had "missed the boat."[92] Several factors rendered spurious the fears of those who were worried about Communist intentions. First, as we have seen, the Communists were an important component of the resistance movements, but they were by no means a majority of the resisters. Communists and their sympathizers who were important leaders in the various resistance movements were by no means all doctrinaires who placed the interests of their party before the patriotic duty they had assumed.

Had the Communists attempted a takeover, the non-Communist movements and the majority of the French population would surely have sided with de Gaulle.[93] The General's popularity alone was enough to make the Communists think twice about any coup, and his positive actions to tame the Communists were another reason for

---

tasks of feeding the people, reopening the schools, restoring transportation and communications. As indicated by these documents and the reports cited in Coles and Weinberg, *Civil Affairs*, passim, the resisters usually did a commendable job. Charles-Louis Foulon, *Les commissaires de la république* (Fondation nationale des sciences politiques, multigr., Paris, 1973), is a superb thesis covering the actions of the Commissioners of the Republic with profound insight into all aspects of the liberation.

[90] Bidault, *D'une résistance*, p. 55.

[91] De Gaulle, *Mémoires de guerre*, vol. 3, pp. 10–17.

[92] *Histoire du parti communiste français*, vol. 2 (Paris, 1962), p. 271. This work was written by a group of anonymous dissenters form the regular party apparatus.

[93] *Combat*, no. 42, December 1943, had warned that a bloody civil war would result if the Communists tried to seize power.

their remaining in line. De Gaulle shrewdly used the Communists in the CFLN and the Provisional Government but firmly refused them any key post that might have allowed events in France to parallel the later Communist takeovers in Eastern Europe.[94]

Further, the presence of Allied troops in France and later in Germany meant that it would have been sheer madness for the Communists to make a power grab at the liberation. They could not possibly have succeeded in forcing a revolution in France, and assuming the slightest realism on the part of their leaders they undoubtedly knew it.[95] Also, the French Communists' relation to Moscow makes it unlikely that they ever seriously considered revolutionary action. The party apparatus in France was evidently following guidelines laid down by Stalin and would do nothing contrary to the desires of the Soviet Union. A civil war in France might have meant the collapse of the western front, which was contrary to Russian interests.

De Gaulle's inclusion of Communist ministers in the CFLN tied the party to the Provisional Government's decisions, and when Maurice Thorez, head of the French Communist party, returned from Moscow in November 1944, his speeches clearly indicated the Communists' intention to support the Gaullist regime.[96] Thorez ordered party members to comply with the decrees incorporating the FTP into the French Army and dissolving the *milices patriotiques* (local

---

[94] Gordon Wright, "Reflections on the French Resistance," *Political Science Quarterly* 77, no. 3 (September 1962): 344–45.

[95] In *Le Parti communiste français dans la Résistance* (Paris: Éditions Sociales, 1967), pp. 336–37; Jean Gacon, "La premiere 'expérience de Gaulle' Août 1944–Janvier 1946," *Recherches Internationales* no. 44–45 (July–December 1964), p. 244; and countless other officially sanctioned accounts, which are too numerous to list here, the Communist party has always officially maintained that it never considered trying to seize power at the liberation. See Jacques Fauvet, *Histoire du parti communiste français*, vol. 2 (Paris: Fayard, 1965), pp. 141–43; and Rieber, *Stalin and the French Communist Party*, p. 157, who are both convinced, as is this author, that the party did not try to take power at the liberation as some have alleged.

[96] Maurice Thorez, *S'Unir combattre travailler* (*rapport* of the secretary general of the PCF to the session of the Central Committee on 21, 22, 23 January 1945), pp. 10–11, 18. The actions of isolated Communists at the liberation in resisting these orders and quarreling with Gaullist authorities can be attributed to individual zealousness. Later splits in the party, which resulted in the expulsion of several of these "leftists," seems to substantiate this hypothesis. An interesting discussion of Thorez's return to France appears in *Le Monde*, 27 November 1969.

Joyful Parisians at the Place de la Concorde celebrating the liberation of Paris in August 1944.

militia groups often dominated by Communists). The party's immediate aim was to rely on its resistance record to build a mass-based party capable of playing a leading role in the government.[97]

---

[97] Rieber, *Stalin and the French Communist Party*, pp. 160–66. In his "Rapport Beige," at the end of November 1943, Jacques Bingen wrote: "The Communist Party feels at once strong and weak. It has faith in the future triumph (*within five years*) of communist ideas in France. However it knows that a coalition of the rest of France against it, above all if General de Gaulle put his weight in the balance, could possibly be fatal to it in the near future and delay the triumph of Communism. There is a

By and large the resistance movements overcame all internal dissensions that might have threatened the triumph of the liberation. But in one area where they were generally in agreement, the purge of collaborators, the resisters seemed to sweep France to the brink of tragedy. In speaking of the purge at the liberation we are dealing with the actual liquidation of thousands of Frenchmen at the hands of their fellow countrymen. The later institutional purge was less stringent than might have been expected.[98] In the unsettled atmosphere of the liberation sentences were delivered in various circumstances: by FFI courts martial or those designated by official Gaullist agents with differing degrees of respect for judicial procedure; or, less happily, by individuals or groups without any authorization but the guns in their hands.

It is impossible to arrive at a satisfactory number of the actual victims of the purge. Robert Aron's figure of forty thousand—or one in every one thousand Frenchmen—is most often cited,[99] but recent investigation indicates that this total is at least double and perhaps four times the actual number.[100] After an uneventful tour of southern France, the region where the purge was most widespread, one contemporary observer wrote: "The rumors of disorder of which we heard so much in Paris and indeed elsewhere seem to be largely explicable by a human tendency to retail exaggerated stories."[101]

---

good chance that the P. C. and its friends will participate in de Gaulle's government." (My italics), Archives, CHG.

[98] One example—Paxton, *Parades and Politics at Vichy*—demonstrates that most of the former officers of the Army of the Armistice maintained their rank in the new French Army. Similarly, M. Paul, *Histoire des PTT*, vol. 3, p. 616: "It seems that when all things are considered, most of the *comités d'épuration* were not merciless."

[99] Robert Aron, *Histoire de l'épuration*, vol. 1 (Paris: Fayard, 1967), p. 433. This total includes executions by groups of former miliciens and all types of unauthorized groups and individuals. Not all of the deaths are attributable to the resistance movements' actions.

[100] Peter Novick, *The Resistance versus Vichy* (New York: Columbia University Press, 1968), Appendix C, Summary Execution Statistics, pp. 202–8. Novick's study of the purge provides several important correctives to interpretations in Aron's various works. Extensive investigations on a *département* by *département* basis, carried out by the *Comité d'Histoire de la deuxième guerre mondiale*, indicate that Aron's figures are greatly exaggerated. The *Comité's* findings are analyzed in Marcel Baudot, "La résistance française face aux problèmes de repression et d'épuration, Revue d'histoire de la deuxième guerre mondiale," No. 81, 21e année, January 1971.

[101] Crane Brinton, "Letters from Liberated France," vol. 2, no. 2, p. 141.

Secondhand descriptions of the purge were usually more exciting than the reality.

It is easier and perhaps more important to assess the resistance movements' part in the purge than to arrive at a precise cost in blood. The movements never made any secret of their desire for revenge on the Germans and their French collaborators. Very early in the Occupation the clandestine newspapers began printing blacklists of persons they intended to punish.[102] Later more personal notices appeared in collaborators' mailboxes in the form of miniature coffins.[103] In issuing orders in case of an Allied embarkation, *Combat* reminded its readers, "DON'T FORGET TO HATE!"[104] Ominous warnings were directed to *attentiste* Frenchmen:

> It Will Soon Be Too Late
> Victory is approaching. There are still Frenchmen who have done nothing to hasten the event. Warning! There is not much more time. It is not enough to listen to the radio from London or to read *Combat*, one must fully involve himself, take risks, be ready to fight. In the new France, a man will be judged by his acts. . . . We are accepting workers of the eleventh hour. *Soon it will be noon!*[105]

After the invasion of France had begun, no equivocation remained: "Everyone who is not with us is against us."[106]

With a notable lack of concern for calm, detached judicial procedure, the Comité Central de la Résistance pronounced sentence on one of the most hated collaborators before the CFLN authorities had completed his trial in Algiers. In September 1943 the *Comité* declared: "Pierre Pucheu, former Minister of the Interior at Vichy . . . has been condemned to death by the French people."[107] Obviously these actions of the resistance movements helped to inflame passions at the liberation, but a strong case for the resisters' exercise of restraint can also be made.

------

[102] These lists appeared in *Le Franc-Tireur* in 1942, *Libération* and *Combat* in 1943, and lists become more and more frequent in all of the underground journals by 1944.

[103] Aron, *Histoire de Vichy*, p. 595.

[104] *Combat*, no. 47, 1 September 1943.

[105] *Combat*, no. 48, 25 September 1943.

[106] *Combat*, no. 58, July 1944.

[107] *Le Franc-Tireur*, 20 September 1943.

In March 1944 the MUR journals reported that the CNR disapproved of the printing of lists of people to be "gotten" at the liberation.[108] Justice was not to be dealt with simply by whim. Collaborators were to be given fair trials where all the evidence could be considered.[109] De Gaulle, the CFLN, and the movements all repudiated "personal justice."[110] A major theme of the resisters at the liberation was the need to restore republican order immediately. Yves Farge, a leading resister and a *commissaire de la république* at Lyon, issued a proclamation urging caution in the dispensation of justice. "Beware of premature judgments and the frenzy of passion. Especially, do not forget that the great majority of French civil servants have merely done their duty, and often they have had to hide their thoughts in order to serve."[111] At the liberation of Toulouse, the *commissaire de la république*, Pierre Bertaux, proclaimed:

> Let your joy be profound, but also let it remain sober. Too much blood has already flowed, too many tears have been shed, for us to risk giving a spectacle of disorder, indiscipline or profligacy. No pillaging. No individual acts of violence. The traitors will be punished according to the laws of the Republic.[112]

The resisters did not want the purge to look like "a bloody farce."[113] Particularly in southern France the resistance movements were often the only organized bodies capable of restoring law and order. They established official courts that insisted on valid and sufficient evidence, and they apparently made every effort to avoid excesses of shotgun justice.[114]

---

[108] *Combat*, no. 55, March 1944.

[109] *Combat*, no. 54, February 1944, noted that the trials of Pétain, Flandin, and Peyrouton would be delayed until all evidence was available after the liberation.

[110] The instructions given to the *commissaires de la république* were very clear on this point. See the directives dated January 1944, appended to J. P. Bloch, *Le Vent souffle sur l'histoire*, pp. 307–20. Pierre Bourget and Charles Lacretelle, *Sur les murs de Paris 1940–1944* (Paris: Librairie Hachette, 1959), p. 199, reproduces a poster of a local liberation committee forbidding private individuals to shave heads, make arrests, and so on, merely on the basis of suspicions.

[111] Farge, *Rebelles*, p. 191.

[112] Ville de Toulouse, *Bulletin Municipal*, October 1944, p. 78.

[113] Farge, *Rebelles*, p. 226.

[114] Aron, *Histoire de la libération*, pp. 138–39.

The phenomenon of the purge cannot be understood without a consideration of the circumstances that surrounded it. The French had suffered through four long years of Nazi occupation. The resisters had suffered hunger and humiliation, had often seen their families and best friends tortured or executed, while those who collaborated with the enemy often had lived in high style, heedless of the plight of their oppressed countrymen. Some, such as the hated Milice and the informers, had actually helped the Gestapo track down patriotic Frenchmen. Certainly the Nazi suppression of the Resistance would have been far less effective without the help of French spies. Hatred and passions were bound to explode during the liberation.

Such circumstances do not justify the purge, but they do help to explain the outbreak of a sort of terror during the liberation period. Naturally many resisters were caught up in this vicious circle of violence. Indeed, somewhat surprisingly and to the credit of the resistance movements, summary executions were rare and usually limited to the most notorious collaborators.[115] Stanley Hoffmann has suggested that the executions of collaborators in the summer and fall of 1944 were not so much evidence of civil war as "examples of ritual murders."[116]

Often the "deeply felt need for emotional release on the part of a population which for four years had been swallowing its resentment"[117] was gratified by methods less drastic than murder. Occasionally women suspected of sleeping with Germans were shaved bald and paraded nude through the streets of a village. The author of the best study of the purge in France has speculated: "It is more than likely that many girls who were shorn were, unbeknown to themselves or their barbers, the instrument of salvation for miliciens and collaborators who might otherwise have died to appease the rage of their fellow citizens."[118] The little clique of serious collaborators was a very small part of the French population. By symbolically removing this cancer through the purge, the resisters and the vast majority of the country now rallied behind them used the collaborators as scapegoats responsible for all the nation's ills.[119]

In sum, the purge was a sad capstone to the resistance epoch, and

---

[115] See Novick, *The Resistance versus Vichy*, chap. 4: "Justice at the Crossroads," and Baudot, "La résistance . . . problèmes . . . d'épuration," pp. 41–47.

[116] Stanley Hoffmann and others, *In Search of France* (New York: Harper & Row, 1965), pp. 35–36.

[117] Novick, *The Resistance versus Vichy*, p. 68.

[118] Novick, *The Resistance versus Vichy*, p. 69; see also p. 78.

[119] Hoffmann, *In Search of France*, pp. 35–36.

it wrought a heavy toll. Although the occasional mistakes and summary executions are to be regretted, given the circumstances, they probably could not have been avoided. The resistance movements surely stimulated much of the anticollaborationist sentiment, and yet certainly without the efforts of de Gaulle and the resistance movements to control it, the extent of the violence would have been far greater.

By the winter of 1944 one of the most heroic adventures in French history was over. When one considers their extraordinary military and political accomplishments, the resisters would seem to have had every cause for satisfaction. Yet curiously, even before the collapse of their political movement the MLN[120] in postwar politics, the disenchantment of many resisters with the outcome of the liberation was evident. Perhaps, as one of them later remarked: "There are no victories without disillusionments."[121] But often the resisters' disappointment stemmed from more specific reasons.

In the months preceding the liberation, the clandestine newspapers had begun to formulate an image of the kind of future French society the resisters envisaged. The theme "From Resistance to Revolution" appeared frequently,[122] and the desire for a solid, incorruptible Republic was universally proclaimed. An alleged betrayal of these ideals led to bitter resentment in many resisters.[123] One explanation for this disappointment lay in the very nature of the ideas the resistance movements formulated.

The resisters' projects for the future were usually rather vague, lacking specific detail; they were couched in highly moral tones. A beautiful illustration of the idealistic language the resisters used appeared in *Combat*'s first call to the Resistance: "Now, the Country is in Danger. She demands volunteers. Respond to her call. Let us organize together the Crusade of Truth against Falsehood, Good against Evil, Christianity against Paganism, of Liberty against Slavery."[124] This style persisted throughout the Occupation as the movements looked beyond liberation. In September 1942 *Combat* wrote:

---

[120] See chap. 5.

[121] Interview with M. Étienne Bauer, 5 January 1970.

[122] See Georges Cottier, *De la Résistance à la révolution* (Neuchatel: Éditions de la Baconnière, 1945), for numerous excerpts from the clandestine press.

[123] Pierre Hervé's tract, *La Libération trahie* (Paris: Éditions Bernard Grasset, 1945) coined the representative slogan "The Liberation Betrayed" for the disconsolate resisters.

[124] *Combat*, no. 1, December 1941.

"We want a Just France . . . an Honest France."[125] Lying in public was to be a crime in the new France.[126] The revolution was to be "the dawn of a new civilization."[127] On the eve of the liberation of Paris this revolution still lacked precise definition. France was "a spirit to safeguard . . . a certain sense of the absolute and the universal . . . a certain conception of right and the primacy of morality over politics . . . an affirmation of the requirements of conscience."[128]

The important role the working class played in the Resistance led the resisters to emphasize the major concern the new France would have for improving worker status. Before the liberation Francis Closon, a Gaullist agent, wrote: "I believe that, as a matter of principle, we must not let slip by any occasion to include the workers in the responsibilities of power, if for us the word 'revolution' has any meaning."[129] For other themes the resisters quite often harkened back to the French Revolution. Indeed, their ideas can perhaps be most simply understood as an attempt to adapt the ideals of the Revolution to the twentieth century. This fundamental aspect of the resisters' ideas was evident in *"Pour une nouvelle révolution française,"* published in the clandestine *Cahiers Politiques*. The article contains an excellent statement of the political ideal of the Resistance.

> What revolution?
>
> We repeat: a new French Revolution. A revolution which will take up the broken thread of 1789 and clearly trace out . . . the inevitable consequences of our principles of long ago and our present aspirations: a true democracy, freed from the moneyking, a power derived from the people but strong and stable, the equitable disposition, by the nation, of our common riches, a dignified life for free workers, the sharing of economic responsibilities by all and no longer only by the few. In short, more liberty, more equality, more fraternity, in a renewed national community, which has regained the place which belongs to it in a reconciled family of nations.[130]

---

[125] *Combat*, no. 34, September 1942.

[126] Ibid.

[127] Ibid.

[128] *Résistance*, 7 August 1944, quoted in Bruneau, *Essai d'historique*, p. 19.

[129] Closon, "Rapport," no. 2, 10 October 1943, Archives, CHG.

[130] *Les Cahiers politiques*, no. 2, June ? 1943 (no. 1 was April 1943, and no. 3 was August 1943). *Les Cahiers* were produced by the Comité Général d'Études, whose role was to formulate plans for the future administration and institutions of France.

Many of the preceding excerpts from clandestine publications indicate that the penetrating judgment of a recent intellectual history of modern France is quite valid:

> For all the heroism and sacrifice that went into it, the social thought of the Resistance lacked specific content. Most of the time, it did not go beyond a reiteration of the principles of fraternity, moral regeneration, and the transcending of factional quarrels. The economic policy the Resistance writers advocated lay somewhere between a nondogmatic socialism and the techniques of the welfare state: in this sphere alone their thought left a visible trace on official practice in the postwar years. Elsewhere the social doctrine of the Resistance was more a state of mind—a mystique—than a tangible program.[131]

André Malraux concurred. "As a whole, the men of the Resistance were liberal patriots. Liberalism is a sentiment, not a political program...."[132]

Yet the plans of the Resistance were not simply shallow and verbose. The mystique of the Resistance if intangible was nevertheless powerful. The humanistic spirit that the resisters bequeathed to France was certainly preferable to the cynicism and "lesser evil" philosophy exhibited by some leaders at Vichy which might have been France's spiritual heritage had the Resistance not rejected such moral relativism.[133] The resistance movements' ideas were diverse, derived from men of all political shades. Resisters were usually in complete agreement only on what they were *against*.[134] But if they were unable to agree on precise formulas for the future, the resisters' common rejection of specific alternatives was not simply a negative phenomenon.

A remarkable generosity was implicit in the ideas of the Resistance. Not only did the movements decry the bogies of anti-Semitism, anti-

---

[131] H. Stuart Hughes, *The Obstructed Path* (New York: Harper & Row, 1968), p. 161.

[132] André Malraux, *Anti-Memoirs* (New York: Holt, Rinehart and Winston, 1968), p. 85.

[133] Paul Farmer, *Vichy Political Dilemma*, p. 352; Stanley Hoffmann, "Collaborationism in France during World War II," *The Journal of Modern History* 40, no. 3 (September 1968): 375–95; and Wright, "Vichy Revisited," pp. 512–14.

[134] Michel, *Les courants de pensée*, pp. 7, 15.

communism, and anticlericism,[135] but a surprising reconciliation toward the German people also emerged during the Occupation. At first the clandestine journals instinctively and understandably demanded revenge on Germany. But as the Occupation continued, some editors distinguished between the Germans and the Nazis. By the liberation *Combat* envisioned Franco–German cooperation as the necessary basis for a secure peace.[136] Some resisters, recalling the Versailles settlement after World War I, stressed the dangers of a vindictive peace. Finally, a realization of the dangers of a chauvinistic nationalism led resisters to dream of a federation of Europe with reduced national sovereignty for the member nations.[137] This thought later found a reflection in the Common Market.

Postwar France did not always live up to the lofty standards that the resisters had set for her, and many who had given so much for those ideals were understandably disappointed when French politics returned to "normalcy."[138] But French society's failure to translate their ideals into reality is only part of the explanation of the resisters' disillusionment. The clandestine journals that expressed these ideals were written by a very small group of men who rarely knew the names or identities of most of their followers. The spirit of their editorials may be assumed representative of the majority of the movements' militants, but specific programs for the future were certainly individual projects.[139] It is critical to recognize that the immediate fight was the central concern of the resistance movements.[140] The small amount of space in the underground press devoted to plans for the future compared to the amount filled with immediate concerns is suggestive of their relative importance to the resisters.

---

[135] See Henri Michel, *Les courants de pensée*, for an exhaustive and very perceptive examination of the whole spectrum of resistance thought. The "Second Section" concentrates on the ideas expressed by the resistance movements (pp. 119–44).

[136] *Combat*, no. 55, March 1944.

[137] *Les Cahiers de libération*, September 1943, pp. 7–15; also Walter Lipgens, "European Federation in the Political Thought of Resistance Movements during World War II," *Central European History* 1, no. 1 (March 1968).

[138] See the testimonies of several leading resisters in "Huit Ans Après," *l'Observateur* (No. spécial, 3e année, no. 119, 21 August 1952, and no. 120, 28 August 1952).

[139] Michel and Guetzévitch, *Les Idées*, pp. 8–11.

[140] Michel, *Les courants*, p. 2; and Cerf-Ferrière, *Chemin clandestin*, p. 78.

The majority of active resisters held no political aspirations. They had joined the resistance movements because their patriotism and humanism had demanded their participation. When France was free from German occupation and its traditional republican liberties were restored, most resisters wanted simply to return to work as factory hands, university professors, artists, or whatever their former positions had been.[141] Undeniably many resisters were dismayed that ideas such as those expressed in the CNR Charter were not more fully reflected in postwar legislation. Nevertheless, the later cynicism and indifference to the Fourth Republic's fate represented the disillusionment, not simply of the resisters, but of society at large faced with the inertia of postwar French politics and society.

Beyond the realm of ideas, a more concrete explanation for the resisters' deception lay in the misunderstanding that almost always accompanied their direct encounters with General de Gaulle. We have seen that from their first contact, relations between the interior resistance movements and de Gaulle's agents were often strained, but the resisters' resentment was usually directed toward the intermediary *délégués*, who occasionally intervened in matters that the resisters felt were under their own jurisdiction. Months before the formation of the National Resistance Council in May 1943, the Resistance had accepted de Gaulle as the symbol of their struggle and the standard-bearer of French national interests. When local resisters overturned Vichy and throughout France installed their own men in critical administrative positions, they were acting in de Gaulle's behalf. More precisely, they felt that the General's government was legitimate because they, the true representatives of the French people, had chosen to follow de Gaulle.[142] Nor was there any doubt about the people's will. The resisters neither proposed nor even considered any other

---

[141] Jean Bruller (Vercors), *The Battle of Silence*, pp. 272–73, 282–85, notes his desire for anonymity after the war. Hughes, *The Obstructed Path*, pp. 232–35, draws an interesting contrast between Sartre and Camus. For Sartre the extreme moral commitments demanded in clandestine life were the norm. But Camus, not an existentialist like Sartre, felt that war and the Occupation were something hellish, beyond the human norm. To commit oneself totally to a cause was but a temporary affair demanded by extreme circumstances.

[142] See chap. 3; also the arguments of Marie Granet in *Ceux de la Résistance (1940–1944)* (Paris: Les Éditions de Minuit, 1964), pp. 67–71 and passim; and especially Granet, *Un Journal socialiste clandestin pendant l'occupation, Libération-Nord*, p. 22.

candidate to lead the Provisional Government. Consequently, at the liberation de Gaulle's apparent disregard for their sensibilities understandably offended them.

No sooner had Paris been liberated than General de Gaulle informed the National Resistance Council that it had done a good job but was no longer needed.[143] CNR President Georges Bidault was taken into the Provisional Government as foreign minister, and the other members were given seats in the Consultative Assembly. The Council, under a new president and revised membership, continued to meet and to petition de Gaulle, urging implementation of the CNR Charter, but the General refused to meet with the body as a whole or to grant it any special consideration.[144] The central organ of the interior Resistance no longer had any power or official status, and it soon became "little more than a debating society."[145]

Similarly, de Gaulle curtly snubbed the ambitions of the Departmental Liberation Committees to assume an active role in French reconstruction. Following two smaller gatherings at Vizelle and Valence, most of the CDLs in southern France were represented at Avignon, where a congress of the *"États généraux des C. D. L. de la zone sud"* was held 7–8 October 1944.[146] After having fought so long and seen so many of their comrades killed in the struggle to liberate France, it was not surprising that the resisters were reluctant to turn over their powers to others before their desires for the transformation of French society had been enacted. Thus at Avignon they proclaimed themselves the "guardians of the will to execute the program of the Resistance."[147] The resisters denied any intention of substituting the CDLs for the government and rejected the idea that they might be considered organs of opposition to the government or "political troublemakers."[148] Referring to the recurrent rumors of an animosity between the Resistance and de Gaulle, they reaffirmed their complete confidence in the head of the Provisional Government.[149] But they did wish to be included in some institutional framework that would allow them to serve as a link between the people of the provinces and the central government in Paris.

---

[143] De Gaulle, *Mémoires de guerre*, vol. 2, pp. 318–19.
[144] De Gaulle, *Mémoires de guerre*, vol. 2, pp. 318–19, and vol. 3, p. 39.
[145] Rieber, *Stalin and the French Communist Party*, p. 168.
[146] See *États Généraux . . . Procès-Verbaux des Délibérations*.
[147] *États Généraux*, pp. 26–27.
[148] See *États Généraux*, pp. 10, 27.
[149] *États Généraux*, pp. 10, 154, and passim.

For some time the CDLs, assisting the commissioners and prefects, had held complete authority over their regions. Confronted with numerous, very serious problems and having minimal resources at their disposal, they had done a remarkably good job of administration.[150] With only the most general directives for guidance, they had often displayed a refreshing sense of individual initiative. Their experience suggested to them that the highly centralized French administration might be improved by an expansion of regional control, which would foster such initiative at the lower levels and allow for greater flexibility.[151] Thus, they demanded a fuller representation for the regions in proposing that one representative from each of the eighty-six CDLs be included in the Consultative Assembly.[152]

Despite their protestations of loyalty, de Gaulle clearly viewed the existence of the CDLs as a potential danger to his authority. When the resisters invited him to their congress at Avignon, the General refused to come or to send an official government representative. In a letter to the *commissaire de la république* at Lyon, he responded to the CDLs' resolutions at Valence in a most unequivocal manner. After acknowledging his satisfaction that the CDLs had pledged to support him, de Gaulle reminded them "that the attributions of the Departmental Committees were clearly defined by Article 19 of the ordinance of 21 April, that the Committees have a consultative role and that the regional commissioner and the prefect must consult them, but must not allow them any executive power."[153] As to the government's relation to the people, de Gaulle continued:

> The Government keeps in close touch with public opinion and the Resistance through conferences with the Provisional Consultative Assembly which will soon be meeting and up until that time through the National Resistance Council.
> General de Gaulle considers the members of the departmental committees as good and faithful companions in the

---

[150] See Coles and Weinberg, *Civil Affairs*, passim, reports from various areas across southern France that French had administration well in hand.

[151] *États Généraux*, p. 153, and passim; and document communicated to the author by M. Alban Vistel, "Région de Lyon, Affaires économiques, Ravitaillement: Y. Savoy à N. A. P. (Région et Zone Sud)," 18 May 1944, in personal papers of Alban Vistel.

[152] *États Généraux . . . Procès-Verbaux des Délibérations*, pp. 128–35. When delegates from the CNR advised the representatives of the CDL against demanding such representation, the provincial resisters voted them down.

[153] *États Généraux*, pp. 20–22.

struggle against the enemy and his accomplices, and he ad-
mires their courage; but nevertheless he affirms the necessity
for everyone, in the national interest, to play the role and do
his duty in the place which is assigned to him by law.[154]

Needless to say the Committes were dismayed by de Gaulle's an-
swer to their proposals,[155] but they soon relinquished their authority
to the official administrative bodies. The CDLs' effacement was
speeded up when Maurice Thorez returned from Moscow and directed
the Communists to comply with General de Gaulle's orders. In a
speech in Paris Thorez declared that the CDLs "must not substitute
themselves for municipal and departmental administration. No more
than the C. N. R. has substituted itself for the Government."[156]

The resisters' contacts with de Gaulle on a personal level only
added to the disappointment occasioned by his disregard for their
organizations. During an inspection tour of the liberated cities of
southern France in September 1944, de Gaulle seemed awkward and
ill at ease in the presence of the resistance chiefs and their irregular
military units.[157] In one of the more celebrated incidents, the General,
apparently upset by the alleged proliferation of self-made officers at
military reviews he attended, quipped to one young man who was
without insignia of rank: "What is the matter with you, don't you
know how to sew?"[158] Incidents of this sort and de Gaulle's aloofness
stood in unhappy contrast to the enthusiasm with which his coming
had been greeted. Yves Farge, the *commissaire de la république* at

---

[154] *États Généraux*, pp. 20–22.

[155] *États Généraux*, p. 23. The delegate from the CDL of the Rhône
remarked: ". . . if the Head of the Government thinks he can understand
the aspirations of the grand masses of this country by listening to the
voices of the Consultative Assembly, which is not yet meeting, or by the
voice of the *Conseil National de la Résistance*; personally I believe that
this is not sufficient." His remarks were seconded by wild applause and
shouts of "Perfectly right!"

[156] Thorez, *S'Unir*, p. 23.

[157] Paul-Marie de la Gorce, *De Gaulle entre deux mondes*, pp. 351–57.
De Gaulle's own account is found in *Mémoires de guerre*, vol. 3, pp. 10–21.

[158] Jean Lacouture, *De Gaulle* (Paris: Éditions du Seuil, 1969), pp. 138–
39. Ravanel, "Le récit du colonel Ravanel," pp. 7–9, explained that so
many FFI officers were at Toulouse to greet de Gaulle because they had
been waiting for some time for his visit. Everyone who could come from
the surrounding areas came into Toulouse to see de Gaulle and to affirm
their support for him. Consequently, they were shocked and dismayed by
his behavior.

Lyons, recalled: "I was pained and revolted to see . . . that an opaque screen was developing between the head of the government and the country."[159]

One of de Gaulle's most perceptive biographers, Paul-Marie de la Gorce, has suggested that the General's temperament was a major factor in the awkwardness of his contacts with the Resistance in southern France.[160] A northerner from Lille, de Gaulle was by nature cold, austere, and restrained, and his military background had impressed on him the virtue of order and regulation. The warmth, excitement, and exuberance of the liberated citizens of Marseille and Toulouse were perhaps incomprehensible to de Gaulle. In any case he was overly ready to see chaos and disorder behind their spontaneous enthusiasm.

But surely more than differences in temperament separated de Gaulle from the resisters. After all, his reason for visiting southern France was clearly "to reduce to nothing, if possible, the authority emanating from the resistance groups or the *maquis* and to reestablish everywhere the normal hierarchies of the State."[161] With this goal in mind it is difficult to imagine how de Gaulle might have arrived at a sympathetic understanding of the resisters' ambitions.

The amazing growth of the Communist party under the Occupation and its undeniable popularity at the liberation certainly played a part in de Gaulle's reticence toward the resisters. Reports from his agents within France and the opinions of some of his advisers may well have given him an exaggerated impression of the Communists' influence over the Resistance.[162] The rivalry between COMAC (the Resistance's military directory composed of two Communists and one non-Communist) and General Pierre Koenig, whom de Gaulle had appointed commander-in-chief of the FFI, must have increased these suspicions about the Communists' intentions.[163] The COMAC often expressed opinions that many Communist and non-Communist resistance leaders shared—for instance, the repeated demands for an

---

[159] Farge, *Rebelles*, p. 317.

[160] De la Gorce, *De Gaulle entre deux mondes*, pp. 351–57.

[161] De la Gorce, *De Gaulle entre deux mondes*, p. 351.

[162] Closon, "Rapport," 10 November 1943, and "Rapport," no. 4 (Closon) of 1 April 1944, pp. 8–9, Archives, CHG. See attitudes reflected in Passy, *Missions secrètes en France*, pp. 258–60; Soustelle, *Envers et contre tout*, pp. 306–9; and De Gaulle, *Mémoires de guerre*, vols. 2 and 3, passim, for several indications of de Gaulle's suspicions.

[163] See Kriegel-Valrimont, *La Libération*, and Marie Granet, *Ceux de la Résistance*, chap. 3, pp. 154–87, and appended documents.

immediate distribution of parachuted weapons and the resistance forces' persistent desire to direct operations from within France during the liberation. Hence de Gaulle's apprehensiveness about the Communists probably disposed him to distrust the resistance movements in general.[164] As de Gaulle undoubtedly viewed the matter, restoration of the state by a reduction or elimination of the irregular authority of the resisters in southern France was directly linked to checking Communist influence on French politics.[165]

A final consideration of Charles de Gaulle's personality may offer a further explanation for his ostensible ingratitude toward the resistance movements. In discarding their organizations de Gaulle was by no means rejecting the resisters' aspirations for a renovation of French society. There can be no doubt about the sincerity of his conviction that many serious inequalities had to be rectified, and his later actions as head of the Provisional Government testified to this dedication to reform.[166] But de Gaulle's revolution was to be a gradual process, ordered by the state. The exuberant manner of the Resistance threatened to produce unnecessary tensions that the central authority could not control, whereas de Gaulle wanted "to prevent uncontrollable overturnings by proceeding voluntarily with the inevitable changes."[167]

In retrospect it seems rather sad that de Gaulle did not envisage a schema that might have incorporated the Resistance more fully within his plans for the reconstruction of France. But he seemed determined to carry alone to fulfillment the enormous task he felt he had begun alone on 18 June 1940. In an extremely revealing passage of his *Mémoires de guerre*, de Gaulle offered a description of his associates on the Comité Français de la Libération, which included several leading representatives of the interior resistance movements. He concluded:

---

[164] Marie Granet, *Un Journal socialiste clandestin pendant l'occupation, Libération-Nord*, pp. 18–20, and Granet, *Ceux de la Résistance*, mentions that some of the movements were also worried about the Communists' apparent domination of COMAC and the impression that this control might have on de Gaulle.

[165] De la Gorce, *De Gaulle entre deux mondes*, p. 351.

[166] The reader of de Gaulle's *Mémoires de guerre*, p. 18, when the General describes his reflections after visiting Lille, is readily convinced of de Gaulle's sincerity.

[167] De la Gorce, *De Gaulle entre deux mondes*, p. 355.

In sum, seeing around me courageous companions of enormous good will, I was filled with esteem for all and with friendship for many of them. But at the same time, listening to their souls speak, I came to wonder if, among all of these men who spoke of revolution, I was not, in truth, the only revolutionary.[168]

This attitude on the part of the man they had chosen to serve was undoubtedly the most important reason for the resisters' immediate disillusionment with the liberation.

In conclusion, we should not allow the resisters' postwar disappointments to obscure their very real accomplishments. The resistance movements, with the MUR in the vanguard, had after all played no small role in regaining the traditional liberties of Frenchmen and in restoring France's tarnished international image. Because of their actions Frenchmen were able to decide freely their future destiny. Their major goal was unquestionably the liberation of France, and they contributed significantly to it. In the political realm they had carried out a completely successful overthrow of Vichy, eliminated any pretext for an Allied military government, and assured the installation of a Gaullist administration. In the first turbulent weeks after the liberation, they had given France a solid, functioning administration, confounding those who had predicted utter chaos. Despite the occasional excesses of the purge, the resisters' role had generally been one of moderation and justice. If some were bitterly disappointed when postwar France failed to become the new world of their dreams, nevertheless the Republic would move toward realization of many of their ideals.

As Henri Frenay once said of Charles de Gaulle,[169] it was perhaps too much to expect that the resistance movements, having assured the liberation of France, could as successfully act as the agents of renovation for their country. Possibly it was inevitable that the resisters' enthusiastic amateurism would give way to order and to administration "as usual." Still, for some a certain nostalgic regret must remain that because of de Gaulle's distrust of the movements, as well as the resisters' own internal divisions, an opportunity for a genuine trans-

---

[168] De Gaulle, *Mémoires de guerre*, vol. 2, p. 153.

[169] Henri Frenay, "De Gaulle et la Résistance," *Preuves* 70 (December 1956): 84.

formation of French society was somehow missed. Nevertheless, the resisters' legacy of activism in the service of an idealistic humanism remains an inspiration for future generations who seek to better the lot of their fellowmen. Seldom in her long history had France been so well served as by these men. None were more deserving of the Republic's highest accolade: *"Ils ont bien mérité de la patrie."*

Map of France
after the Armistice

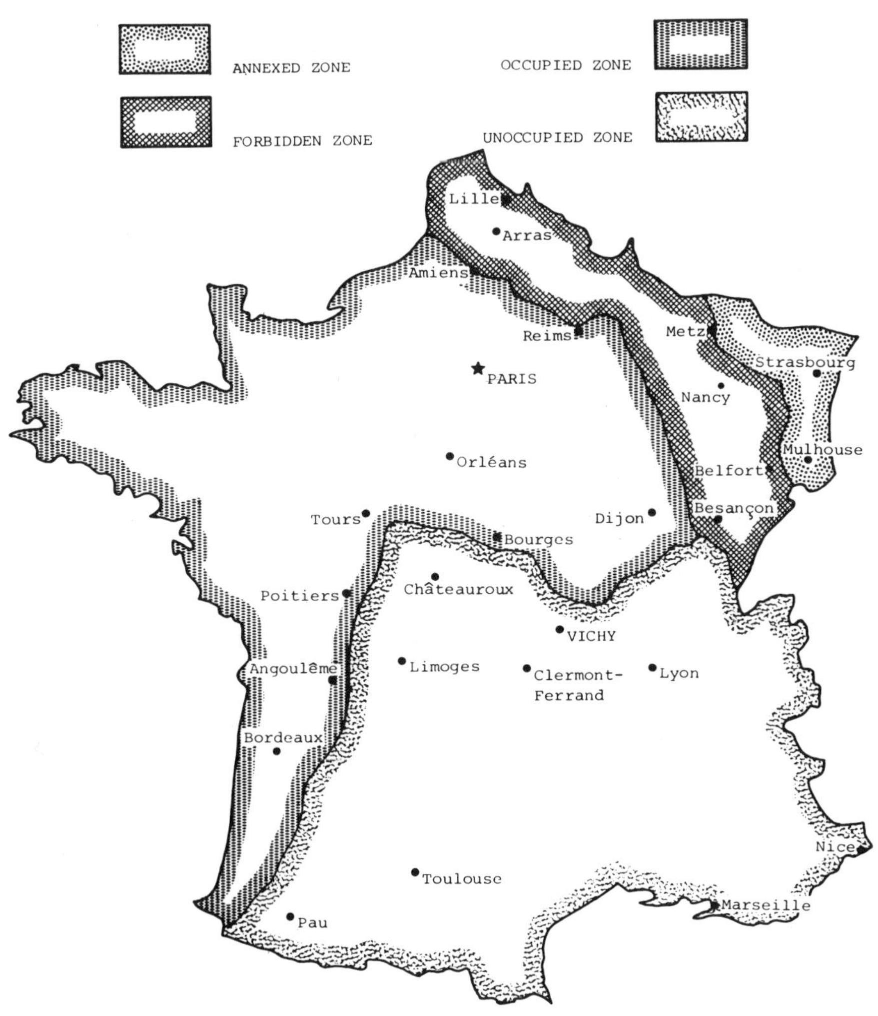

Organization of the French Resistance, Spring 1944

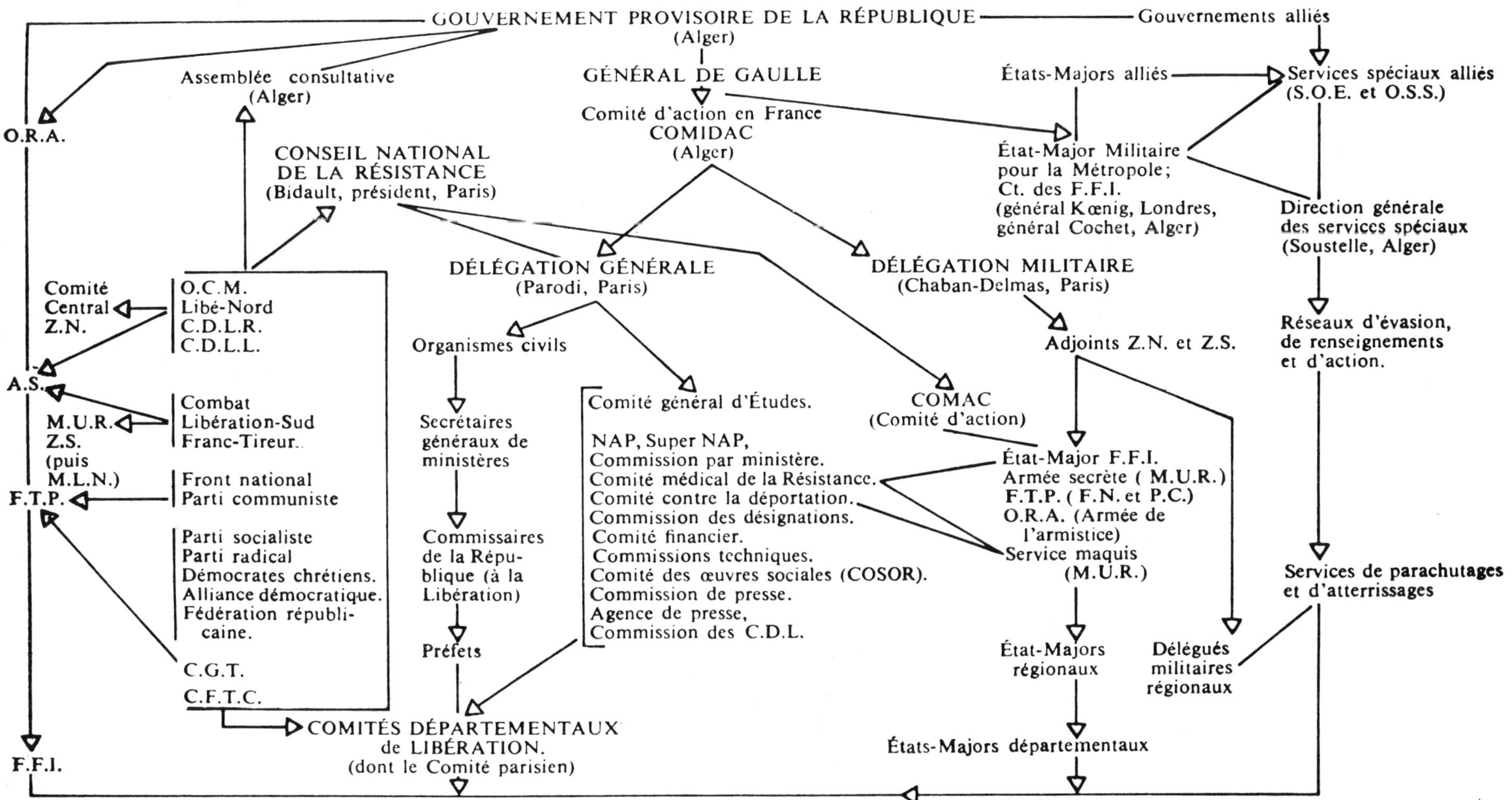

Sigles : O.R.A., Organisation de Résistance de l'Armée (de l'Armistice); A.S., Armée secrète; F.T.P. Francs-Tireurs et Partisans; O.C.M., Organisation civile et militaire; C.D.L.R., Ceux de la Résistance; C.D.L.L., Ceux de la Libération; C.G.T., Confédération générale du travail; C.F.T.C., Confédération française des travailleurs chrétiens; N.A.P., Noyautage des administrations publiques; la Direction des services spéciaux résulte de la fusion du B.C.R.A. et des services de l'Armée de l'Armistice; Z.S., zone sud; Z.N., zone nord; F.F.I., Forces Françaises de l'Intérieur; M.U.R., Mouvements Unis de Résistance; M.L.N., Mouvement de libération nationale.

Glossary

AMGOT—Allied Military Government of Occupied Territories. Administration by the Allied military authorities, which the French feared might be instituted in France at the liberation.

AS—*Armée Secrète.* The Secret Army, military formations of the resistance movements, grouping all of their paramilitary units. The Secret Army was a distinct organization, which did not include the Maquis, the FTP, or the Groupes Francs, though all of these groups theoretically merged into the FFI before the liberation.

BCRA—*Bureau Central de Renseignements et d'Action.* The Free French organization primarily responsible for receiving military intelligence and directing supply of the movements from London.

BIP—*Bureau d'Information et de Presse.* Central press service of the interior resistance.

CAD—*Comité d'Action contre la Déportation.* Organization directing the fight against the STO.

CAS—*Comité d'Action Socialiste.* Clandestine Socialist organization responsible for the reconstitution of the party in the underground.

CC—*Comité Central des Mouvements de Résistance.* Coordination committee for the MUR and the five other major movements; included no party or trade union representatives.

CCL—*Commission des Comités de Libération.* A CNR commission responsible for establishing regional and local committees of liberation in all parts of France.

CDL—*Comité Départemental de Libération.* Departmental resistance councils, including members of parties, movements, and syndical organizations that were represented on the CNR.

Ceux de la Libération. One of the five major resistance movements in the northern zone.

Ceux de la Résistance. One of the five major resistance movements in the northern zone.

CFL—*Corps Francs de la Libération.* Designation given in 1944 to a fusion of the MUR's military groups (Maquis, Groupes Francs, AS, etc.) into one organization.

CFLN—*Comité Français de la Libération Nationale.* Top organization of the exterior French Resistance, formed in June 1943 with the fusion of de Gaulle's CNF and Giraud's forces. Named itself the French Provisional Government shortly before the liberation.

CGE—*Comité Général d'Études.* A consultative body for the Gaullist Délégation Général in France; a group of experts who discussed projects for immediate action at the liberation as well as problems of postwar France.

CNF—*Comité National Français.* The directing organization of the Free French in London before their fusion with the Giraudists to form the CFLN.

CNR—*Conseil National de la Résistance.* Chief coordinating and executive organization of the interior French Resistance. Formed 27 May 1943; included representatives of movements, parties, and trade unions. A five-man bureau did its major work.

COMAC—*Commission d'Action Militaire.* CNR commission that claimed authority over all interior resistance military formations.

Combat. The largest resistance movement in southern France; part of the MUR.

Commissaire de la République. Gaullist agents with major responsibilities for restoring order and installing the new administration in France during the liberation period.

Défense de la France. One of the five largest resistance movements in northern France.

Délégation Générale. Organization that represented first the CNF and then the CFLN in France. Central organ of de Gaulle's agents in France.

Délégué Générale. Head of the Gaullist delegation in France.

DMN—*Délégué Militaire National.* Representative in France of the exterior French military command; under him were zonal, regional, and departmental representatives (DMZ, DMR, and DMD).

FFI—*Forces Françaises de l'Intérieur.* The united underground military formations, including the AS, elements of the former Armistice Army, the Groupes Francs, the Maquis, and the FTP, although the FTP often refused to take orders from the FFI command.

Front National. The Communist-dominated resistance movement, operating in both zones but most important in northern France.

FTP—*Francs-Tireurs et Partisans Français*. Military arm of the Communist movement, Front National.

Franc-Tireur. One of the three largest southern resistance movements; part of the MUR.

Groupes Francs. Élite sabotage forces of the MUR.

Libération-Nord. One of the five largest northern resistance movements.

Libération-Sud. One of the three largest resistance movements in southern France; part of the MUR.

Maquis. Bands of escapees from the STO, who formed as guerrilla units in mountain and forest regions of France. Most of these formations became part of the FFI during the liberation.

MLN—*Mouvement de Libération Nationale*. Designation for an attempt to federate all of the resistance movements in France under one organization. When the Front National and several other northern movements refused to join, some leaders of the MUR, along with several northern movements, retained the tag MLN in an abortive attempt to found a resistance-based political party.

MOF *Mouvement Ouvrier Français*. Composed largely of members of the two major French trade unions, CGT and CFTC, organized to oppose the *relève* and the STO.

Milice Patriotique. Short-lived local militia organizations under the command of the CDLs.

MRP—*Mouvement Républicain Populaire*. A new, mainly Catholic, political party, born of the Resistance and formed after the liberation.

MUR—*Mouvements Unis de la Résistance*. A federation of the three major resistance movements in southern France, Combat, Libération and Franc-Tireur.

NAP—*Noyautage des Administrations Publiques*. Resistance organization responsible for sabotaging the Vichy administration from within.

OCM—*Organisation Civile et Militaire*. One of the five major resistance movements in northern France.

ORA—*Organisation de Résistance de l'Armée*. Resistance organization formed by officers belonging to the remnants of the Armistice Army, which was disbanded after the invasion of southern France in November 1942.

OSS—*Office of Strategic Services*. The American intelligence service.

Relève. Scheme whereby three volunteer French workers went to Germany in exchange for the return of one prisoner of war.

SOE—*Special Operations Executive*. British intelligence and sabotage organization.

STO—*Service du Travail Obligatoire*. Forced labor draft for French workers to be transported to Germany.

Bibliography

1. DOCUMENTS: UNPUBLISHED

Archives of the Comité d'histoire de la deuxième guerre mondiale in Paris
(The Comité d'histoire began collecting interviews, *témoignages*, and
documentary material concerning the Resistance and Occupation
shortly after the end of World War II. Its holdings are now quite
extensive, including some 1,500 testimonies from former resisters,
numerous collections of private papers and documentation originating
from the Gaullist organizations in London and Algiers, as well as a
fine library of memoirs and secondary materials. The archives of the
Comité d'histoire are an essential starting place for research concern-
ing the Resistance in France.) :
Papers of Alban Vistel
Papers of Gilbert Grandval
Papers of Henri Guillermin
Papers of Georges Oudard, which include reports of Jacques Bingen,
Émile Blamont, Pierre Brossolette, Albert Camus, Yvon Morandat,
Jean-Paul Sartre, and Claude Serreules.
Propaganda Files
National Archives in Washington, D.C.:
Captured German Documents:
T-501: Rolls 93, 94, 96, 97, 101, 106, 117, 139, 144, 156, 166, 184, 191.
T-78: Rolls 443, 444, 452, 457.
T-77: Rolls 788, 829, 833, 846, 850, 1027.

Records of the Organization of Strategic Services (OSS)
Personal papers of Alban Vistel, communicated directly to the author.

2. DOCUMENTS: PUBLISHED

Bulletin Municipal, Ville de Toulouse, Numéro spécial consacré à la libération de Toulouse, October 1944, Imprimerie Gaussel et Cie., Marseille.

Bulletin Officiel du Commissariat Régional de la République, Gouvernement Provisoire de la République, Région de Limoges, December 1944 and January 1945, Charles-Lavauzelle et Cie., Paris, 1945.

Cahier Bleu (Directives élaborées par la Résistance Métropolitaine, promulgées à Alger en 1944, puis à Paris lors de la libération de la France), Numéro spécial hors série de L'Echo de la Presse et de la Publicité.

Conseil National de la Résistance, "Rassemblement du 7 Octobre 1944 au Vélodrome d'Hiver," République Française.

Cottier, Georges. *De la Résistance à la Révolution.* Neuchatel: Éditions de la Baconnière, 1945.

De Gaulle, Charles. *Discours et messages.* vol. 1 *(Pendant la guerre Juin 1940–Janvier 1946).* Paris: Éditions Berger-Levrault, 1946, Librairie Plon, 1970.

États Généraux des C. D. L. de la Zone Sud à Avignon les 7–8 Octobre 1944, Procès-Verbaux des Délibérations. Avignon: Imprimerie Rullière Frères, 1944.

États Généraux de la Renaissance Française (les 10, 11, 12, 13, 14 Juillet 1945), *Conseil National de la Résistance: Proclamations et Serment du Palais de Chaillot Résolution adoptée en séance plénière.* Paris: Entreprise Française de Presse, 1945.

Foreign Relations of the United States, Diplomatic Papers, 1942, vol. 2: *Europe;* 1943, vol. 2: *Europe;* and 1944, vol. 3: *The British Commonwealth and Europe.* Washington, D.C.: United States Government Printing Office, 1962, 1964, 1965.

Geo London, ed. *Le Procès Pétain.* Lyon: Roger Bonnefon, 1945.

Journal Officiel de la France Combattante Lois et Décrets. Année 1–3, 1941–1943.

Kriegstagebuch des Oberkommandos der Wehrmacht (1940–1945), Band 4: January 1944–22 May 1945, Bernard & Graefe Verlag für Wehrwesen, Frankfurt am Main, 1961.

Michel, Henri and Boris Mirkine-Guetzévitch. *Les Idées politiques et sociales de la résistance.* Paris: Presses Universitaires de France, 1954.

The Papers of Dwight David Eisenhower: The War Years. vols. 1, 2, 3, and 4. Baltimore, Md.: Johns Hopkins University Press, 1970.

Pétain et les allemands (Mémorandum d'Abetz sur les Rapports Franco-Allemands). Paris: Éditions Gaucher, 1948.

Trial of the Major War Criminals before the International Military Tribunal. Vols. 6 and 10, 1947; vols. 15 and 21, 1948. Nuremberg.
Verordnungsblatt des Militärbefehlshabers in Frankreich, vol. 1 (July 1940–December 1941) and vol. 2 (January 1942–February 1943).

3. Témoignages and Interviews

Charles d'Aragon. *Témoignage*, 1955.
Emmanuel d'Astier. *Témoignage*, 1947 and 1949.
Lucie Aubrac (Samuel). *Témoignage*, 1945.
Raymond Aubrac. *Témoignage*, 1947.
Claude Aveline. *Témoignage*, 1945.
Jacqueline Bernard. *Témoignage*, 1950 and 1956.
Antoine Avinin. *Témoignage*, 1945.
Anne-Marie Bauer. Interview, November 1969
Étienne Bauer. Interview, 5 January 1970.
Georges Bidault. Interview, 25 March 1970.
Jean Bloch-Michel. *Témoignage*.
Claude Bourdet. *Témoignage*, 1946.
René Capitant. *Témoignage*, 1957.
René Cerf-Ferrière. *Témoignage*, 1956.
Eugène Claudius-Petit. *Témoignage*.
Francis Closon. *Témoignage*, 1950.
Pascal Copeau. Interview, 23 January 1970.
Alfred Coste-Floret. *Témoignage*, 1955.
Paul Coste-Floret. *Témoignage*, 1955.
Francis Cremieux. *Témoignage*, 1957.
Jacques Debû-Bridel. Interview, 22 April 1970.
Henri Frenay. *Témoignage*, 1948, 1955, and 1956.
Jean Georges Gotteland. *Témoignage*.
André Hauriou. *Témoignage*, 1947.
Henry Ingrand. *Témoignage*, 1949 and 1956; and Interview, 11 March 1970.
Max Juvenal. *Témoignage*, 1947; and Interview, 8 June 1970.
Francis Leenhardt. *Témoignage*.
Jean-Pierre Lévy. *Témoignage*, 1946.
Roger Massip. *Témoignage*, 1946.
François de Menthon. *Témoignage*, 1955.
Edmond Michelet. *Témoignage*, 1950 and 1956.
Joseph Jacques Hervé Monjaret. *Témoignage*, 1946 and 1963.
Yvon Morandat. *Témoignage*, 1946.
Pascal Pia. *Témoignage*, 1946.
Auguste Pinton. *Témoignage*.
Louis Terrenoire. *Témoignage*, 1947.
P. E. Viard. *Témoignage*, 1950.
Alban Vistel. Interview, March 1970.
Georges Zerapha. *Témoignage*, 1947.

4. Memoirs

Asher-Ravanel, Serge. "Le récit du colonel Ravanel," *L'Express*, 26 March 1959, pp. 7–9.

D'Astier de la Vigerie, Emmanuel. *De la chute à la libération de Paris.* Paris: Librairie Gallimard, 1965.

————. *Rapport Général sur la situation des Partis et des Mouvements de Résistance, sur le rôle actuel de la Résistance et l'incidence des elections.* Paris: Bibliothèque nationale [4⁰L⁵⁹b 6].

————. *Sept fois sept jours.* Paris: Librairie Gallimard, 1961.

————. *Sept Jours en Exil.* Paris: Jacques Haumont, 1946.

Bénouville, Guillain de. *Le Sacrifice du matin.* Paris: Robert Laffont, 1947.

Bertaux, Pierre. "Comment je suis devenu résistant," *Histoire de notre temps* numéro 1 (Spring 1967). Paris: Librairie Plon, pp. 185–212.

Bidault, Georges. *D'une résistance à l'autre.* Paris: Les Presses du Siècle, 1965.

Blum, Léon. *L'oeuvre de Léon Blum,* vol. 5: *Mémoires, La prison et le procès,* and *À l'échelle humaine.* Paris: Éditions Albin Michel, 1955.

Bouthillier, Yves. *Le drame de Vichy.* 2 vols. Paris: Librairie Plon, 1950 and 1951.

Camus, Albert. *Carnets (Mai 1935–Fevrier 1942).* Paris: Éditions Gallimard, 1962.

————. *Carnets (Janvier 1942–Mars 1951).* Paris: Éditions Gallimard, 1964.

Cerf-Ferrière, René. *Chemin clandestin.* Paris: Julliard, 1968.

Choltitz, Dietrich von. *Soldat unter Soldaten.* Zurich: Europa Verlag, 1951.

Churchill, Winston. *The Second World War: The Hinge of Fate* and *Closing the Ring.* vols. 4 and 5. Boston: Houghton Mifflin Co., 1950 and 1951. (Bantam paperback edition used here.)

Cooper, A. Duff. *Old Men Forget.* London: Hart-Davis, 1954.

Crusoé (Lemaigre Dubreuil). *Vicissitudes d'une victoire.* Paris: Les Éditions de l'Ame Française, 1946.

De Beauvoir, Simone. *La force de l'âge.* Paris: Éditions Gallimard, 1960.

Debré, Michel. *Un Grand Mouvement préfectoral (Extrait de la Revue: Les Cahiers Politiques,* No. de Fevrier–Mars 1946. Paris: Imp. Curial–Archereau, 1946.

Debû-Bridel, Jacques. *La Résistance intellectuelle.* Paris: Julliard, 1970.

De Gaulle, Charles. *Mémoires de guerre.* 3 vols. (*L'Appel:* 1940–1942; *L'Unité:* 1942–1944; and *Le Salut:* 1944–1946). Paris: Librairie Plon, 1954, 1956, 1959.

Eisenhower, Dwight D. *Crusade in Europe.* Garden City, New York: Doubleday and Co., 1948.

————. *Eisenhower's Own Story of the War.* New York: Arco Publishing Co., 1946.

Farge, Yves. *Rebelles soldats et citoyens.* Paris: Éditions Bernard Grasset, 1946.

Faure, Petrus. *Un témoin raconte.* St. Etienne: Imp. Dumas, 1962.

Galtier-Boissière, Jean. *Mon journal pendant l'occupation.* Paris: La Jeune Parque, 1945.

Giraud, Henri. *Un seul but La Victoire.* Paris: René Julliard, 1949.

Grenier, Fernand. *C'était ainsi . . . (Souvenirs).* Paris: Éditions Sociales, 1959.

Groussard, Colonel. *Chemins secrets.* Paris: Éditions Bader-Dufour, 1948.

Hauriou, André. *La Socialisme humaniste (Vers une doctrine de la résistance).* Algiers: Éditions Fontaine, 1944.

Hervé, Pierre. *La Libération Trahie.* Paris: Éditions Bernard Grasset, 1945.

Jonchay, Colonel du. *La Résistance et les Communistes.* Paris: Éditions France–Empire, 1968.

Juvenal, Max. *Un Résistant Parmi tant d'autres parle à la jeunesse de son pays.* Paris: La Fédération Nationale des Anciens de la Résistance, 1965 (Supplément au Journal No. 79, Janvier–Fevrier 1965).

Kriegel-Valrimont, Maurice. *La Libération.* Paris: Les Éditions de Minuit, 1964.

Lecoeur, Auguste. *L'Autocritique Attendue.* Paris: Éditions Girault, 1955.

————. *Le Parti Communiste Français et la Résistance.* Paris: Librairie Plon, 1968.

————. *Le partisan.* Paris: Flammarion, 1963.

Leproux, Marc. *Nous . . . les terroristes.* Monte-Carlo: Éditions Raoul Solar, 1947.

Le Troquer, André. *La parole est à André Le Troquer.* Paris: Le Table Ronde, 1962.

Malraux, André. *Anti-Memoirs.* New York: Holt, Rinehart and Winston, 1968.

Massiet, Raymond. *La préparation de l'insurrection et la bataille de Paris.* Paris: Payot, 1945.

Mayer, Daniel. *Les Socialistes dans la Résistance (souvenirs et documents).* Paris: Presses Universitaires de France, 1968.

Murphy, Robert. *Diplomat Among Warriors.* Garden City, New York: Doubleday and Co., 1964.

Nal, Commandant Louis. *La Bataille de Grenoble (Mémoires posthumes présentés et annotés par Joseph Perrin).* Paris: Éditions des deux Miroirs, 1964.

Nocher, Jean. *Les Clandestins (La vie ardente et secrète de la Résistance).* Paris: Librairie Gallimard, 1946.

Ouzoulias, Albert. *Les Bataillons de la Jeunesse.* Paris: Éditions Sociales, 1969.

Passy, Colonel (André Dewavrin). *Souvenirs.* vol. 1, *2e bureau Londres.* Monte-Carlo: Éditions Raoul Solar, 1947; vol. 2, *10 Duke Street Londres.* Monte-Carlo: Éditions Raoul Solar, 1948; vol. 3, *Missions secrètes en France.* Paris: Librairie Plon, 1951.

Pierre-Bloch, Jean. *Mes Jours Heureux.* Paris: Éditions du Bateau Ivre, 1946.

————. *Le Vent Souffle sur l'Histoire.* Paris: Éditions S. I. P. E. P., 1956.

Pineau, Christian. *La Simple Vérité.* Paris: René Julliard, 1961.

Rémy (Gilbert Renault). *Comment Meurt un Reseau*. Monte-Carlo: Éditions Raoul Solar, 1947.

————. *Les mains jointes*. Monte-Carlo: Éditions Raoul Solar, 1948.

————. *Mais le Temple est Bâti*. Monte-Carlo: Éditions Raoul Solar, 1950.

————. *Mémoires d'un agent secret de la France Libre*. Paris: Aux Trois Couleurs, 1945.

Schumann, Maurice. *Honneur et Patrie*. Paris: Éditions du Livre Français, 1946.

Soustelle, Jacques. *Envers et Contre Tout*. Vols. 1 and 2. Paris: Robert Laffont, 1947 and 1950.

Speer, Albert. *Inside the Third Reich*. New York: Macmillan Co., 1970.

Stucki, Walter. *La fin du régime de Vichy*. Neuchatel: Éditions de la Baconnière, 1947.

Textes & Documents. No. 20, 4ᵉ Trimestre 1964: "*La Résistance Française*."

Tillon, Charles. *Les F. T. P*. Paris: René Julliard, 1962.

Trouillé, Pierre. *Journal d'un préfet pendant l'occupation*. Paris: Éditions Gallimard, 1964.

Vercors (Jean Bruller). *The Battle of Silence*. New York: Holt, Rinehart and Winston, 1968. See also his famous clandestine novel, *The Silence of the Sea*. New York: Macmillan Co., 1944.

Virieu, Xavier de. *Radio Journal Libre (Juillet 1943–Août 1944)*. Paris–Lyon: Éditions Jean Cabut, 1947.

Vistel, Alban. "Fondéments spirituels de la Résistance." Esprit, 20ᵉ Année, No. 195 (October 1952): 480–92.

————. *Héritage spirituel de la Résistance*. Lyon: Éditions LUG, 1955.

————. *La nuit sans ombre*. Paris: Librairie Arthème Fayard, 1970.

5. Clandestine Newspapers, Resistance Pamphlets and Special Tracts

Action

Bulletin d'Information (P. C. Zone Sud)

Bulletin d'Information du Front National de Lutte Pour la Libération de la France

Bulletin Intérieur de l'A. S. (Région Toulouse)

Bulletin Intérieur des Mouvements Unis de la Résistance

Les Cahiers Français (also called *Les Documents*). Vols. 1 and 2, nos. 1–59. Comité Français de la Libération Nationale

Les Cahiers de Libération

Combat

Documents (édités par le Comité Directeur du Front National)

Fighting France Pamphlets. No. 1, Pierre Tissier, "The Nazification of Vichy France." No. 2, Georges Boris, "French Public Opinion Since the Armistice." London: Oxford University Press, 1942.

France Forever, Nos. 1–56, December 1943–December 1944.

La France Libre

La France Veut . . . Une Grande Armée Nationale et Républicaine, brochure "Édité par la Commission Militaire Nationale du C. N. R." (Les débats de l'Assemblée Consultative Provisoire sur l'intégration et l'utilisation dans l'armée des cadres issus des FFI). Paris: Atéliers Roc.

Le Franc-Tireur

F. N.: Un événement politique considérable.

Les Lettres françaises

Libération

Parti Communiste français pamphlets: Julien Airoldi, "*Épuration Rapide Complète*" (Rapport présenté au Congrès des C. D. L. en Avignon, le 7 octobre 1944); Florimond Bonte, *La Politique extérieure de la France et l'indépendance Nationale* (Discourse prononncé le 21 novembre 1944 devant l'Assemblée Consultative); *Haute Trahison Crime des Trusts,* "*La France accuse!*" Paris: Éditions du parti Communiste; Maurice Thorez, "*S'Unir, Combattre, Travailler*" (Rapport of the Secretary General of the P. C. F. to the Session of the Central Committee on 21, 22, 23 January 1945).

Paulhan, Jean. *Lettre aux directeurs de la Résistance.* Paris: Les Éditions de Minuit, 1952.

Le Populaire

La Revue Libre

Rouge Midi

Socialisme et Liberté

L'Université Libre

Vérités

La Voix du Peuple (Organe Régional illégal du Parti Communiste du Rhône)

6. GENERAL WORKS: BOOKS

Adam, Gérard. *La C. F. T. C. 1940–1958 histoire politique et idéologique.* Paris: Librairie Armand Colin, 1964.

Amoretti, Henri. *Lyon Capitale, 1940–1944.* Paris: Éditions France-Empire, 1964.

Amouroux, Henri. *La Vie des Français sous l'Occupation.* Paris: Librairie Arthème Fayard, 1961.

L'Année Politique, 1944–1945. Paris: Éditions du Grand Siècle, 1946.

Arnoult, Pierre. *Les Finances de la France et l'Occupation Allemande 1940–1944.* Paris: Presses Universitaires de France, 1951.

Arnoult, P. and others. *La France sous l'occupation.* Paris: Presses Universitaires de France, 1959.

Aron, Robert. *Histoire de l'Épuration.* Vol. 1. Paris: Librairie Arthème Fayard, 1967.

__________. *Histoire de la libération de la France juin 1944–mai 1945.* Paris: Librairie Arthème Fayard, 1959.

————. *Histoire de Vichy 1940–1944.* Paris: Librairie Arthème Fayard, 1954.

Aury, Bernard. *La Délivrance de Paris.* Paris: B. Arthaud, 1945.

Bankwitz, Philip Charles Farwell. *Maxime Weygand and Civil-Military Relations in Modern France.* Cambridge: Harvard University Press, 1967.

Barnes, Peter Franklin. *The French Movements of Resistance* (Portrait of a Transient Elite). B.A. Honors Thesis, Harvard College, 1962.

Bastid, P. *Les Grands procès politiques de l'Histoire.* Paris: Librairie Arthème Fayard, 1962.

Baudoin, Madeleine. *Histoire des Groupes Francs (M. U. R.) des Bouches-du-Rhône de septembre 1943 à la libération.* Paris: Presses Universitaires de France, 1962.

Baudot, Marcel. *L'opinion publique sous l'occupation.* Paris: Presses Universitaires de France, 1960.

Beau, Georges and Léopold Gaubusseau. *R. 5 Les S. S. en Limousin, Périgord, Quercy.* Paris: Presses de la Cité, 1969.

Bellanger, Claude. *Presse Clandestine 1940–1944.* Paris: Librairie Armand Colin, 1961.

Bernard, Henri. *Histoire de la Résistance européenne (la quatrième force de la guerre 1939–1945).* Verviers: Marabout Université, 1968.

Bloch, Marc. *L'Étrange défaite.* Paris: Société des Éditions Franc-Tireur, 1946.

Borchers, Major E. *Abwehr contre Résistance.* Paris: Amiot-Dumont, 1949.

Bourget, Pierre and Charles Lacretelle. *Sur les murs de Paris 1940–1944.* Paris: Librairie Hachette, 1959.

Bruneau, Françoise. *Essai d'historique du mouvement né autour du journal clandestin "Résistance."* Paris: S. E. D. E. S., 1951.

Calmette, Arthur. *L' "O. C. M." Organisation Civile et Militaire: Histoire d'un Mouvement de Résistance de 1940 à 1946.* Paris: Presses Universitaires de France, 1961.

Canlorbe, Pierre. *Le Service de Santé de la Résistance.* Paris: Reboul & fils Imprimerie, 1945.

Caute, David. *Communism and the French Intellectuals, 1914–1960.* New York: Macmillan Co., 1964.

Chastenet, Jacques. *De Pétain à de Gaulle.* Paris: Librairie Arthème Fayard, 1970.

Coles, Harry L. and Albert K. Weinberg. *Civil Affairs: Soldiers Become Governors.* Washington, D.C.: Office of the Chief of Military History, Department of the Army, 1964.

Collins, Larry and Dominique Lapierre. *Is Paris Burning?* New York: Simon and Schuster, 1965.

Colton, Joel. *Léon Blum.* New York: Alfred A. Knopf, 1966.

Dansette, Adrien. *Histoire de la Libération de Paris.* Paris: Librairie Arthème Fayard, 1946.

Debû-Bridel, Jacques. *De Gaulle contestataire.* Paris: Librairie Plon, 1970.

————. *Les Partis contre Charles de Gaulle.* Paris: Aimery Somogy, 1948.

__________. *Sous la Cendre*. Paris: Gallimard, 1951.

De la Gorce, Paul-Marie. *De Gaulle entre deux mondes*. Paris: Librairie Arthème Fayard, 1964.

Delarue, Jacques. *Histoire de la Gestapo*. Paris: Librairie Arthème Fayard, 1962.

__________. *Trafics et Crimes sous l'Occupation*. Paris: Librairie Arthème Fayard, 1968.

Delperrie de Bayac, Jacques. *Histoire de la Milice*. Paris: Librairie Arthème Fayard, Paris, 1969.

Denis, Henri. *Le Comité Parisien de la Libération*. Paris: Presses Universitaires de France, 1963.

Documents sur les Maquis Limousin. "Anciens du Maquis Limousin." Paris: Presse de l'Imprimerie E. Desfossés Néogravure, 1946.

Doysié, Abel. *La Résistance dans la Région de Limoges*. (A large, mostly manuscript dossier found in the Bibliothèque of the Comité d'histoire de la deuxième guerre mondiale.)

Duquesne, Jacques. *Les Catholiques Français sous l'Occupation*. Paris: Éditions Bernard Grasset, 1966.

Durand, Paul. *La S. N. C. F. pendant la guerre*. Paris: Presses Universitaires de France, 1968.

Durand, Yves. *Vichy 1940–1944*. Paris: Bordas, 1972.

Elliott-Bateman, Michael, ed. *The Fourth Dimension of Warfare*. Manchester, Eng.: Manchester University Press, 1970.

Eschalier, Jacques. *Étude de Presse Clandestine: Le Journal "Libération" Zone Sud 1941–1944*. Faculté des Lettres et des Sciences Humaines de Paris, Année scolaire 1961–1962. Diplôme d'Études Supérieures—Histoire Contemporaine.

European Resistance Movements 1939–1945. 2 vols. London: Pergamon Press, 1960 and 1964.

Farmer, Paul. *Vichy Political Dilemma*. New York: Columbia University Press, 1955.

Fauvet, Jacques. *Histoire du Parti Communiste Français*. Vol. 2: *Vingt-cinq ans de Drames, 1935–1965*. Paris: Librairie Arthème Fayard, 1965.

Ferry, Fresnette. *Le Problème constitutionnel et l'opinion publique en France de 1940 à 1946*. Thèse présentée devant la faculté de Droit de l'Université de Paris, July 1947.

Fiat, Robert. *L'Insurgé (1940–1944) Un Mouvement de Résistance Un Journal*. Essai d'Histoire for Diplôme d'Études Supérieures d'Histoire, 1961.

Foot, Michael R. D. *SOE in France*. London: Her Majesty's Stationery Office, 1966.

Foulon, Charles-Louis. *Les commissaires de la république*. Paris: Fondation nationale des sciences politiques, multigr., 1973.

Fourcade, Marie-Madeline. *L'Arche de Noé*. Paris: Librairie Arthème Fayard, 1968.

La France et Son Empire dans la Guerre. 3 vols. Paris: Éditions Littéraires de France, 1947.

Frenay, Henri. *Méthodes d'un Parti ("Alerte aux Démocrates")*. Paris: Les Éditions Universelles, 1945.

Funk, Arthur Layton. *Charles de Gaulle, The Crucial Years, 1943–1944*. Norman: University of Oklahoma Press, 1959.

Garcon, Maurice. *Plaidoyer pour René Hardy*. Paris: Librairie Arthème Fayard, 1950.

Les grandes énigmes de la Résistance. 3 vols. Paris: Éditions Les Amis de l'Histoire, 1968.

Granet, Marie. *Ceux de la Résistance (1940–1944)*. Paris: Les Éditions de Minuit, 1964.

————. *Défense de la France*. Paris: Presses Universitaires de France, 1960.

———— and Henri Michel. *Combat*. Paris: Presses Universitaires de France, 1957.

Greene, Nathanael. *From Versailles to Vichy*. New York: Thomas Y. Crowell Co., 1970.

Guyot, Claude. *Historique du Comité Départemental de Libération de la Cote-d'Or*. Besançon: Néo-Typo, 1962.

Halin, Hubert. *Europe Unie, Objectif majeur de la Résistance*. Bruxelles-Paris: Éditions de l'URPE, 1967.

Herval, René. *Bataille de Normandie*. 2 vols. Paris: Éditions de "Notre Temps," 1947.

Histoire du parti communiste français. Vol. 2. Paris, 1962. (Written by anonymous party members.)

Hobam, Nicolas. *Quatre années de lutte clandestine en Lorraine*. Nancy: Nicolas Hobam, 1946.

Hoffmann, Stanley. *Decline or Renewal? France since the 1930s*. New York: Viking Press, 1974.

Hoffmann, Stanley and others. *In Search of France*. New York: Harper & Row, 1965. (Copyright Harvard University Press, 1963.)

Hostache, René. *Le Conseil national de la Résistance*. Paris: Presses Universitaires de France, 1958.

Hughes, H. Stuart. *The Obstructed Path*. New York: Harper & Row, 1968.

Jäckel, Eberhard. *Frankreich in Hitlers Europa*. Stuttgart: Deutsche Verlags-Anstalt, 1966.

Kriegel, Annie. *Les Communistes français*. Paris: Éditions du Seuil, 1968.

Lacouture, Jean. *De Gaulle*. Paris: Éditions du Seuil, 1969.

Ligou, Daniel. *Histoire du socialisme en France*. Paris: Presses Universitaires de France, 1962.

Luther, Hans. *Der französische Widerstand (gegen die deutsche Besatzungmacht und seine Bekämpfung)*. Tübingen: Institut für Besatzungsfragen, 1957.

Lyon Sous la Botte. Lyon: Éditions de La Plus Grande France, 1944.

Marabuto, Paul. *Les partis politiques et les mouvements sociaux sous la IVe République*. Paris: Librairie du Recueil Sirey, 1948.

Marshall, Bruce. *Le Lapin blanc*. Paris: Librairie Gallimard, 1953.

Mémorial de "l'Insurgé" (Témoignages et documents rassemblés par Marie-Gabriel Fugère). Lyon: Imprimerie Nouvelle Lyonnaise, 1968.

Michel, Henri. *Bibliographie critique de la Résistance*. Paris: Institut Pedagogique National, 1964.

__________. *Les Courants de pensée de la Résistance*. Paris: Presses Universitaires de France, 1962.

__________. *La Guerre de l'ombre (La Résistance en Europe)*. Paris: Éditions Bernard Grasset, 1970.

__________. *Histoire de la France libre*. Paris: Presses Universitaires de France, 1963.

__________. *Histoire de la Résistance*. Paris: Presses Universitaires de France, 1950.

__________. *Jean Moulin l'unificateur*. Paris: Librairie Hachette, 1964.

__________. *Vichy, Année 40*. Paris: Robert Laffont, 1966.

Milward, Alan S. *The New Order and the French Economy*. London: Oxford University Press, 1970.

Morgan, Claude. *Yves Farge*. Paris: Les Éditeurs Français Reúnis, 1954.

Moulin, Laure. *Jean Moulin*. Paris: Presses de la Cité, 1969.

Noguères, Henri. *Histoire de la Résistance en France*. Vols. 1, 2, and 3. Paris: Robert Laffont, 1967, 1969, and 1972.

Novick, Peter. *The Resistance versus Vichy*. New York: Columbia University Press, 1968.

Ozouf, René. *Pierre Brossolette*. Paris: Librairie Gedalge, 1946.

Le Parti communiste français dans la Résistance. Paris: Éditions Sociales, 1967.

Paul, Marcel. *Histoire des PTT pendant la deuxième guerre mondiale (1939–1945)*. 4 vols. Paris: Ronéotypé by Ministère des P. T. T., 1967.

Paxton, Robert O. *Parades and Politics at Vichy*. Princeton, N.J.: Princeton University Press, 1966.

__________. *Vichy France*. New York: Alfred A. Knopf, 1972.

Piquet-Wicks. *Quatre dans l'Ombre*. Paris: Gallimard, 1957.

Pogue, Forrest C. *The Supreme Command*. Washington, D.C.: Office of the Chief of Military History, Department of the Army, 1954.

Présidence du Conseil, Comité d'Histoire de la 2ᵉᵐᵉ Guerre Mondiale. *Chronologie de la Résistance Française (1940–1945)*. Paris: April 1959.

Reile, Oscar. *Geheime Westfront (Die Abwehr 1935–1945)*. Munich: Verlag Welsermühl, 1962.

__________. *Macht und Ohnmacht der Geheimdienste*. Munich: Verlag Welsermühl, 1968.

Reitlinger, Gerald. *The SS Alibi of a Nation, 1922–1945*. London: William Heinemann Ltd., 1956.

Rémond, René. *La Droite en France (De la Première Restauration à la Vᵉ République)*. Paris: (Aubier) Éditions Montaigne, 1963.

Rieber, Alfred J. *Stalin and the French Communist Party 1941–1947*. New York: Columbia University Press, 1962.

Rossi, A. (Angelo Tasca). *Les communistes français pendant la drôle de guerre*. Paris: Éditions Les Iles d'Or, 1951.

__________. *La guerre des papillons, quatre ans de politique communiste (1940–1944)*. Paris: Éditions Les Iles d'Or, 1954.

__________. *Physiologie du parti communiste français*. Paris: Éditions Self, 1948.

Rougeron, Georges. *Le Département de l'Allier sous l'État Français (1940–1944)*. Montluçon: Imprimerie Typocentre, 1969.

__________. *La Résistance dans le Département de l'Allier (1940–1944)*. Montluçon: Typocentre, 1964.

Schoenbrun, David. *The Three Lives of Charles de Gaulle*. New York: Atheneum, 1968.

Shirer, William L. *The Collapse of the Third Republic*. New York: Simon & Schuster, 1969.

Siegfried, André. *De la IIIᵉ à la IVᵉ République*. Paris: Bernard Grasset Éditeur, 1956.

Spears, Sir Edward. *Two Men who saved France (Pétain and de Gaulle)*. London: Eyre & Spottiswoode, 1966.

Stead, Philip John. *Second Bureau*. London: Evans Brothers Limited, 1959.

Tanant, Pierre. *Vercors, Haut-lieu de France*. Paris: B. Arthaud, 1966.

Tesson, Philippe. *De Gaulle Iᵉʳ*. Paris: Éditions Albin Michel, 1965.

Thornton, Willis. *The Liberation of Paris*. New York: Harcourt, Brace & World, 1962.

Tollet, André. *La Classe Ouvrière dans la Résistance*. Paris: Éditions Sociale, 1969.

Tournoux, Jean-Raymond. *Pétain and de Gaulle*. London: William Heinemann, 1966. (Copyright Librairie Plon, Paris, 1964.)

Touzeau, Jacques. *La Propagande radiophonique en France pour la relève et le Service du Travail Obligatoire*. Diplôme d'Études Supérieurs for Faculté des Lettres et Sciences Humaines de Nanterre, Université de Paris.

Umbreit, Hans. *Der Militärbefehlshaber in Frankreich 1940–1944*. Boppard am Rhein: Harold Boldt Verlag, 1968.

Verdier, Robert. *La Vie clandestine du parti socialiste*. Paris: Éditions de la Liberté, 1944.

Vidalenc, Jean. *L'Exode de mai-juin 1940*. Paris: Presses Universitaires de France, 1957.

Vigneras, Marcel. *Rearming the French*. Washington, D.C.: Office of the Chief of Military History, Department of the Army, 1957.

Viorst, Milton. *Hostile Allies: F. D. R. and Charles de Gaulle*. New York: Macmillan, 1965.

Wahl, Anthony Nicholas. "De Gaulle and the Resistance (The Rise of Reform Politics in France)." Ph.D. diss. in Political Science, Harvard University, 1956.

Warner, Geoffrey. *Pierre Laval and the eclipse of France*. New York: Macmillan Co., 1968.

Werth, Alexander. *France 1940–1955*. Boston: Beacon Press, 1966.

White, Dorothy Shipley. *Seeds of Discord (De Gaulle, Free France and the Allies)*. Syracuse, N.Y.: Syracuse University Press, 1964.

White, Theodore H. *Fire in the Ashes: Europe in Mid-Century*. New York: William Sloane Associates, 1953.

Williams, Philip M. *Crisis and Compromise*. London: Longmans, Green and Co., 1964.

Wright, Gordon. *France in Modern Times*. Chicago: Rand McNally & Co., 1960.

————. *The Ordeal of Total War 1939–1945*. New York: Harper & Row, 1968.

————. *The Reshaping of French Democracy*. New York: Reynal & Hitchcock, 1948.

————. *Rural Revolution in France*. Stanford: Stanford University Press, 1964.

7. General Works: Articles

Adeline, Général. "La Libération de Bordeaux." *Revue Historique de l'Armée*. 17e année, no. 4 (December 1961): 141–54.

Aragon, Charles d'. "Éloge funèbre du M. R. P."*Esprit*, no. 4 (April 1968): 629–41.

D'Astier, Emmanuel. "Les cent jours de 'Rex.' " *Le Nouvel Observateur*. No. 5, 17 December 1964, pp. 16–17.

Baudot, Marcel. "La Résistance française face aux problèmes de repression et d'épuration." *Révue d'Histoire de la deuxième guerre mondiale* 81, 21e année (January 1957): 23–47.

————. Compte rendu de Robert Aron, *Histoire de l'épuration, Revue d'Histoire de la deuxième guerre mondiale* 71 (July 1968): 104–10.

Bechmann, Roland (Lescot). "Le Vercors." *L'Armée Française*, no. spécial (June–July 1948): 3–15.

Bernard, Jacqueline. "The Background of *The Plague*: Albert Camus' Experience in the French Resistance." *Kentucky Romance Quarterly* 14, no. 2 (1967): 165–73.

Bidault, Georges. "Hommage à Jean Moulin." *Revue d'Histoire de la deuxième guerre mondiale* 1 (November 1950): 1–5.

Bloch-Lainé, Fr. "Le Financement de la Résistance." *Revue d'Histoire de la deuxième guerre mondiale* 1 (November 1950): 6–19.

Bourdet, Claude. "Histoire de la Résistance française." Conférence faite le 3 Mai 1960, printed in *Après-Demain*, nos. 30–33.

————. "La Politique intérieure de la Résistance." *Les Temps Modernes*, nos. 112–113 (1955): 1837–62.

Brinton, Crane. "Letters from Liberated France." *French Historical Studies* 2, no. 1 and no. 2 (Spring and Fall 1961): 1–27 and 133–56.

Buckmaster, "Ici Londres (Mes agents secrets)." *Caliban*, no. 24 (February 1949): 17–22.

Bulletin Intérieur des Amicales "Combat." May and July 1947.

Cahiers du Communisme, no. 4–5, April–May 1965, pp. 92–95.

Calmette, A. "La Libération de Bordeaux (août 1944)." Éditions Bière, Bordeaux, 1947.

Cobban, Alfred. "Vichy France." In A. and V. Toynbee, eds., *Survey of*

International Affairs 1939–1946: Hitler's Europe. London: Royal Institute, 1954, pp. 338–434.

Costa de Beauregard, Colonel. "Vercors 1944." *L'Armée*, no. 6 (September 1960): 7–20.

Coulet, François. "14 juin 1944, de Gaulle débarque." *Miroir de l'Histoire* 209 (May 1967): 97–105.

Courtin, René. "Charles de Gaulle, Hier et Aujourd'hui." *Foi et Vie*, no. 6 (November–December 1955): 534–47.

Defrasne, Colonel. "L'Epopée du Vercors, 1942–1944." *Revue Historique de l'Armée*, 22e année, no. 2 (May 1966): 127–40.

Defromont-Leschevin, Annie. "Le Mouvement F. T. P. F. dans le Valenciennois." *Revue du Nord*, vol. 51, no. 203 (October–December 1969): 743–55.

Dogan, Mattei. "Political Ascent in a Class Society: French Deputies, 1870–1958." In Dwaine Marvick, ed., *Political Decision Makers*. New York: Free Press of Glencoe, 1961.

Etiemble. "Y avait-il Collaboration en France?: Justice pour les 'collabos.'" *Évidences* no. 26 (June–July 1952): 9–14.

Even, Commandant. "La Retraite Allemande des Cotes de Provence à Lyon." *Revue Historique de l'Armée*, no. 3, 15e année (August 1959): 99–108.

Fauvet, Jacques. "Les débuts de la IVe République." *Miroir de l'Histoire*, no. 206 (February 1967): 43–51.

Feral, F. et A. Ressigeac. "Notice Explicative de la Carte de la Résistance F. F. I. en Tarn-et-Garonne." December 1963.

France Forum, no. 58 (July–August 1964).

Frenay, Henri. "De Gaulle et la Résistance." *Preuves*, no. 70 (December 1956): 78–84.

Friedlaender, Saul. "Berlin et le jeu americain à Vichy." *Revue suisse d'histoire*, no. 13 (1963): 339–71.

Fumet, Stanislas. "Y avait-il Collaboration en France?: La fonction de l'écrivain." *Évidences*, no. 26 (June–July 1952): 14–19.

Gacon, Jean. "La Première 'Expérience de Gaulle' Août 1944–Janvier 1946." *Recherches internationales*, no. 44–45 (July–December 1964): 235–54.

Galtier-Boissière, Jean. "Histoire de la Guerre, 1939–1945." *Crapouillot* 4 and 5 (1949 and 1950).

Gilles, Capitaine. "Il y a vingt ans. Un épisode glorieux de la Résistance (La véritable histoire de la concentration des Maquis d'Auvergne)." *Revue de la Haute-Auvergne* 39, 66e année (July–September 1964): 141–74.

Girardet, Raoul. "Notes sur l'Esprit d'un Fascisme Français 1934–1939." *Revue Française de Science Politique* 5, no. 3 (July–September 1955): 529–46.

Goutard, A. "Pourquoi et Comment l'Armistice a-t-il été 'accordé' par Hitler?" *Le Revue de Paris* (October 1960): 79–95.

Granet, Marie. "Dessin Général des Maquis." *Revue d'Histoire de la deuxième guerre mondiale* 1 (November 1950): 51–72.

__________. "Un Journal socialiste clandestin pendant l'occupation, Libération-Nord." Two brochures, Imprimerie S. E. P., Arras (suppléments to *La Revue Socialiste*, nos. 192, 193, 1966).

Gubbins, Sir Collin. "Resistance Movements in the War." *Journal of the Royal United Service Institution* 93, no. 570 (May 1948): 210–21.

Guérin, E. "Les ingénieurs des télécommunications dans la résistance." *Télécom*, no. 11 (May 1966): 34–38.

Heilbronner, A. "La France économique de 1939 à 1943; Le ravitaillement en France." *Revue d'Economie Politique* (1948): 1644–83.

"Histoire du parti communiste." *Crapouillot* 55 (January 1962).

Hoffmann, Stanley. "Aspects du Régime de Vichy." *Revue Française de Science Politique* 6 (1956): 44–69.

__________. "Collaborationism in France during World War II." *The Journal of Modern History* 40, no. 3 (September 1968): 375–95.

__________. "The Effects of World War II on French Society and Politics." *French Historical Studies* 2, no. 1 (Spring 1961): 28–63.

Hoop, Jean-Marie d'. "La main-d'oeuvre française au service de l'Allemagne." *Revue d'Histoire de la deuxième guerre mondiale* no. 81, 21ᵉ année (January 1971): 73–88.

Hughes, H. Stuart. "The Problem of Limited Collaboration." *Confluence* 3, no. 2 (June 1954): 172–83.

Kogan, Norman. "American Policies towards European Resistance Movements." *Deuxième Conference Internationale d'Histoire de la Résistance* (Milano, 1961).

Kuisel, Richard F. "The Legend of the Vichy Synarchy." *French Historical Studies* (Spring 1970): 365–98.

Levy, G. M. "Un épisode crucial de la Résistance française en mai–juin 1944: La Concentration des maquis d'Auvergne." *Revue Historique de l'Armée* no. 3 (1968): 43–62.

Liebmann, Leon. "Entre le mythe et la légende: 'L'anti-capitalisme' de Vichy." *Revue de l'Institut de Sociologie de Bruxelles* 1 (1964): 109–48.

Lipgens, Walter. "European Federation in the Political Thought of Resistance Movements during World War II." *Central European History* 1, no. 1 (March 1968).

Lyet, Colonel P. "Comment furent libérés Toulon et Marseille." *Revue Historique de l'Armée* 14ᵉ année, no. 4 (1958): 155–66.

Martin-Chauffier, Louis. "Quand naisait 'Libération.'" *Le Figaro Littéraire* no. 972 (3–9 December 1964), pp. 1, 19.

Mathis, Capitaine. "Comment furent actionnées, par l'état major français de Londres, les Forces Françaises de l'Intérieur." *Revue Historique de l'Armée* no. 2 (May 1959): 39–60.

Metral, Alphonse. "Les Glières 1944." *Revue Historique de l'Armée* 22ᵉ année, no. 2 (May 1966): 119–24.

Michel, Henri. "L'aide apportée aux Alliés par la Résistance clandestine française." *Revue des Travaux de l'Académie des Sciences Morales & Politiques,* 115ᵉ année, 4ᵉ Série (1962): 63–79.

————. "The Psychology of the French Resister." *Journal of Contemporary History* 5, no. 3 (1970): 159–75.

————. "La Résistance dans les P. T. T.: La Source K." *Revue des PTT* (June 1963): 11–16.

————. "La Révolution Nationale latitude d'action du gouvernement de Vichy." *Revue d'Histoire de la deuxième guerre mondiale* no. 81, 21ᵉ année (January 1971): 3–22.

————. "Sur Pétain et Vichy." *Revue d'Histoire de la deuxième guerre mondiale,* no. 23 (July 1956): 32–50.

"1939–1944: la vie de la France et des Français." *Historia,* 3 volumes hors série 13, 14, 15 (1969).

Noguères, Henri. "Vichy dans la Résistance." *Miroir de l'Histoire,* no. 216 (December 1967): 81–89.

l'Observateur, "Huit Ans Après." No. Spécial, 3ᵉ année, no. 119 (21 August 1952) and no. 120 (28 August 1952).

"Origines et Missions du M. R. P." Numéro Spécial of *Forces Nouvelles,* Paris, 1952.

Paris Match Numéros 791–94 (June 1964).

Passy, Colonel (André Dewavrin). "Le Colonel Passy." *Le Nouvel Observateur,* no. 83 (15–21 June 1966): 4–5.

————. "Entre alliés, pas de secret." *Le Figaro Littéraire,* 2–8 June 1969, pp. 15–16.

————. "M. R. D. Foot, n'attaquez injustement les 'Français Libres.'" *Le Figaro Littéraire,* 16 June 1966.

Paul, Pierre. "La Libération de Lyon, 3 septembre 1944." *Revue Historique de l'Armée,* no. Spécial (May 1958): 169–77.

Piquet-Wicks, Eric. "Un héros clandestin." *Historia* 25, no. 148 (March 1959): 247–56.

Poiteau, Capitaine. "Guerilla en Montagne." *Revue Historique de l'Armée,* no. 3 (1968): 163–80.

Revue d'Histoire de la deuxième guerre mondiale, no. 1, année 1, 1950; no. 3, année 1, 1951; nos. 10–11, année 3, 1953; no. 30, année 8, 1958; no. 35, année 9, 1959; no. 47, année 12, 1962; no. 49, année 13, 1963; nos. 54, 55, and 56, année 14, 1964; and no. 61, année 19, 1966.

Revue Historique de l'Armée, no. 4 (1969).

Roure, Rémy. "Y avait-il Collaboration en France?: Le temps de la honte." *Évidences,* no. 26 (June–July 1952): 19–24.

————. "Valeur de la Résistance." *Terre Humaine,* no. 22 (October 1952): 28–31.

Sawyer, John E. "The Reestablishment of the Republic in France: The de Gaulle Era, 1944–1945." *Political Science Quarterly* 62 (September 1947): 354–80.

Siegfried, André. "The Rebirth of the French Spirit." *Foreign Affairs* 23, no. 4 (July 1945): 556–66.

Soucy, Robert J. "The Nature of Fascism in France." *Journal of Contemporary History* 1, no. 1 (1966), 27–55.

"Souvenirs et Témoignages sur l'Insurrection de Paris." *Les Cahiers Français* (October 1964): 14–31.

Spears, Sir Edward. "De Gaulle à Londres." *Miroir de l'Histoire* no. 207 (March 1967): 27–37.

Tillon, Germaine. "Première Résistance en Zone Occupée." *Revue d'Histoire de la deuxième guerre mondiale*, no. 30 (April 1958).

Victor, Joannes and Germaine Willard. "La Résistance Française et la Seconde Guerre Mondiale." *Cahiers du Communisme*, no. 7–8 (July–August 1965): 70–78.

Villon, Pierre. "Les exigences de l'internationalisme et notre politique en 1939–1940." *Cahiers du Communisme* (May 1957): 687–701.

————. "De Gaulle et la Résistance: L'Histoire contre la Legende." *France Nouvelle*, no. 667 (7–13 August 1958).

————. "Juin–Août 44." (1 *La bataille contre l'attentisme* & 2 *Pourquoi Paris n'a pas brûlé!*) (September and November 1964), pp. 57–69, 59–76.

Wright, Gordon. "Reflections on the French Resistance." *Political Science Quarterly* 77, no. 3 (September 1962): 336–49.

————. "Vichy Revisited." *Virginia Quarterly Review* 34 (1958): 501–14.

Index

LE FRANC-TIREUR

Organe des Mouvements de Résistance Unis
LIBERTÉ · ÉGALITÉ · FRATERNITÉ

Mai 1940 - Mai 1943

La victoire a changé de camp !

Tunis et Bizerte !

Pour célébrer l'anniversaire du Vichy

libération
l'hebdomadaire de la Résistance française

DE GAULLE
Aller jusqu'au

Quatrième Année

La déportation

AOUT 1942

combat

Je détruirai la France. (Hitler)

Je tiens les promesses, même celles des autres. (Pétain)

Dans la guerre comme dans la paix le dernier mot est à ceux qui ne se rendent jamais - Clemenceau

ORGANE DU MOUVEMENT DE LIBÉRATION FRANÇAISE

PAS UN HOMME POUR L'ALLEM...

DERNIÈRE NOUVELLE

ALERTE DANGER

La police fait imprimer...

SOUVERAINETÉ FRANÇAISE

H. F.

L'Afrique du Nord et De GAULLE

PRISONNIERS DE L'AXE !

Nouvelles des F...

LIBÉRATION

ORGANE DES MOUVEMENTS DE RÉSISTANCE UNIS

Un seul chef : DE GAULLE ; une seule lutte : POUR NOS LIBERTÉS

Autres Organes des Mouvements de Résistance Unis
COMBAT
FRANC-TIREUR

La Jeunesse française répond : Merde

le Rassemblement du Peuple

SABOTEZ LA CONSCRIPTION des esclaves au service d'Hitler

Français, sabotez le recensement pour la déportation

"COLLABORATION" COMBAT

Pour un 14 Juillet de Comb...